"I feel like the midwife who helped birth a baby who grew up to become a combination of Joan of Arc, Wonder Woman, Mother Teresa, and Beverly Sills. When I suggested to Sandy Rios over coffee one morning that she write her autobiography, I had no inkling of what a truly great idea that was. What a remarkable life Sandy has lived and shares with us in these pages. *God's Velvet Hammer* is the perfect description of this amazing woman who is unflinching in her devotion to God and country—and she does it all with a smile in her voice. Sandy and her life story are gifts you will want to take to heart and share with everyone you know."

—Cleta Mitchell, Senior Legal Fellow, Conservative Partnership Institute, Washington, DC

"You will not be able to put down *God's Velvet Hammer*. You will laugh. You will cry. You will be inspired. You will, I am sure, never forget Sandy Rios."

—Gordon Chang, author of *The Coming Collapse of China*

"This is a remarkable story of a woman who fought many battles standing for righteous ideals amid deep disappointment, betrayal, and personal sorrow. But it is also a story of the faithfulness of God, whose presence sustained her, and gave her both courage and joy. My wife and I have known Sandy for many years as a woman who always puts principle above profits and faithfulness above affirmation. She was witness to many critical historical and political events of the past and met many household names in the evangelical world, some of whom compromised because of cultural and political pressure, others stood firm. One message came through to me. God does not abandon us even when our support structures are pulled from beneath us."

—Dr. Erwin W. Lutzer, Pastor Emeritus, Moody Church, Chicago

"Sandy Rios is proof that one life can make a difference for both time and eternity. Her variety of life and ministry experiences share a common thread of what God can do through a life totally yielded to Him. Be prepared to laugh, cry, be challenged and encouraged by Sandy's life. Most of all, any reader will be inspired to be more like Jesus!"

—Hutz H. Hertzberg, chief education officer
Turning Point Academy Schools

"Sandy Rios's captivating life story makes for a must-read book. Sandy's life experiences and memorable interactions with a remarkable range of folks have both tested and empowered her. She is a modern-day Deborah, that biblical figure known for her steely toughness and complete trust in God!"

—The Honorable J. Kenneth Blackwell, U.S. ambassador
(Ret.) United Nations Human Rights Commission,
vice president Council for National Policy

"Sandy Rios has been a strong and impassioned voice on radio ever since I've known her. But I had no idea what was behind that passion until *God's Velvet Hammer*. There's a reason why she's not boring on radio, and this book explains why. You won't be disappointed."

—Dr. Robert Jeffress, Senior Pastor, First Baptist Church, Dallas

"My friendship with Sandy Rios began several years ago when my dear Carol was in the last stages of cancer. When I later remarried, Sandy met Rosemary and our friendship with Sandy continued. Our paths have intersected many times since then. Let me cut to the chase: Sandy Rios's life makes James Bond or Indiana Jones's lives look boring. She has done it all. It is stunning that one person could have experienced so much. When I was a young man, an older man taught me, 'Always respect experience'—meaning honor and learn from those who have experienced much. Sandy is one of those. When I am with her in a group, she is the one who asks the most thought-provoking and penetrating questions. Succinctly stated, learn from her. Read what she writes. She is fiercely committed to God and country. And she is my friend."

—Dr. Jim Garlow, founder and CEO, Well Versed

"Sandy Rios is a national treasure. A passionate patriot, a fearless freedom fighter, and a truly great communicator, she has for decades been at the forefront of the conservative movement and its efforts to protect our country against all enemies, foreign and domestic. Her life story, brilliantly captured in this memoir, describes the trajectory of the struggle of our time—to protect and strengthen our constitutional Republic, in which she has played, and continues to play, an indispensable and leading role."

—Frank Gaffney, executive chairman and founder of Center for Security Policy (centerforsecuritypolicy.org)

"Sandy Rios has been an impassioned, godly, uncompromising voice on radio and on the platform ever since I've known her. Her friendship and support to me and the people of Virginia has been invaluable. But I had no idea what adventures and trials made her what she is today. *God's Velvet Hammer* is a wild read full of God's providential twists and turns in a great human life. It will explain it all."

—Dave Brat, U.S. Congress 2014–2019, vice-provost and dean of the School of Business at Liberty University

"Sandy Rios's new book, *God's Velvet Hammer,* stands alone for her omnium-gatherum of life and her calling to write them. They must be read. Sandy's life has spanned the globe, all the while engaging with the leading personalities of our age. God has moved Sandy in a mighty way along an exhilarating smorgasbord of life—a rich, full, challenging, and humbly triumphant life. Sandy Rios is a woman with a beautiful heart. *God's Velvet Hammer* will warm your heart and strengthen your faith as it has mine."

—Steve King, U.S. Congress (Ret) 2003–2021

"*God's Velvet Hammer* is one of the most transparent and fascinating books I have ever read. I have known Sandy Rios for over a decade but as I read her account of her life, I realized I did not really know her at all. Her modesty and humility have prevented her from sharing her most exciting life story. Here is a woman who has endured great difficulties and yet at the same time met and worked with some of the most incredible household names. Thank you, Sandy, for sharing the captivating story of your incredible life and providing the readers a chance to get to know you."

—Lt. Gen. (Ret.) Jerry Boykin, U.S. Army

"This is a time for heroes. Sandy is one for Mercy and me. Sometimes heroes are called up in the most unlikely of ways. But Sandy is a hero because she stays strong, focuses on Our Savior, and never disregards others even when the lights shine bright. We value her friendship, love her example, and now we get to read the juicy stories—what a life!"

—Matt Schlapp, chairman of ACU, director of CPAC

"It's been an honor to work alongside Sandy in policy fights for many years, as I've always known I could count on her to infuse backbone, common sense, and even humor into whatever federal issue or policy we faced. But I had no idea what incredible experiences forged those things in her life until this book, *God's Velvet Hammer*!"

—Ken Cuccinelli, 46th Attorney General of Virginia, Acting Deputy Secretary, Department of Homeland Security

GOD'S
Velvet Hammer

*How an Ordinary Girl Was Called
to Do Extraordinary Things*

SANDY RIOS

FIDELIS
PUBLISHING

FIDELIS PUBLISHING ®

ISBN: 9781956454383

ISBN (eBook): 9781956454390

GOD'S VELVET HAMMER
How an Ordinary Girl Was Called to Do Extraordinary Things

© 2023 Sandy Rios

Cover Design by Diana Lawrence

Interior Layout/Typesetting by LParnell Book Services

Edited by Amanda Varian

Order at www.faithfultext.com for a significant discount. Email info@fidelispublishing.com to inquire about bulk purchase discounts.

Fidelis Publishing, LLC Winchester, VA • Nashville, TN fidelispublishing.com

Manufactured in the United States of America

10 9 8 7 6 5 4 3 2 1

This book is dedicated to my mother, Lois Wilson.

A woman someone once called a "thoroughbred" . . .
a great lady . . . godly and steadfast
and above all . . . faithful.

Contents

Preface

Doesn't it seem presumptuous to write a book about your life? I've always thought so. When my daughter, Sasha, was still home with me, many people urged me to write about her life and my struggles as the mother of a severely disabled child. But the last thing I wanted to do was relive the heartbreak of that in a play-by-play account.

As my life changed and brought me into a sphere I would never have dreamt possible—the world of radio and television, travel to remote places and communist strongholds and then to Washington, DC, and the world of politics and media—I was offered opportunities to write, but was so busy trying to save the world, I had no time to write about it.

It was while serving as president of Concerned Women for America, a publisher named Gary Terashita reached out to me. Others had reached out, but for some reason, my conversation with him stayed with me. I kept his card and in the back of my mind thought maybe someday I would write a book.

Recently a steady stream of friends and acquaintances began to encourage me to write. And strangely enough, in interviews on my radio show with two good friends, LTG Jerry Boykin and Congressman Steve King, both gave glowing accolades to their publisher, Gary Terashita of Oliver North's Fidelis Publishing. That seemed like more than a coincidence to me. Was this a prompting from God? I felt I must find out.

As I began to notate the events of my life, I found a strange joy and excitement I never expected, and my husband's enthusiasm was contagious. We laughed uncontrollably as I told him of strange adventures in strange places he previously never heard about. Lost in India; Checkpoint Charlie in Berlin; singing with the U.S. Army Band; smuggling Bibles into China; cohosting the first American broadcast from Radio Moscow; being inside North Korea on 9/11; going nose-to-nose with Bill Maher; cohosting CNN's *Crossfire*; making friends with a Spanish countess, a model and pioneer in the OSS. Not so funny, my severely disabled daughter, the breakup of my first marriage, and my untimely end at Concerned Women for America.

In this book you will read about the execution of John Wayne Gacey, the inside story on the Clinton Impeachment, the background story of the Born-Alive Infant Protection Act, anecdotes on Mike Ditka and the Chicago Bears, embarrassing moments, and crazy mistakes.

I knew God's hand was on my life, but recalling the clear ways and incredible moments He directed me brought me overwhelming joy.

This is not a story of success and ambition, but of calling.

Like Paul writing about his qualifications to preach—his shipwrecks, beatings, imprisonments—consider this a story of my own shipwrecks, adventures, and heartaches. A trial by fire preparing me for a mission the natural me could never have accomplished.

Like the apostle Paul, my story is HIS story. The shipwrecks had meaning, the closed doors a blessing, the heartaches and setbacks were character builders preparing me to be part of the greater story of God's plan of redemption for this world.

I am an ordinary girl who has led an extraordinary life. Why would God call such an insignificant little girl from an insignificant little town to go to battle for Him in the world's arena? As I write and you read, maybe we can figure it out together.

Sandy Rios
September 2023

1

Berlin

It was 1972 and the Vietnam War was raging. My new husband drew the number thirty-five in the American military draft lottery. Since service was inevitable, he enlisted rather than wait to be called. He was sent to one of the most politically dangerous places on the globe, Berlin, Germany. Just twenty-five years earlier Berlin was the crown jewel of the Third Reich. That once gorgeous, now thoroughly bombed-out, showplace became our home.

At the ripe old age of twenty-two, I was rummaging around for paper in a desk drawer in a Berlin Brigade office. That's when I came across a color brochure that pierced my heart and set the course of my life. It was one of many experiences making Berlin a crucible in which major forces of my future converged and congealed in dramatic ways.

The Wall

After World War II ended, Germany was divided into East and West. The Russians were allowed by General Dwight David Eisenhower to conduct the final brutal assault against the Third Reich and take Berlin. As a result, Stalin was granted all of East Germany, while the Western half, to be known as West Germany, was shared by the Allies: England, America, and France. Berlin was tucked inside East Germany, just 100 miles from the Russian border. And since the city had been Hitler's showpiece, it too was divided into Eastern and Western sectors. Eventually the Western sector was surrounded by one hundred miles of white concrete and barbed-wire wall. There were actually two walls separated by a corridor known as the "Death Strip" which was carefully guarded and enforced by 50,000 land mines.

There were 7,000 East German soldiers manning the wall on 302 towers strategically placed 250 yards apart. All of this was done, not to keep West Germans out, but to keep the unfortunate German citizens who lived in the East from fleeing for freedom to the West. So, if you can imagine a small circle within a larger land mass, surrounded on all sides by forces who hated democracy and freedom, you will see why living there was stressful and isolating.

The wall dividing Berlin down the middle and isolating us on all sides was a result of an act of sheer terror by what became the Communist/East German/Soviet Bloc in November of 1961. Without warning the wall went up one morning after unsuspecting Germans living in the West left for work in the East or were visiting family for the day. By the end of that day, those Germans were suddenly and painfully cut off from loved ones and livelihoods for the next twenty-eight years.

Every week we lived there, people either died while escaping the East or were killed for trying. Some jumped from windows overlooking the wall. Others concocted elaborate devices in which to hide. A few clung to the underbelly of vehicles leaving, but not many survived. One little boy fell into the Wannsee River that ran down the middle of Berlin and drowned because no one would save him for fear of the guards who were stationed in the towers with "shoot to kill" orders.

From 1961–1989 over 100,000 Germans citizens tried to escape. More than 600 were shot. At least 140 were killed.

One Christmas, my Scottish friend Morag and I climbed a wooden structure on the west side of the wall to sing a Scottish/American version of "Silent Night," and shout "*Frohliche neues jahr!*" (Happy New Year!) to the East German Guards. We heard them laugh in response.

But this was no laughing matter. Checkpoint Charlie was the American guard post at what was the gateway to East Berlin. I was able to get permission to cross over on several occasions in my little orange Volkswagen. After much paperwork, I would drive to Checkpoint Charlie with a friend, and be greeted by the American MPs. We were always expected. I was handed a card with my photograph and the following message in English, Russian, German, and French: "YOU ARE LEAVING THE AMERICAN SECTOR"

I was given a letter and instructed to immediately ask for a Russian officer if problems arose and to hand him the letter. The MPs set a time by which I was to return and told me that under NO circumstances should I roll down my window until I passed through to the other side. That's when carefully zig-zagging through the 500 feet of tank barriers and barbed wire separating Checkpoint Charlie and the entrance to East Berlin began. Once into the barriers, an East German soldier would peer through my tightly closed window to which I pressed my identity card. He then menacingly stared at my face, then at the card, then at my face again. All the while East German guards in the towers had their guns pointed at us, as the stern officer motioned me on.

Entering East Berlin was a surreal experience. In spite of bombed-out sections of West Berlin still remaining, it was a vibrant, beautiful city. The streets were full of cars and commerce. East Berlin on the other hand was neither. The streets were silent. Only a few quirky little Russian cars occasionally passed. It cost an entire year's salary to purchase a car in East Germany, and people there were so very poor. In fact, there were few of them to be seen—anywhere.

East German inflation was so bad in the early '70s that one American dollar could buy twelve East German Marks. We ordered

Chateaubriand for $1.25. We bought Christmas windmills and Nut-crackers and candles in cheaply made cardboard boxes, something like our recycled materials now, for next to nothing. It was sad to me.

Everywhere we looked there were soldiers—Russian and East German. The tension was palpable. As we ate in a restaurant, there was no conversation, no laughter. The only sound we heard was the clicking of forks. No one made eye contact. We might catch a furtive glance, but that was always followed by a quick head down toward the plate. The same dynamic seemed to be everywhere. On one occasion my husband, who belonged to the West Berlin Charlottenburg Sports Club, was competing in a track meet against the East Germans in the Olympic Stadium. There was no sound, no cheering. Spectators on the risers were silent.

My new beautiful black friend, Metda, and I must have made quite a spectacle shopping together in East Berlin. We held hands as we ran across the street, both of us with our long straight hair of the seventies flying. I wore red, white, and blue striped bell bottoms with patent leather shoes adorned by stars.

I wasn't unserious—I was just expressing, perhaps in my youthful way, love for my country. It took my breath away to drive back into West Berlin at the end of the day to see the colors, hear the sounds, and taste . . . FREEDOM.

Growing up with the Reality of Communism

West Berlin at that time contained more spies than any city on the globe. While shopping one day with my friend Lois in the Kurfürsten-damm (the downtown shopping district), I was watching her precious little red-headed, two-year-old son, Brody, when a large Russian man who looked like he'd just walked out of Central Casting came over to talk to me. He had the quintessential bushy, dark hair, and thick, wild eyebrows, but was dressed immaculately in a black woolen overcoat with a fur collar. He smiled at Brody and, thinking I was his mom, commented on how much he missed his children back in Russia. In my innocence, I said something like, "Oh, it's nice that you could visit us on our side today!" He bristled and snapped at me, "This is not YOUR side! We are just letting you stay here!" and marched off.

Only a decade earlier as a high school freshman, I felt the fear and danger of Communism as the world, including my small town, stood still during the thirteen-day standoff between the United States and the Soviet Union known as the Cuban Missile Crisis. The U.S. and Russia were armed with enough nuclear weapons to destroy the world, and both were prepared to use them in their own defense. During those two weeks we went about our daily lives as much as we could while watching with dread as Soviet ships, blockaded by U.S. warships, anchored threateningly, not far from the coast of Florida.

When the Soviets eventually backed down, the whole world, including my school, my family, my friends, and I breathed a sigh of relief. The Cold War was an ever-present and personal issue as I was growing up. In 1959, when I was ten, I saw Nikita Khrushchev take off his shoe at the U.N. General Assembly, pound it on the podium, and shout to America, "WE WILL BURY YOU!" We were perpetually on the brink of nuclear war.

I understood the dangers of communism. I understood WWII and the earlier fight to the death with the Nazis. My father was an engineer with Patton's Third Army, and patriotism and love of country were regular fare at our dinner table and at my school. We said the Pledge of Allegiance daily and couldn't graduate eighth grade without passing proficiency exams on the Constitution. We knew our incredible history backward and forward. Love of country was not propaganda or jingoism. Love of our country was the natural response to a very real historical and beautiful story tracing itself not only to good men, but to men who also served and honored God. It was clear and it made sense. We understood freedom even if we had never lived without it.

But my time in Berlin gave me a taste of oppression and life without freedom I never forgot.

5

Little did I know one day I would travel and work in Russia, China, Vietnam, and North Korea. Or that I would be placed in a position to actually fight against the oppression of Communism with words in a desperate attempt to warn America of its dangers.

What Racism?

My East Berlin travel buddy, Metda, was my first black friend. Her husband, Sergeant Matt Chubbs, was the head of American Youth Activities for the Berlin Brigade. My husband worked with Matt as director of the sports division. Metda was a beautiful, hilarious girl who provided an important transition for me from passionately defending black Americans who were then terribly treated to actually knowing them.

Metda and I both loved clothes and fashion—thus the shopping trip together. We would brush each other's hair, examine each other's skin and remark at the differences. We laughed so much as we made these discoveries. Once Matt and Metda's three-year-old daughter, Michelle, stayed with us while they traveled to London. Metda left her with me with hair neatly styled in pom-poms on top of her head. But I could not for the life of me get a brush through Michelle's hair. When after five days they returned, she was happy and well-loved, but her hair looked like a wild bush sat atop her head. I was embarrassed, but it WAS funny, and the four of us got a good laugh—at my expense.

Hated the Nazis—Loved the Germans

There were so many wonderful, quirky things about living in Berlin. The German people are indeed war-like. I'll give you some examples:

Germans don't believe in waiting in line. Once Willie and I traveled to London with the Charlottenburg Sports Club of Berlin so they could compete in a track meet. My husband was a member, and I the only tagalong girl. We didn't speak much German, but our friend, Christian Zierfogel, also a member, translated for us. (Christian spent a lot of time in our apartment where we often discussed the existence of God. He was an atheist, and when we left Berlin, in a very moving gesture, he gave me his family Bible.) We literally walked all over London. The guys were runners, for heaven's sake, so no taxis for them. As we were moving about the city, they noticed the Brits "queuing up" for those tall, red double-decker buses. They found it amusing that they would line up single file and wait patiently. Germans NEVER did that. So those eighteen lanky runners decided it would be hilarious if they formed a "queue" at the bus stop, placing me right behind them, then wait for the unsuspecting Brits to line up behind me. When the bus came, the first half of the line (the runners) evaporated, leaving a dozen or so polite British citizens and me standing too far away from the bus to actually catch it. I confess I DID laugh when I realized what they had done.

To get on a German bus was like fighting a skirmish in a battle. Polite, small-town me, learned very quickly that I would be standing on the same street in Berlin for years if I didn't fight, elbows engaged, to get on that bus. And the bus drivers were always at war with the passengers. The stops and starts were abrupt. There was much yelling back and forth and always a contest between the impatient driver and the people as they attempted to get on or off. You could never get off fast enough for a German bus driver. One day after I exited a big bus, I turned to watch as an old man with a cane slowly descended the stairs. The bus driver pumped his hydraulic brakes in impatient simmering rage. As the old man stepped onto the pavement, the driver proceeded to close the doors—on the old man's cane! I looked just in time to see the old German man wresting his cane from the door, then beating the side of the bus with it as it drove away.

This was Germany. If you touched fruit or vegetables in a market, you got your hand slapped. If you got too close to a painting in an art gallery, you got a tongue-lashing from an employee. I should know. It happened to me.

But I honestly got used to it and saw the wonderful side of the German people. We lived in a large, three-story home with the family Mueller. Heir Mueller Senior lived on the first floor with his wife, Heir Mueller Junior with his wife and family on the second, and we, the Rioses, lived on top in the attic-like but cute, Bavarian/style apartment. We had no heat at night in the winter and no screens on the windows to stop mosquitoes in the hot summers. I would stay in bed as long as possible in the mornings, shivering under Army blankets until I could get the courage to run to a hot, steamy shower. After closing the bright red kitchen door and turning on the oven, I spent the rest of the winter day reading in my very cozy kitchen.

We learned to love the Muellers. It was from the Mueller Juniors I learned an important German phrase, *"Darf ich mir ihren Staubsauger borgen?"* Everyone traveling to Germany MUST learn this phrase: "May I borrow your vacuum cleaner?"

Heir Mueller Senior was a prisoner of war (POW) in America during the First World War. He loved Americans as did his son. He had a thick crop of white hair and always wore dark blue or black turtleneck sweaters. We made homemade ice cream for them in the backyard once and I baked a chocolate Bundt cake with a macaroon center that I was eager to share with Heir Mueller. I will never forget sitting at the table, watching him eat German-style, fork down, head close to the plate in one constant forking motion. Finishing cake and ice cream in record time, he set down his plate, looked at me, and announced *"Zu sus! Zu sus!"* (Too sweet!). Looking at his barren plate, I didn't believe him for a moment.

We were mysteriously robbed one night. We were only a few days from returning to the States temporarily so my husband could train with the U.S. Army Track Team in Colorado. (He ran in the Mexico City Olympic Games in 1968, but the draft interfered with his participation in the fateful '72 Munich Games.) That week I caught a severe case of mumps, no doubt from students I was teaching at the Berlin American schools. On the last night after a going-away party with friends, we returned home late to find the gate and doors ajar—our apartment robbed. Heir Mueller Junior got his gun and carefully went through our apartment. As we waited in the hallway, looking down over the winding staircase, I thought I was in a movie scene as I saw two German detectives slowly climbing those stairs, smoking pipes, and wearing long black leather coats—sort of a blend of Nazi and Sherlock Holmes chic.

The day we left Berlin, I cried as I hugged my German friend Heir Mueller in the hallway of his house. His kindness touched me so much that I remember him well to this day.

My Friend Morag

My journey as a follower of Christ I will leave to a later chapter, but let me just say, I came to Germany on the heels of a renewed faith. I was worried there might not be much Christian ministry in post-war Berlin, but within just a few weeks of arriving I found something life-changing.

I attended Bible study in the home of the Commandant of Spandau Prison, Colonel Eugene Bird and his wife, Donna. Spandau Prison was the residence of the last remaining Nazi war criminal, Deputy Führer Rudolf Hess. The Allies rotated every two weeks commanding Spandau. Colonel Bird was the American commandant. The Birds' home was designed by Hitler's architect, Albert Speer. Colonel Bird and Donna had recently become Christ-followers through the ministry of Dr. Norman Vincent Peale. Donna was injured in a surgery gone bad and was paralyzed from the waist down, but her radiant face and insightful comments on the Word of God were a blessing to us all. (Colonel Bird was later unceremoniously dismissed as commandant for developing a friendship with Hess and writing a book about his life while he was commandant.)

Our teacher was a Scottish lady from Edinburgh named Morag Surguine. She would sit in a chair as fifty women from all over the world sat on the floor at her feet and drank in her powerful verse-by-verse instruction.

"Speak, Lord, in the stillness, while we wait on Thee. And hush our hearts, in expectancy," Morag would pray each week in her lilting Scottish accent with the rrrrrolling r's. I sat on the floor next to her—always. She was ten years older than I, but we became dear friends—and eventually sisters. When thirty years later I moved to DC, alone and single, God gave me Morag who lived only minutes away.

I grew under Morag's teaching—solidified my faith and understanding of who it is I served and what I believed. Much like my love for country grew from actual knowledge of who she was and how she began, my love for God increased and my passion to serve Him was honed into shaping the kind of life I would choose to live.

My Bumbling Faith

Before that interim trip back home to the States, I prayed God would give me someone on that plane to share my faith in Christ with. My life had been so altered that I wanted a chance on the long flight to have that important conversation with anyone willing to listen.

I was sick with mumps as I boarded the plane with huge, swollen jowls, covered on either side by my long hair. (This was the prehistoric way we handled illness. We carried on.) I wondered how in the world I was going to manage the nearly twenty-four-hour journey, much less have that conversation. My assigned seat was not on the aisle, but one seat in, on the long middle row of the jumbo jet. Not a soul was assigned any of those empty seats down the long row to my left. Eventually an elderly German man carefully made his way down the aisle and sat in the one empty seat next to me. He spoke no English and I could only speak German in present tense. (This was going to be interesting.)

Somehow through rudimentary German and pointing, I managed to find out that very day was his seventy-seventh birthday! I notified the flight attendant who happily appeared with a little cake and two bottles of liquor! There was only one problem. (All of you

Catholics, Presbyterians, Methodists, and heathens will find this story humorous, but please hear the earnestness of a young Baptist girl who was raised to believe drinking of any kind was a sin.)

My seatmate was so thrilled and enthused to share his celebration with me. I, on the other hand, was mortified at the thought of drinking even a drop of liquor. At first I tried my broken German: "*Ich bin Eine Baptisten—und Ich Nicht Drinken Alcohol.*" (Don't learn that phrase—it doesn't exist in German.) Needless to say, he did not understand and when I politely shook my head "no," he began to get angry. Remember, Germans are an aggressive people.

I looked frantically for an interpreter. On the other side of the aisle, across from my seatmate was a Greek woman reading a book. Awkwardly bending around him to the right, across the aisle, I said "*Entschuldigung, bitte. Sprechen sie English?*" "Yes," she replied. Mump swollen, verbally fumbling me then tried to explain to her that I was a Christian and could not drink alcohol, and would she please explain this to my German friend? "That's ridiculous!" she barked at me in English. "I'm not telling him that!" and promptly went back to her book.

Still no passengers were in the aisle to my left, the Greek woman was mad at me on the right. Flummoxed, I looked behind my seatmate to discover a very pretty German girl about my age who did in fact speak English. I asked her to translate and, to my great relief, she sweetly obliged. My old German friend settled down as I struck up a conversation with my new friend behind me. Because of the nature of the translation, she asked me about my faith and I spent the next hour sharing with her—swollen jowls and all—the power of God to change lives.

Part of my learning curve in studying God's Word was to discover that some sins are cultural, not biblical, and that we don't measure our faith by the keeping of arbitrary rules, but by growing an inward holiness on those biblical principles that are nonnegotiable.

And Then There Was Music

I was a singer. I auditioned to sing with the U.S. Army Band in 1973. They were planning a production of *Fiddler on the Roof* and I won the part of Hodel. I was excited. But then suddenly the rights to *Fiddler* fell through and the producers announced we were instead going to perform *Golden Rainbow*, a musical set in Las Vegas. "I've Got to Be Me" was one of the songs from that musical made famous by stars, Steve Lawrence and Eydie Gormé. The costumes for the dancers and for me were being shipped to us from the Ice Capades.

Oh, brother. I froze. How could I don a skimpy little ostrich-feathered, sequined costume, and sing a song about who knows what? I was in Bible study, for heaven's sake, and the renewal of my faith didn't include this. Like the forbidden liquor on the plane, this was a challenge.

When the costumes arrived, they were indeed covered with sequins and ostrich feathers, but thankfully, my dress was modest. We performed *Golden Rainbow* in the beer tent of the German Octo-berfest fourteen nights straight. The band was wonderful, the guys so very much fun, and I enjoyed every minute of it.

One night as the dancers and I were changing in a special back-stage tent, we were abruptly visited by Colonel Gail Halverson, the Commander of Berlin Tempelhof Airport. Also known as the "Candy Bomber," he dropped candy out of his plane to hungry German children during the Berlin Airlift of 1948–49. Colonel Halverson entered our tent with his entourage without warning. With glowing accolades, he thanked us profusely for our performance as the dancers clutched at their partially clothed bodies. The entire time he was speaking, his gaze was fixed over our heads. It was hilarious. After he exited the tent, we burst out laughing. Obviously, no one warned him what was behind that curtain, but being the devout Mormon gentleman he was, he made the best of it.

As our performances were coming to a close, the director of the European Armed Forces Entertainment Division took me aside and told me if I wanted to go to New York, he would help me make connections. He thought I had great talent and could become famous. I was obviously flattered and humbled, but then . . . he offered to take me home that night.

Even at twenty-two I realized this was a fork in the road. How I loved to sing and perform, but did I want THAT kind of life? Did I want to be faithful to my husband, raise children, have a home, and honor God as I promised? The answer was "yes!" and with that, I consciously turned my back on the only professional singing I knew existed: the world of pop and musical theater. It could never be, I thought—with sorrow—but no regret.

My Heart's Desire

Even as a little girl playing with my dolls, I longed to be a mother. I babysat constantly and was mesmerized by every little person I saw. When we had been married for two years, the possibility of making that dream come true became my focus. But God seemed to have other plans. After trying many things, the gynecologist told me I had an infantile uterus and would never be able to conceive. For months I mourned and wept, observing how every American soldier's wife and every woman I knew for that matter seemed to be pregnant or already a mother. The grief was real and later helped me understand the pain of all the childless women God has brought into my life since.

After a few months more, God blessed me with a pregnancy. I was beyond excited. I couldn't sleep. I imagined every single step unfolding before me. One night I had a vivid dream I remember to this day. I was lying in my Army blanket–covered bed in our bedroom in Berlin when a little girl with long, dark hair came to my bedside. It was a poignant moment and I can still feel now what I felt then . . . the marvel at this small, beautiful child.

I arrived back in America in 1974 seven months pregnant. But that part of my story will come later.

Back to the Drawer . . .

But the drawer—the drawer I opened while I was in Berlin Brigade? Remember, the year was 1972 and back home, unbeknownst to me, a battle was also raging over the right for women to have an abortion.

Abortion was a dirty word when I was growing up. We knew in concept what it meant, but not really what it involved. So, when I opened that drawer looking for paper, and instead pulled up a color brochure, what caught my eye were the bodies of dismembered babies, descriptions of saline solution, and the brutal act of tearing babies apart limb by limb. Like a pornographic image men try to erase from their minds, that image burned in my heart so deeply, I could NEVER forget. And when at last I returned home to the United States, I found myself right in the middle of that incredible debate.

In just two short years, my life was set on a course I couldn't have imagined. The choices I made and things I learned, as disparate as they seemed to be, eventually merged into a life calling my young self could never have imagined.

> *Now to Him who is able to do exceedingly, abundantly*
> *above all that we could ask or think . . .* (Ephesians 3:20)

2

The Road to Berlin

Paved with White Privilege?

If you can visualize Henry Fonda as a poor Oklahoma farmer with his struggling family in John Steinbeck's *Grapes of Wrath*, you will have an idea of what old photos of my parents and grandparents resembled. My dad and mom were born and raised in Oklahoma during the drought of 1930–1936, known as the Dust Bowl.

During that horrible period, many families lost their farms, and children labored in the fields like adults to keep food on the table. I remember my mom telling me about how hobos would come to the back door begging for food and were never turned away. Whatever her family could spare was given freely to those wandering strangers.

My father, Wallace, and his twin brother, Walter, were born on October 12, 1920, to Fanny Bland and Benjamin Franklin Duckworth. Both grandparents made their way to Oklahoma Territory on covered wagons after the Civil War. My grandmother, Fanny, whose family migrated from Georgia, was a severe-looking woman who wore her long hair pulled back in an equally severe bun. Perhaps that stern look could be traced back to the Cherokee Indian part of our family. No one could tell a story—or pray for that matter—like my grandma. She wrote beautiful poetry and bore eleven children.

Grandma Duckworth was a great cook. On the Sabbath she allowed each of her nine living children to invite a friend for Sunday Dinner. The counters were lined with homemade pies. Once "Big Boy" and "Little Boy," as my father and his brother were known to the family, were challenged to eat as much pie as they could. My dad put down two and a half pecan pies and promptly got sick. He wasn't able to eat pecan pie for many years after.

The boys worked on the farm, and later my dad in a dairy, rising at 4 a.m. to milk the cows. But none of them ever went hungry. They slept several children to a bed by placing some at the head, feet down and the rest at the foot, feet up.

At Christmas one year, my grandfather, Benny, splurged and bought a bright red wagon for his mischievous twins. It was an extraordinary present for so humble a family, and Big Boy and Little Boy couldn't wait to take it for a spin. After Christmas dinner they ran outside and decided it would be great fun to tie it to a cow's tail. But the cow proceeded to bang the wagon from side to side in rebellion, breaking their brand-new wagon into pieces.

When times got tougher, my dad left home to work in the CCC, the Civilian Conservation Corps, to send money back home to the family. He was fifteen. The CCC was established during Roosevelt's New Deal for the purpose of building much-needed infrastructure and at the same time helping desperate Depression Era families survive.

My dad was a hard worker but had a mind of his own. The CCC Camps operated with military-like discipline. He went AWOL because they wouldn't let him leave to attend his older brother's wedding. He had by then worked to send back enough money for the family to buy a car. But when he returned home, wild man that he was, his parents wouldn't allow him to drive it. Instead, his kinder, gentler brother, "Little Boy" who stayed behind, got the wheels.

My mom's story is far sadder. Her family of six girls and two boys was smaller, but they were often hungry. My mom was about seven when, out of desperation, her father, Albert "Hap" Wilson, and his wife, Minnie, moved from farming the land in Oklahoma to San Luis Obispo in Northern California to pick fruit. Migrant workers, their story mirrored the one John Steinbeck later told in his famous novel, then movie, *The Grapes of Wrath*.

After Minnie delivered her ninth baby, she developed what was known then as "childbirth fever." For days she languished with fever as high as 107 degrees. A neighbor took the baby boy, Milton, to care for him. I will never forget my mother describing the scene as my grandfather gathered the children around a pot-belly stove to prepare them for their mother's death. But my grandmother survived, permanently damaged from the fever.

Minnie's family drove out in a Model T Ford across the often impassible rutted, dirt roads leading from Oklahoma to California, (a journey of about 1,566 miles each way on today's highways) to retrieve their beautiful daughter/sister and her virtually orphaned children. The family who took baby Milton begged to be allowed to keep him, but my grandfather refused to separate the family. He loaded his very loved but brain-injured wife and children into the already crowded car and made the long and difficult journey back to Oklahoma. (Milton, who my mom adored and cared for from the time he was a baby, later served in the Korean War. He was killed in a car accident shortly after he returned home.)

My mother and her older sister took on the care of the other children including the new baby. They scrubbed clothes on a washboard with soap they made from fat and lye. Clothes were sewn from empty fabric flour sacks, decorated with small flowers. The sisters worked the cotton fields by tying the little ones to the end of the row they were picking. The only time my mom could be a child was on rainy days when she would stay home and play with her dolls.

Still, they found ways to enjoy life. "Hap" Wilson, with a mop of hair and big dimples, was the best shot in the county. He supplemented the family income with mink furs. When radios became available, Grandpa bought one of the first. People from all over the county came to listen to the radio at the Wilsons' humble home. Beautiful and shapely, my mom and her five sisters lined up in a family photo looking like pin-up girls of the 1930s and '40s.

Years later at my parents' fiftieth wedding anniversary, with kids and grandkids, aunts and uncles gathered around the table, I asked my dad what he had seen in my mother. "Whee-whe-oh!" he wolf-whistled, outlining the figure of a shapely woman with his hands, as the room burst out laughing.

My mom loved to dance, sang at political events, played traveling softball and basketball, and was valedictorian of her class. Well, she *would* have been. In those days agrarian kids had to miss months of school to help on the farm. Mother was nineteen when she left high school, just before she was to graduate.

My dad on the other hand, never graduated from the eighth grade. He was always embarrassed by that, but life was hard and survival took precedence.

My mom and dad met at a rodeo and were married six weeks later. That might seem odd, but my dad wasn't one to wait for anything. Once, he arranged a time to pick up my mother for a date. Early that afternoon, she washed and pin-curled her hair, climbed up on the roof of the barn so the reflecting heat of the metal roof could dry it, and brought along her fiddle for good measure. When my famously impatient dad showed up two hours early, both of them got quite a surprise.

They were married by a justice of the peace with only my dad's parents as witnesses. After the wedding on May 29, 1940, they got in the car and drove 611 miles to Southern Illinois where an oil boom offered desperately needed work. Daddy had fifty dollars, an army blanket, and a car.

My dad became a roughneck in the oil fields. It was dangerous work, but it paid well. My parents lived in what were called "lease houses," small, framed temporary homes. But on December 7, 1941, everything changed as Pearl Harbor suffered a surprise attack and

President Franklin Delano Roosevelt declared war on Japan. My dad was twenty-one and was drafted almost immediately.

My mom, whose childhood was robbed by work, heartache, and the care of little brothers and sisters, did not want children. But as war loomed, she desperately wanted a part of my dad in case he never returned. On December 3, 1942 Mother gave birth to LaDonna Lois, my future big sister. Determined to spend as much time as possible with my dad, they followed him from camp to camp. At his final training base, Ft. Polk, Louisiana, they stayed in a lean-to tent attached to a trailer with no running water, plumbing, or heating. They had one hot plate and all three slept together on one cot.

When my father shipped out to England, it was the last time he was to see his wife or my sister for nearly three years.

My dad was in the Army Corp of Engineers in General Patton's Third Army. He helped build bridges for American combat troops to cross—sometimes in the midst of a battle. One nail-biting night while his unit was moving in small boats in the middle of a river, they were caught in the crossfire of Allies on one side, Germans on the other.

Another time, he was sitting in the back of a transport truck as suddenly he saw a German plane move toward them from behind to strafe the convoy. The men on either side of him were killed, one falling over on his lap.

He saw combat and death and the liberation of Auschwitz Concentration Camp. He once was court martialed for driving a big truck over a dozen British bicycles while drunk. He shot craps and won enough money to buy their first home. He was a rugged character, a man of his times. Good looking and tougher than nails, he came home to my mother and sister safe but restless.

I, a Post-War Baby Boomerette

On September 17, 1949, seven years after my sister's birth, I was born into a very different circumstance. The world was at peace, and there was work to be had. Possibilities were endless. Without formal education, my father found his way back into the oilfields. Hard work was his stock and trade. He was an ambitious man, determined to make the best of it.

My earliest memories are of a home in a tiny place with only a post office and a general store, known as Concord, Illinois. We lived in a house with a big porch in back. With no indoor plumbing, my mother bought me a little white porcelain potty with a red rim. I spent a lot of time on that porch gazing at the cow pasture where our very mean cow, Elsie, lived. Once my dad's twin, Uncle Walter, by then a successful businessman, came to visit from California with his family. When he braved the cow pasture to take my cousin Ramona to the outhouse, she got down from the three-seat bench, looked back at the hole and said, "Ew, Daddy. Look how much I did!"

My first glorious taste of classical music came from my mom's 78 rpm recording of Tchaikovsky's *Nutcracker Suite*. I listened, entranced over and over again, dancing on my toes so diligently that my visiting grandmother thought there was something wrong with me.

My mom didn't want us to grow up to be "country." She and Daddy took his gambling earnings to build a house, and moved us to the big city of Carmi, Illinois, population 6,000. I was only four but can still remember that home and the Saturday morning they delivered our first television. Imagine the awe of watching *Howdy Doody* and *Captain Kangaroo* for the first time!

But it was in that house that so much more changed for my family. My mom sewed all of our clothes, our coats, our drapes, and upholstered our couches. She spent her life in poverty, making do with flour sacks. When one morning she visited the fabric store and was able to buy several Simplicity Patterns with beautiful fabrics to make dresses, she was filled with overwhelming gratitude. My mom was not a Christ-follower at that time, but she knew about Him. She was driving the car home as the sunshine came through the windows, and in an act based on what she did know, thanked God from the bottom of her heart for the overwhelming blessings. It was right then that she dedicated her life to serving Him.

After that, each morning she got up early and dressed in her beautiful robe. I would always see her in a chair, reading her Bible. (I remember my mom at seventy-eight, sitting at a table, erect and noble like the lady she always was, teaching from that Bible to her Sunday school class.) Mother began to change, but my dad wasn't having it. For ten years she was one person and now she was another. He rebelled and recoiled. On Sunday nights while Mother was in church, he whisked me away to the drive-in movie. He called me his "buddy." This went on for a full two weeks until one night, sitting in an adjacent chair, I witnessed my mom and dad and a pastor on their knees in front of our couch. They were praying as my dad asked God for forgiveness for the many things he had done and committed his life to Jesus as well.

Daddy quit drinking and joined my mom at church. He joined the choir. Famously shy, his ears would turn red as he processed in his robe to the choir loft. They attended Bible study and Sunday school, and church. Soon my sister, LaDonna, wanted to follow Jesus too. Our family was transformed. My dad was thirty-seven, my mom thirty-six.

It was in that atmosphere of teaching, preaching, and music that a struggle began to develop deep inside me. The Bible is clear. Each person must confess their own sins and establish a relationship of their own with God through His Son, Jesus. Children are not grafted in—their personal sins not automatically forgiven based on the choices of their parents. Like the birth of a new baby, each spiritual birth is separate, beautiful, and unique.

My mom wasn't keen on children making this decision. What sins could an eight-year-old girl have committed? Sins are serious like murder and adultery and stealing. Sinning is something adults did, she thought. But Jesus showed us through His teaching that what the holiness of God requires is an issue of the inner man—an attitude of obedience in the heart. "Out of the abundance of the heart the mouth speaks" (Matthew 12:34).

I rebelled against God in other ways. When I felt the nudge of the Holy Spirit, I fought back. Whatever it was, I didn't want . . . THAT. I would be hearing hymns sung in church all around me, feeling God calling me to respond, but I didn't want that. We drove the long road to California that summer over Route 66. Sitting in the back seat next to my sister, I felt God calling me again, but I didn't want that. We arrived at my dad's twin brother's house where we visited Disneyland, Knott's Berry Farm, and the wonders of the California of the '50s, but God would not leave me alone. For more than a year I fought without the ability to verbalize or even understand what was happening.

One night my sister was gone for the night. We always slept together, cuddled first on one side, then the other. I was afraid of the dark. As the house got silent, I could hear the loud rumbling of my dad's snore, hour after hour. I couldn't sleep. Then whatever it was that had been visiting me relentlessly came again into that room where I was alone in the dark. Just like Jacob, I wrestled and fought. I didn't want to surrender my will, but finally in a moment of exhaustion, I prayed a profound prayer. "God, if You will just let me sleep, I will say 'yes!'" Immediately I fell into a deep slumber. I woke up early the next morning, jumped out of bed singing hymns, and ran into the kitchen to tell my mom I had become a Christian!

That strange but powerful experience never left me. I felt God's presence in varying degrees from that day on. I disobeyed at times, failed Him miserably on others, but never forgot what He did for me and how He called me no matter what mess I made of my life later.

"Preacher"

As corny as it sounds, I loved God as a little girl. I studied and memorized His Word and tried to persuade my friends in my own awkward way that Jesus loved them too! The neighborhood kids called me "Preacher." It wasn't a compliment.

One day my fourth-grade teacher, Miss Patton, was teaching us about the beginnings of the world. She explained that some scientists thought the earth was formed from particles thrown off from the sun. I was learning more each and every day about my new faith, and I wanted Miss Patton to understand too. I raised my hand and said, "Oh, no, Miss Patton! God created the earth!" From that day forward I was not her favorite student. Once, she said I broke the law by reading a note she wrote to my mother. In front of the entire class, she scolded me and said I could be arrested for reading other people's mail. I was mortified and hurt. But as I look back on it, I realize it was just a hint of what God had in store for me.

At my first pre-teen party I was shocked to see kids—KIDS!— "making out" all over the house. In my discomfort, I did the only thing I knew to do. I went to the piano and played hymns. You can imagine how popular I was.

My big sister, LaDonna, left for secretarial school when I was ten, and got married soon thereafter. She looked like and had the grace of a model, along with incredible gifts for typing and shorthand. She later became the executive assistant to CEOs of Chrysler, Panasonic, and later Florida Power. Because of our age difference, I spent most of my growing up years as an only child.

My mom got sick when I was twelve. She entered menopause, and the drop in estrogen caused sleeplessness and depression. It was normal, but my mom thought that like her mother, she was "losing her mind." My otherwise strong and steady mom begged me not to leave her in the mornings to go to school. She cried at every mealtime. My dad would leave the table to comfort her, as I sat there alone, stomach churning, staring at my plate.

My dad and I drove in a terrible snowstorm to take her to St. Louis to be hospitalized for shock treatments. I still remember holding my dad's big hand as we walked away from the facility. He was such a tall man, dressed in his long black overcoat and fedora, the tears streamed down his cheeks. I virtually lost my mom for the next few years. After she came home, she was quiet, distant, able to do the physical care, but she was absent emotionally.

Without the power and presence of God I don't know how people bear these things.

Behold, Politics!

Discussions at our dinner table were often political. My parents cared about national issues and stayed informed. I remember arguing with kids on the playground during the 1960 presidential election over Nixon vs. John F. Kennedy. Evangelical Christians were concerned about having a Catholic in the White House because of the potential influence of the Pope over his decisions.

Kennedy prevailed, however, and I became a great fan of his press conferences. He was so very clever. He made me laugh and he made me think. I was a fourteen-year-old freshman in high school, teasing my hair in the band room mirror when the principal came over the loud-speaker to announce that Kennedy had been shot. The entire school body was ushered into the auditorium where our giant, muscular principal, Mr. Jones, announced in his deep, dramatic voice, "The President . . . is dead."

That assassination was followed in short order by the assassination of his brother, Robert Kennedy, and then of Dr. Martin Luther King Jr. Cities were burning. There were marches in the streets. Black Americans were being fire-hosed by police and sometimes hung from tree limbs. But in spite of the horror of that, Dr. King personified the powerful but measured control of a godly man—not weak, just determined to deliver his people in the right way. I often visited my sister in Atlanta, Georgia, where I witnessed "Whites Only" drinking fountains. "Whites Only" diner counters. Separate bathrooms, space for blacks only at the back of the bus. It was wrong and I could not bear it.

Carmi was located in White County. It was so far south in Illinois it almost seceded during the Civil War. We had one black family. My parents used nouns that wouldn't be acceptable today, but in their time they were NOT racists, and I was not taught to think less of anyone for their skin color. I didn't even know about skin color. When I was little, my dad's sister took me to a grade school basketball game. As we sat in the bleachers, I found myself drawn to a black girl named Florence. We played with dolls, and were having a wonderful time, when my aunt grabbed me by the arm and filled my ear with words I had never heard. She WAS a racist, as were many of my dad's family. When we got home my parents affirmed my decision and scolded my aunt. Later in college, I got into a terrible argument with my dad's twin brother who was saying horrific things about blacks. I'm not proud of that moment. I should have done it more respectfully, but the injustice welled up inside me and I couldn't contain myself.

My sister in Atlanta was dating a Palestinian man who hated America. We watched the news each night as America's Anchor Man, Walter Cronkite, delivered the body bag count of American soldiers killed in the Vietnam War. Scene after scene of burning cities and riots filled the screen. (I learned years later that Walter Cronkite was no objective newsman. He was in fact an anti-war, pro-abortion activist who greatly contributed to the poisoned narrative of the war and the bogus inflated claims about coat-hanger abortions polluting the debate of the day.)

I was thirteen the first time when, as we were watching the news, I heard Ali Fouad shout, "Come on America, destroy yourself!" I was enraged, but totally incapable of verbally fighting back with him. He was a man and I a mere child. But I never forgot that.

I was just coming off the heels of my mom's illness when I entered high school at fourteen. I thought I was ugly and fat and certainly not hip like the other girls. I loved cheerleading, knew every move, every cheer, and practiced incessantly in front of the television. But when the time came to audition, I didn't think wearing a short skirt and dancing like that was something God would want me to do. The dilemma was solved for me when I learned you couldn't be a cheerleader and a student council member, and I wanted to be on student council!

As I stood in line to give my first campaign speech, I nervously noticed my competitors actually had things written out. *You mean I can't just talk?* I panicked to myself. Quickly I conjured up a few sentences, but in my nervousness confusingly merged them into one silly finale. ". . . and if you ALL vote for me, I'm sure I'll get it!" The crowd roared with laughter. I didn't even realize what I said. Imagine my surprise when I was elected! During the next four years I managed concession stands, revamped homecoming, and ran school elections.

A Beauty . . . Not

I never thought I was pretty. I wasn't raised in a home that treated my sister or me like a princess. My dad taught me to be brave, not beautiful. He made me do things I didn't have courage to do, like driving his stick shift truck over the rough, divided boards of Possum Bridge when I could barely reach the pedals. Or at ten driving his boat alone down the center of creepy, smelly, Old River, to dock it for the fall. I could see my dad occasionally through the trees, driving his truck on the service road thirty feet above the river. But when I hit a trout line, the engine blew and like Peter walking on the water, my heart sank. Eventually my dad shouted from the shore to use the oar—THE OAR.

I was never told I was pretty. I was told I talked too much and too loudly and I was going to be fat like Robert (a very fat little friend). I knew my parents loved me, but they were not ones for flattery or silliness. They insisted on honesty and taking responsibility for my actions, but looks were never emphasized. My mom dressed us all beautifully, so appearance was important, but not the centerpiece of achievement.

So, imagine my surprise in high school when ballots were cast for homecoming queen. I was overseeing the counters when the tabulation showed I had been nominated. It took my breath away as I silently thanked God for such a wonderful, unexpected gift.

Home from college for the summer when I was nineteen, I was arm-twisted into entering the Miss White County Fair competition.

Me? Parade on stage in a gown? In a bathing suit no less—to be judged on my beauty. That was unfathomable to me. There wasn't even a talent division in the contest which might have made more sense. Nevertheless, I reluctantly entered.

I had spent the summer working at the Jack & Jill Dress Shop. What fun. Bobbie Brooks was one of my favorite manufacturers, so picture me opening every fresh, new box of the latest fashions. I ended the summer in significant debt. But back to the beauty contest . . .

I made one of the five finalists which threw me into the "hand in the glass bowl" question segment. When the announcer read my question dramatically, "WHAT would you do . . . if you had a million dollars?!!!" I quickly replied, "Pay off my bill at the Jack & Jill Dress Shop." The crowd roared. I didn't win the contest, but I did get a taste of my future!

I was nominated for more queen courts in high school and college, but was, always in my heart and mind, defined by my dad's view of me. Years later, feeling very insecure after my divorce, I vulnerably asked my dad, "Am I pretty?" "You wouldn't win any beauty contests," he replied. Ouch.

And then about ten years after that, when he was in his eighties, one morning we were sitting at the kitchen table when for some reason my dad, out of the blue and in passing, commented that I was pretty. Involuntarily, I burst out crying and said, "Daddy, do you know that that's the first time in my life you've ever said that to me?" The grieved look on his face told me he had no idea how that omission affected me through the years.

For the rest of his life, he complimented my work, my accomplishments, and my appearance.

In his last ten years, he excitedly gathered the residents of his nursing home to watch his daughter's frequent appearances on television. And I was so pleased to give him that gift.

Frankly, I was thankful to have been raised to think less of myself than maybe was warranted. Even the simplest achievements and accolades are much sweeter when they surprise you. My mom poured her heart into building my self-esteem based on the biblical principle that we should have an accurate view of ourselves, not an underinflated or overinflated one.

> *I say to every one of you: Do not think of yourself more*
> *highly than you ought to think, but rather think of yourself*
> *with sober judgment.* (Romans 12:3 NIV)

Charles Alexander Gilpin the Third

I loved journalism in high school. One of my poems appeared on the pages of our newspaper, *The Bulldog Barks*. It was inspired by a very hot, boring afternoon, as our history teacher droned on about . . . history.

> *Bee is buzzing 'round the room.*
> *History teacher grabs a broom.*
> *Tries to swat it while it flies*
> *His demand, the bee denies.*
> *Dashing madly 'tween the rows,*
> *Students duck as tension grows.*
>
> *Then the bee makes his retreat . . .*
> *To the rear to meet defeat.*
> *Greeted by an open text,*
> *With history dates, he now is mixed.*
>
> *The moral here is plain to see.*
> *When history's boring, find a bee!*

One of my famous, carefully crafted headlines appeared on the sports page. The Carmi Bulldogs were playing the Bridgeport Bulldogs in basketball. The headline? "A Bulldog Victory Is Certain Tonight!"

We always sat in alphabetical order and Charles Alexander Gilpin the Third sat behind Sandra Duckworth—me. Chuck was the smartest kid in our class. A latecomer to Carmi, he was hilarious and fun, but was, by his own definition an atheist. I loved Chuck. We had a great time in journalism class.

I wanted Chuck to know about Jesus. I cared about him and tried in my own inartful way to paint a picture of how God could so use his many gifts and talents, but Chuck wasn't having it. As we parted our senior year, he wrote in my yearbook, "Best of Luck to Sandra Duck."

Later in college Chuck wrote me a long letter about how he met some Christians at his school in Florida and become a committed Christian. Such news! Then in the next letter I received from him, also in college, he had been diagnosed with terminal cancer. Oh, Lord Jesus. What a thing to endure.

What Anti-Semitism?

Beth Brickman was my best friend. She was funny and clever. The morning of a big test, I would always ask her if she studied. And she would always say, "No! But I read the BEST book!" She was marvelous at telling stories, so I would listen chapter and verse as we made our way to class. Later, after failing out of college, Beth went back to school as a young mother. Majoring in literature, she made straight As and became a beloved teacher.

You might say, together we were a bit mischievous. Eager to start driving, we hopped on her dad's riding mower one afternoon. I clung on from behind as Beth lost control and jumped off. I struggled to pull myself up to the seat to stop the thing before it ran over her mom's beautiful flowers. I didn't succeed.

Beth was a terrible driver. She turned sixteen first and, incredibly, my dad let us take our family car to drag main. (That's what small town teens did in the '60s. We rounded the Dairy Queen then the Dog and Suds and back again. We spent endless hours honking and waving at dark windshields whose driver we recognized by the grill of the car.) That night we had only been gone about ten minutes when Beth drove our car into a ditch.

Shortly afterward, she wrecked her dad's brand-new Lincoln Continental right in front of her house. And speaking of that big two-story brick house, we walked there every day after high school to make fudge or popcorn and dance to the Beatles. Her home became mine as her family always welcomed me. Her dad was our Jewish dentist. "Attilla the Hun," Beth and I called him. Mildred, her mom, was "Little Mil." They had a Great Dane named Roy and a little dog named "Teenie." Dr. Brickman had a fierce temper and a powerful voice. When fighting with his wife you could hear it booming all over the house, "Mildred!!" But he was tender-hearted. He loved Beth so much and he loved me too as her friend. Once when a boy broke my heart, I was sitting in their living room crying. Doctor Brickman went to the front coat closet, pulled out hats from China, Mexico, and all over the world. He donned each and did a corresponding dance wearing each of them prancing through the room, just to cheer me up. It worked.

Once we made funny mouth noises at the table as a family, laughing uproariously. It was a big contrast to my home where work was the ethic and fun hard to find. I could not sit on my bed or decorate my room. When it was time to study, my mom would run to the linen closet and get a white sheet, which she would spread on the couch for me to sit and place my books on. Everything my parents owned, they treasured, and Mother liked things clean! On the rare occasion Beth and I would come to my home after school, my mom, sweet but not "cool," would pull up a chair next to us as we talked. We had one phone in a nook in the dining room. If my boyfriend called, I would lie in the floor, faced tucked as closely as possible to the baseboard, as my parents sat silently in the adjacent kitchen listening to every word.

Beth, by contrast, had a great upstairs bedroom with twin beds. We would chatter into the night, falling to sleep in laughter and great shared secrets. The Brickmans took me to their cottage at Sandy Run where I learned to water-ski. Once our principal, Mr. Jones, was visiting them. He was standing in the kitchen next to "Little Mil" when Beth bent over to feed Teenie, and her bathing suit top fell off. Mortified, we ran to the bathroom and stifled our laughter.

How much I loved the Brickmans. But I wanted to tell them Jesus was a Jew and they were the ones He died for first. When I tried to talk to Beth, I was earnest but bumbling. She agreed to go to church with me once, but years later told me she was so upset by it, she spent all night discussing it with her dad. Her dad. I wanted this man I so loved to understand that Jesus had died especially for the Jewish people and for Him too. Awkwardly and in much prayer, I finally penned a long letter, after I was married, laying out the gospel message and imploring them to consider that they too needed this Savior.

Many years later, when I was home visiting from some far-away place, we sat down to dinner and for the first time ever, Dr. Brickman stunningly asked me to pray. I was so humbled. Did I reach him in some way? Only in heaven will I ever know.

Disobedience

When I was a senior in high school I fell in love with a boy a lot like my dad who wasn't good for me. He was aggressive physically and, in my innocence, I didn't even know what I was fighting. But I fought. I tried to talk to my mom, but she didn't want to hear it. I later learned this area of her life was damaged and unhealthy, and she just wasn't able to help. Denial was her response. I was tormented by the relationship. I lost weight. I was 5'7" and 103 lbs. when I graduated my senior year.

When it came time to choose a college, I decided to go far away—to Oklahoma Baptist University.

Four Lost Years

Before me, no one in my family attended college. My great ambition was to go for at least one year. I was fearful I would flunk out. My parents drove me to Shawnee, Oklahoma, with a U-Haul trailer full of beautiful clothes and unloaded me as quickly as possible. Up to the second floor of Kerr Dorm, into my tiny room with two bunks, and a twin bed, it all went. True to form, my impatient dad couldn't wait to leave. As we stood by the car, he said to me, "Sandra Kaye, we've taught you everything we know. If you don't know how to behave now, there's nothing we can do." And with that, they drove off. I must admit it was a sobering good-bye. But with that simple sentence, Daddy handed me the responsibility for my own life. It had its effect.

I knew no one. I knew nothing about credits or majors. So as I waited in line to register in the outdoor plaza, I had no idea what to expect. As I got to the table the efficient registrar asked me truncated questions like, "Name? Dorm? Major?" "Major—what does that mean?" I asked. Impatiently he gave me examples. My mind was whirling. I was good in math—should it be math? I loved music—but that's too easy, I thought. I loved to read—"English!" I blurted out.

After the shock of being thrown into a new world, I adapted quickly. I made great friends and learned to play cards, which got me into a great deal of trouble for making early morning classes. I pledged a social club (sorority) and brought my mischievousness with me. I played pranks and had a ball. Once, we decorated the barren underground basement of the chapel like a riverboat, covered tables in roll-out gambling boards, painted Coke bottle tops red, white, and blue, and gave participants snacks and soft drinks for their winnings. Dealers wore satin garters, and the stage was a steady stream of entertainment including a chorus line and a girl performing the sultry classic, "Blues in the Night"—me.

I was elected president of Gamma Phi Delta, performed and traveled with the Bison Glee Club, and—after several changes in my major—graduated with a major in voice and a minor in piano. Music wasn't math or English, but it was more rigorous than I ever dreamed. And it was what I loved.

I sang the mysteriously worded "Louie, Louie" in a mini skirt on stage in a talent review. As you might have guessed, I was no longer the same girl, eager to please God I once was. I was ashamed of my past behavior and didn't think God could ever forgive me, so I stopped attending church. I didn't stop loving God or remembering His call; I just didn't think I would ever be worthy of it again.

It was in that spiritual state I met Willie Rios. Dark and handsome, Willie was a charmer. He was Oklahoma champion in the mile, famous for his track and field accomplishments. Famous also for his female conquests. He fascinated me. We had a stormy relationship the four years we were at OBU, then married two weeks after graduation in June of 1971.

We were married in Carmi on a very hot day in June. My famously thrifty dad was very concerned about costs, so I hired a local seamstress from the Baptist Children's Home to make a dress. The final product looked nothing like the *Brides* magazine dress I gave her as a template, but it only cost $50. I chose inexpensive floral fabric for my bridesmaids' dresses which she also made for a whopping $15. My brother-in-law took the pictures. You can see he took the pictures. As we were leaving church for the honeymoon, it was apparent my new husband had no money, so my dad slipped him a fifty-dollar bill.

We spent our honeymoon in St. Louis by the arch. My groom was eager to wash off any indication of marriage from the decorations on our car, so he rose early to clean it. I really don't think he ever wanted to be married, but that's how it all began.

Thirty-five dollars a month was the rent my father charged for us to live in a second floor, two-room apartment he owned. When I was in seventh grade, after taking his savings from working seven days a week in the oil fields, my father bought and established, "Duckworth's Standard Station." Full service—every cute boy in my high school worked there at one time.

Years later at my fiftieth high school reunion, not a few of them told my husband, Bruce, how afraid they were of my dad. (More about Bruce in chapter 12.) They used to joke how my dad ran a service station bell across our driveway that rang inside the house when they brought me home. Daddy then expanded his business to car washes and rental property. Mother worked by his side, keeping the books and cleaning the apartments. It was an incredible thing to see my mom and dad's work ethic.

Willie was without a job, waiting to be drafted, so our pastor decided to make him youth director of our church. Little did he know, neither of our hearts were qualified for that kind of service.

At the end of the summer, we became house parents at the Baptist Children's Home. There were sixteen kids ranging from eight to sixteen years of age. Five days a week we had a cook, but on the other two, it was my job. I was twenty-one and hardly cooked anything in my entire life, but I learned.

What impacted me most was the knowledge that these kids had no one but me to love and care for them. I put them to bed at night, kissed them, and tried my best for them. It was overwhelmingly sad to me how the little I could offer was all they had.

When Willie went off to basic training, I moved back home with my parents. In the same spirit of asking Willie to be youth director, I was asked to teach a Sunday school class of twelve-year-old girls. But the girl who grew up in that church, participated in Bible sword drills, singing and playing hymns was not the same. How could I tell them? How could I explain this to my mother?

I couldn't. Begrudgingly I said "yes." The first lesson was on the tenth chapter of the book of Acts. As I cracked open my neglected Bible and began to read, the words literally leapt off the page at me. In the same bed where I first said yes to Jesus, I spread out every commentary, every translation I could find and began to devour God's Word.

For the first time in my life, I understood forgiveness and grace. I confessed my sins and wept. The burden was lifted, and God granted me what He offers everyone who will come, "Morning by morning . . . new mercies." A fresh start—a new filling of the Holy Spirit. I could not stop.

"I never want to be apart from You again, Father. I'll do whatever You ask. I'll go wherever You want me to go, but I can't live without You!"

It was with that prayer burning in my heart, I took off for Berlin, Germany.

3

Sasha Girl

My dad, the twin, was ecstatic when an Army obstetrician in Berlin suggested I might be pregnant with twins. I, on the other hand, was not. Daddy's bubble sadly burst on that first visit to an American doctor, but I had a bit of a shock myself. I was thrilled to be having a baby but knew nothing about actually having one. In the back seat of my parents' car, I opened the illustrated pamphlet on childbirth and panicked. I looked at the pictures, then at my stomach, then back at the pictures, and realized it was too late to turn back. Such fear came over me I cried out silently, *Dear God, please. Help me!* And in that moment, an inexplicable peace filled me that carried me through a labor worthy of my fears.

In the early morning hours of July 17, 1974, I awoke to the strange sound and sensation only a mother knows of water breaking. My sister's son, Cris, who was like a little brother to me, was sleeping on the floor next to my bed. I went to the bathroom, and looking in the mirror, felt incredible joy and anticipation. I began to sing a song I heard sung in our church when I was a little girl, "My Lord Is Near Me All the Time."

In the early morning darkness, the four of us climbed into the car and headed to Evansville, Indiana, sixty miles away. As I looked up to the beautiful, clear sky, there was a sliver of a new moon with a bright morning star perched on top. Filled with the presence of God, I sang that song all the way to the hospital.

My labor was progressing slowly, so Daddy returned home to get in a day's work. Despite his own enterprises, he was working part-time for Sears, installing heating and air conditioning. When the call came that my labor had intensified and the baby would likely be born before noon, the dispatcher had to explain to my mother that "Mr. Duckworth is in an attic doing the duct work." It was great timing! And speaking of timing, we both had a good laugh between contractions.

Back at the hospital, my sweet mom stayed by my bedside. As the labor progressed, and the pain worsened, she read Scripture and held my hand. When my dad was ushered back into the room, the miserable look on his face as he saw his baby daughter in pain, caused me to say, "Daddy, get out of here. I'll be okay." But I wasn't okay. Long, difficult labors ran in the family—my sister, my mother, her sisters. The only information my mother provided me on childbirth was, "Sandra Kaye, childbirth is the next thing to death." I wasn't disappointed, then, in mine.

My baby was supposed to arrive before noon. I was fully dilated. You could see the baby's head crowning, but she would not come. We could hear the baby's heartbeat thump slowly, then race and then stop repeatedly through the heart monitor. Nurses came and went. One young nurse sat in a chair chewing gum with her feet on my bed, reading the newspaper. But the doctor never visited. I gripped the bedrails—probably bent the bed rails—vomited bile, but still no baby. Finally, as the day was ending, an older nurse came into the room and told me the doctor was going to give me a spinal and use forceps. This very kind nurse had given birth to six children herself. As they wheeled me to the delivery room, I asked plaintively, "Will there be any more pain?" She took my hand and said, "Honey. It will be just like heaven." And it was. The block was administered, the pain left, and as I was giving birth, I jabbered like an elated magpie.

Sasha, named after Dr. Zhivago's little boy in the famous movie, was born just before 9 p.m. "Sasha" was a derivative of Alexandra—the same root as my name, Sandra. It meant "Helper of Mankind." Weighing in at 7 lbs., 13 oz., my Sasha had a beautiful head of dark hair and a scrunched-up face and head to match her difficulties coming into this world.

I wanted to call Willie in Germany to give him the news and share the incredible details, but he could not be found. Finally, my call was returned, but it was late at night in Berlin and he was less enthused by the news than I had hoped.

I developed a severe headache from the spinal tap. So severe, I could only lie flat on my back without a pillow. The only chairs for visitors were at the foot of the bed, so when my milk came in on the second day, I remember how funny it was to have to crook my head to the left and look down and around the huge mounds that had once been my breasts.

Sasha had difficulty nursing. Perhaps this was the first sign of trouble, but how was I to know? Dr. Davis came in to see me and to tell me he was going out of town. During the conversation, out of the blue, he said, "I'm sorry." Not understanding, I jumped in to say something like, "It's not your fault—labors are difficult." Again, he repeated, "I'm sorry." No context. No explanation. It seemed strange to me at the time, but I had no idea what the next days and months would bring.

Sasha was two weeks old when Willie came home from Germany. Only a few months after that, he entered graduate school at Eastern Illinois University in Charleston, Illinois. It was October of 1974. I was in our apartment in married student housing, burping Sasha on my shoulder when her little body stiffened and began to jerk violently. A few minutes later it happened again—then again—and again. She had twelve grand mal seizures that first day.

We rushed her to the emergency room numerous times that day, but no doctor was available. The hospital administrator, holding Sasha,

instead, told me how beautiful she was, and suggested she had probably choked on something. Later in the afternoon, I was conducting a
choir rehearsal at the Methodist church behind our apartment when
Willie appeared frantically at the door with Sasha in his arms, urging
me to come. On that last trip to emergency, still without a doctor, an
ambulance attendant advised us to drive ten miles to nearby Mattoon
where there was a pediatrician.

Dr. Onkar Sharma was a kind, compassionate man who was a
perfect first doctor for so injured a child. He placed her on medi-
cation, but for the next few months the seizures just wouldn't stop.
At five months, Dr. Sharma threw a "Hail Mary," and conducted a
last resort test that required shaving off her beautiful hair. If anything brought home the severity of the situation, that did. I cried
as I held her limp little body in my arms, thinking to myself, *I've
lost my baby.*

A year passed. I conducted a children's choir, made great friends,
and taught Bible study in the home of the future governor of Illinois,
Jim Edgar, and his wife, Brenda, with Sasha lying on a palette next to
me. I prayed and I prayed, believing God could still heal my baby, but
Sasha's condition only worsened.

Still there were wonderful moments. Her face and head sorted
out and she was beautiful. She had long fingers like my mom, dark
black hair like her dad. I adored her, held her, sang to her. But that
first bath. That was really a moment. I studied the baby book carefully,
laid out all the equipment, the Q-tips, cotton balls, baby wash cloth,
hooded soft towel, lotion, blah, blah, blah. Sasha began to cry—well,
scream. As I held her in my arms, bent over the baby book reading its
"twelve steps to bathing an infant," my otherwise soft-spoken mother,
grabbed the book from my hands, and barked, "Close that book and
bathe that baby!" That phrase worked wonderfully years later when in
the morning just before delivering a breakfast speech, the entire thing
disappeared from my computer. With no time to write another, my
mom's words came back to me, "close that book and bathe that baby!"

I got up without any notes and delivered probably one of my finest speeches ever.

I was visiting my parents and my big sis who flew home to Carmi in July of 1975. It was Sasha's first birthday. Willie was in Puerto Rico competing in a race when Sasha began seizing violently. It was the worst ever—and they would not stop. As she turned blue, I tried giving her CPR. Frantically, we jumped in the car to take her to Carmi's tiny hospital. In the emergency room, my dad took her from me and walked the floor as she cried incessantly. My big tough dad loved Sasha. He would hold her in his arms for hours as she slept. For years he did that. The first time I took her to church, he was so eager to show her off, at the end of the final prayer of the service, I opened my eyes to see him standing next to me. Only moments before, when I closed my eyes to pray, he was sitting in the choir loft, fully robed. He wrested her from my arms and whisked her away joyfully to introduce her to everyone.

On that horrible night in the hospital, as my dad walked with Sasha, something in me snapped. For the first time in a year, I felt nothing. I didn't care that she was crying, and I didn't have any interest in holding her. I was in a daze. Some call it shock.

My mom, dad, sister, and I were ushered into the room that was to be Sasha's. As we sat there in stunned silence, like muscle memory, I said, "We have to pray." No one seemed able to pray, so I bowed my head, and without feeling of any kind, labored for sincere words. For a year I begged God for Sasha's healing. I repeatedly emptied my eyes of tears. We prayed for her, over her, anointed her head with oil, called for the elders to pray, but nothing happened.

My prayer then, was this, "Lord, I don't understand. But I trust You." That was it. All that I could manage. It was a short prayer, but it changed my life.

I grew up hearing Bible verses telling us if we believed in faith, God would hear our prayers. If two or more agreed on a request, He would grant it. If someone was sick, the elders were to pray over him/

her, anointing them with oil and they would be healed. Television pastors have made millions preaching only this half-version of what is true about faith. Countless numbers of people have lost faith when their prayers have not been answered. Some have become angry atheists, others, cynics. Still others just quietly go through the motions of faith in God with no hope or real fervor.

With the birth of Sasha, I was thrown into a terribly quandary. My mother and I searched the Scriptures to understand how this could possibly be happening. We believed, and we prayed. I had repeatedly told God my life was His. I would go anywhere—do anything— I never wanted to be apart from Him. But this?

I couldn't sing without crying. I couldn't go a day without crying. I was depressed and grieving, unable to sleep. What happened to all those promises in Scripture?

As I searched the Scripture for answers, I noticed a few passages not emphasized by pastors or teachers as I was growing up. There was Job who lost everything. His children were wiped out in a tornado, his considerable wealth gone in a flash. Boils broke out all over his body, and as he sat in the rubble, trying to get relief from the itching, scratching his body with bits of broken pottery, he declared, "Though He slay me, yet will I trust Him" (Job 13:15).

When Shadrach, Meshach, and Abed-Nego refused to bow to the gods of the Babylonian king, they were thrown into a fiery furnace. That famous Bible story emphasizes how they were miraculously delivered, but what I noticed for the first time was their emphatic declaration BEFORE that deliverance, "Our God is able to save us from this furnace! But if He doesn't, we STILL won't serve your gods!" (see Daniel 3).

Hebrews 11 lists the champions of faith in the Old Testament: Abraham, Moses, Isaac, Jacob, Joseph, and many other heroes of the faith are mentioned. But if you complete the chapter, there is this sentence: "And all these, having obtained a good testimony through faith, did not receive the promise" (v. 39). Wait a minute—so in their lifetimes, most of those faith warriors never actually saw the fruition of what was promised! Nevertheless, they believed.

There was no "name it and claim it" expectation in the faith of Old Testament heroes. No expectation of wealth or health in the New Testament disciples. All died brutal deaths except for one. There were times when God healed or raised the dead, but it was NEVER an expectation or a requirement for real faith.

Then why believe in and serve Him? Because He is the one, true God. He is the God of all Truth. Because He is the Creator of all things. Because He looked down on us with incredible love and compassion, and realized we needed help. He didn't even spare His own Son but allowed Him to be brutally murdered as a payment for our sin. Why wouldn't you trust a God like that? There is more to the story than our lives. We are but an infinitesimal, yet significant part of a much bigger story playing out in the universe which will one day culminate in the redemption of everything. Our heartaches, sorrows, bitter disappointments will go into the mix of God's call on our lives. God wastes nothing. When He doesn't answer our sometimes-desperate prayers, He is not callous and uncaring, He simply has something incomprehensibly greater in mind.

But it took me years to figure that out—at least the twenty my precious Sasha was home with me. When she was eight years old, deeply in sleep in her room as a result of multiple seizures I sat in my living room and wrote "Sasha's Song," which became the title song of my first record album. But more about that part of my life later.

Verse I
I gave you life one summer day. Such joy had never come
    my way
But quickly sorrow came to stay beside us.
My grief was great, my soul was stirred
With questions, doubts and empty words
Of platitudes and promises long treasured.

Would God sustain us through the years
Of heartache, disappointment, tears?
And show to us His strength through fears and failure?

Verse II
My fragile child, so weak, so frail, I bend to softly kiss your
*   pale,*
but silken cheeks, to make you feel my loving.
I know that in that fragile form, beats heart, thinks mind,
*   lives soul.*
In warm and tender ways,
The truth to me is showing
How God sustains us through the years, of heartache,
*   disappointment, tears.*
And shows to us His strength through fears and failure.

BRIDGE
"I may not walk, or run or play, or touch your hand to
*   softly say,*
'I love you, Mommy,' but some day when we're in heaven
I'll fly so free, so whole, that we,
Can spend our time eternally
Embracing, loving, joyfully
Remembering . . . remembering . . . "
How God sustained us through the years, of heartache,
*   disappointment, tears.*
And showed to us His strength through fears and failures!

Seven years earlier, on that traumatic first birthday, we took Sasha to St. Louis Children's Hospital in a wailing ambulance, my dad burning pavement behind us. I sat next to the driver, a great guy named Mark I went to high school with. What a nice gift. As we jetted over the pre-interstate, narrow road, for two hours, cars and trucks parted like the Red Sea, except for one lonely little car. Oblivious to the loud siren and flashing lights of the ambulance towering over him, like Old Mr. Magoo of cartoon fame, the driver stayed his slow course. Mark shouted dramatically into a tiny microphone, "Hey you, in the blue Volkswagen! Move over!" It sounded like the voice of God. The driver swerved off the lane in a manner that made me think indeed he thought it was the voice of God, as Mark and I shared a welcome moment of laughter.

The neurology ward at Children's Hospital was a place for the worst of the worst. Tragedy was all around us, and I was not prepared to think Sasha actually belonged there. But I learned some valuable lessons that would alter my view. Lori was a little five-year-old girl who pranced around the ward on her tiptoes. She frequented the room in her pink cotton pajamas where Sasha's crib sat in the window and sweetly chatted. Lori was a child with hydrocephalus. Eyes wide apart, she had a huge head, deformed hands and feet, and spoke through a tracheotomy. But Lori knew nothing of that. What anyone could see if they had eyes to see it, was an adorable, feminine, cheerful little girl who brightened our days.

"Man looks at the outward appearance, but the LORD looks at the heart." That verse in 1 Samuel 16:7 took on new meaning for me as my world and my perspective shifted to God's view.

We took Sasha to Mayo Clinic in Rochester, Minnesota. I had a consultation with doctors in Pittsburgh, and later UCLA and Beverly Hills. My dad said he would spend every penny he had to find help for her, but there was none to be had.

Our baby girl was greatly damaged. But in spite of that, I remained hopeful.

California Dreaming

As Willie was nearing the end of the Master's program at EIU, his heart and mind turned once again to the Olympic Games. Rather than find a job, he wanted to go to California to train with the Santa

Monica Track Club for the '76 Summer Games in Munich, Germany. The Santa Monica Track Club would become the training center for future nine–Olympic gold medal winner, Carl Lewis. Actor Bruce Dern trained there as well as some of the best track and field athletes in the country.

We left Carmi in a 1974 Oldsmobile Cutlass my dad bought us, expecting to be paid back. We had $500, and a very sick baby. My parents were grief-stricken as we drove out of the driveway to begin the long journey.

Willie assured me the track club would secure us a job and a place to live, but neither of those things happened. Embarrassingly to me, we moved in with my dad's sister and family for six weeks. Willie found a job at minimum wage in a print shop as I searched the papers and drove the streets of Los Angeles, desperately looking for an apartment. It was hard, lonely, and humbling. We couldn't afford much, and landlords did not want children—even little silent, immobile ones.

I finally found a corner apartment twenty blocks from the ocean in Santa Monica. It was a building filled with elderly black widows, not spiders. The apartment manager, Ronnie, was not happy about a white couple living in their midst and no matter how kind I was, she did not return the favor.

Taking pity on us, one of the men affiliated with the club, sent us to a warehouse of discarded furniture. It was a motley collection, but it worked! One blue tufted velvet boudoir chair, faded but beautiful, once belonged to Amanda Blake, Miss Kitty, one of the stars of the television classic *Gunsmoke*.

I managed to scrape together enough money to find some bright yellow paint to cheer Sasha's old used crib. In between coats, I laid the paint can and brushes on the stoop in the back alley. Ronnie threw them all away, and I cried. I couldn't afford to buy more, and somewhere down in her heart, I think Ronnie felt badly.

I found a grand piano quite unexpectedly at a garage sale. I called my dad and told him if he could loan me $500, I would take on piano students and pay him back. He agreed and the piano was placed between the large corner windows of our living room. I spent long hours there and became the accompanist for a string quartet who brought their instruments and filled the place with Rachmaninoff. It was wonderful.

I enrolled Sasha at UCLA. That is, in a special program for young disabled children. Barbara Bach, that beautiful Bond Girl of *The Spy Who Loved Me*, and her famous husband, Ringo Starr, had a little boy in that program. She would come to parent meetings in jeans and a shirt like any other concerned mom. It was encouraging to see people work with our kids and give us some glimmer of hope that progress could be made.

The program was in a large building on the main campus with very wide, long corridors. One day while standing near an entrance, I looked down the long hallway to see a small boy without arms or legs propelling himself down the corridor with his head and trunk, talking all the way.

I was jolted to the core. But then I remembered again God's perspective of looking on the heart and not the appearance. I was learning new lessons at every point on this journey.

We found a small church nearby and began making new friends. The couple we really enjoyed were Paul and Elizabeth Turner, but there was one obstacle. Their daughter, Kathy, only a month older than Sasha, was a normal fifteen-month-old. She was walking, talking, and generally delightful, while Sasha could only lie helpless and virtually silent in a crib. Liz was a musician, Paul a hilariously clever young attorney. I loved their company but wondered if my heart could bear constant reminders of Sasha's limitations. I prayed and asked God to help me. And with full knowledge of the implications, felt Him prompting me to walk toward the sorrow, not away from it. So, I did.

Paul and Elizabeth became incredible friends to me, and Kathy and Sasha became separate little girls we could enjoy in their own unique ways. I made Elizabeth promise NOT to withhold sharing the joy of Kathy's accomplishments with me. It wasn't natural, but it was what God prompted me to do, and it was freeing!

Paul used to call me "Boom-Boom," and faux-bragged frequently about his piano rendition of, "Mr. Frog Is Full of Hops." He imitated voices and kept us in stitches. Years later he became presiding justice of the Los Angeles Superior Court. If ever I needed to call, I would tell staff to inform Justice Turner that "Boom-Boom" was on the line.

Willie's competitions did not go well, and for the first time I was repelled at the thought of him continuing to train. He lost his minimum wage job at a print shop, Sasha was continually sick, and my husband was never home. One night, someone slipped $100 under our front door. I was mortified that this was where we were at financially. When I flew back to Illinois the next summer, I did not want to return to California. But out of obedience to God, I did. Willie promised a change and, in fact did change, and God began to tangibly bring blessing.

Willie was hired to teach Spanish at an exclusive private school overlooking the Rose Bowl stadium. We relocated to beautiful South Pasadena in a cute, little white-framed house off the 405 Freeway. To help us get acquainted, we were invited to a potluck dinner at one of the parents' homes. We drove the winding roads around the hills surrounding the Bowl and came upon what could only be described as a mansion. Wearing my best polyester pantsuit, carrying a home-made cherry pie, I entered the home astonished to see a giant living room. Surrounded by a balcony, there were two great grand pianos center-pieced on the main floor. No one else there was wearing a polyester pant suit.

I hoped I had redeemed my small-town, poor self when I sat to perform a duet version of "The Entertainer," from the wildly popular movie *The Sting*, with another pianist on those grand pianos, Now, that was fun!

It's hard to fathom the way the rich live, even when you have a front-row seat. Every day a chauffeur delivered a McDonald's lunch to one of the students at school. Another's dad rented Disneyland for the evening for his birthday. A few became my piano students. One student, Amanda, lived in another beautiful, gated mansion in South Pasadena proper. Her parents paid me double the rate to drive to their home and give her lessons. She was a sweet, refined eight-year-old.

Once, because Sasha was sick, the chauffeur brought Amanda to me. No doubt the sight of so small a house was shock enough, but when my visiting sister-in-law, Miriam, walked through the living room in an apron, Amanda turned and asked, "Oh, Mrs. Rios. Is that your maid?"

At the end of that school year, we drove back to Illinois to visit family and gather neglected wedding gifts to make California our home. While in Carmi, our friends from Berlin, Tom and Lois Jandris, called from Chicago to invite us up for a visit. It was their little sons, Brody and Ryan, I had babysat for in Berlin. Lois and Tom had never seen Sasha, so off we went.

We stayed in their home and on the morning of the first day, Tom, who was assistant principal at a large suburban high school, told Willie there was an opening for dean of students. Did he want to apply? Next morning Willie donned his yellow polyester suit (polyester was big in those days) and joined the dozens of other applicants. To our amazement he was offered the job and overnight our lives changed.

There were only a few weeks before the start of school, so Willie moved in with the Jandrises and I flew to California to pack and sell what I could. It was exciting. The salary sounded enormous, and we were actually going to be able to buy a home! I felt the hand of God's blessing every step of the way.

There wasn't much to sell except my garage sale baby grand. I ran an ad for $1,000 and sold it at 100 percent profit to an Australian actress named Topsy Barley. Who came to inspect it with her little white dog and two gay companions.

Sasha and I moved back into my parents' home until we could find a place to live near Chicago.

Sweet Home Chicago

We found a three-year-old split-level home we could afford in a community west of Chicago, known as Bolingbrook. It was the thrill of my life to own a home. Once again, my father stepped in to loan us the down payment necessary to purchase it.

We loved our neighbors and friends and discovered the joy of entertaining in our home. Another friend from Berlin, Jim, once called to ask if he could bring his drill team from Michigan to stay for a few nights. Twenty men descended on our house with their weapons, gear, and uniforms. The toilets flushed constantly, the rooms filled with bodies, but we had great fun. They would march down our street, drill in the shared field behind our house, and generally brought a bit of excitement to the neighborhood.

Sasha was three by then and I enrolled her at the Cerebral Palsy Center in Joliet, Illinois. That was no small matter, especially when I scarily loaded her little body into the back of a very large yellow bus each day for the long drive. But her teacher, Elsie Smith, made it all worthwhile. Mrs. Smith was one of the most incredible teachers Sasha ever had. Highly educated, she was a product of some of the finest black colleges of our day. Not many black women her age at that time had even attended college. She had earned several degrees. Mrs. Smith opened my eyes to a whole new world of black academia. But most of all, she inspired and encouraged me. Her husband was a pastor; she a strong believer in Christ. She believed Sasha could be taught to do something and worked diligently to make it so. Mrs. Smith loved on Sasha. She loved on me and gave me the courage to never give up.

At her peak, Sasha could say some two syllable words. "Da-Da!" she would exclaim excitedly when Willie would come home from work. "Ma-Ma!" for me. She could identify body parts. With great difficulty she reached for her nose, her mouth, her tongue on command. She had a wonderful giggle and a piercing cry. She could match pitches on about a five-note range. But gradually after many years of grand mal seizures, she became silent and only subtlety responsive.

It took years to have any official diagnosis . . . thus the visits to so many hospitals and doctors. I was told there were over 1,000 things that could cause seizures. She was tested for literally everything, from that first time Dr. Sharma shaved her head at three months to the most sophisticated hospitals in the U.S. at the time.

"Cerebral Palsy" is a generalized term describing symptoms, but not a cause. It is a catch-all term, like claiming you have a "cold" when it might be allergies or flu. It was the only thing I knew to use for years. I now realize the best way to describe Sasha's condition is simply "severely brain damaged at birth."

When she was five, I thought it was time to have another baby. My parents were dead set against it. They were afraid the baby might have the same problems, and even if not, worried that I could not handle the pressure. But as much as I loved them, I knew having another baby was right.

Jeremy Michael Rios

In the spring of 1980, in my sixth month pregnancy, I was offered a three-month position teaching music at a year-round school just across the street. When I interviewed for the job, the principal asked about my musical experiences and education and happily offered me the job on the spot. We needed the money, and I was ecstatic until he added, "You will be teaching guitar." *GUITAR?* I didn't play guitar! I played piano, clarinet, sang, and conducted, but never played a guitar in my life!

He assured me it was an audio-visual course, and I would be fine. I went home nervous, guitar and manual in hand. My pupils were twelve-year-old seventh graders. I was placed in a temporary classroom with no piano.

One of the great advantages of being a music teacher is the ability to get and hold your students' attention by engaging them in the music. My classroom was filled to the brim with learning-disabled twelve-year-old's, in one class, thirty-six of them! Each was given their own guitar which they immediately began to wield over their heads like weapons. Six months pregnant, I was left to balance my own guitar on what bit of lap I had left and strum, "Hang Down Your Head, Tom Dooley," the only song I knew.

Still, I learned to love the little monsters and, despite the limitations of my ever-expanding belly, managed to teach them other things. Rebuking them for the horrible things they said to each other relentlessly, I taught them respect and kindness as best I could.

I finished my assignment at Jane Addams Middle School and then went into labor at home in the kitchen a few days later. I called Willie at work then went into overdrive. I bent over the bathtub to bathe Sasha and wash her hair (how did I do that?!), prepared and pureed her special food, and was ready to go when he pulled into the driveway.

As we drove to Good Samaritan Hospital in Downers Grove, I read Willie as much of the Lamaze method of coping with birth as I could. My new doctor, unwilling to take any chances, gave me Pitocin to speed the labor. Nicholas Michel Rios was born after a very uneventful eight hours. Well, Michel (Russian like Sasha) was the name I chose for him, but Willie implored me to change it to Jeremy Michael just after delivery.

My parents drove the 300 miles to greet the little dude and arrived only a few minutes after his birth. When the doctor placed him in my arms, his small face was not scrunched, but beautiful. Another baby with big eyes and thick, dark hair, the doctor assured me he was perfect. At eight pounds, six ounces, my dad observed rightly our new baby resembled a rolled roast.

After a short stay in the hospital, we arrived back home to see my parents packing to leave. By then my troubled fifteen-year-old nephew Cris had come to live with them and they were eager to get back home to supervise. Willie went to work and I was left with one little baby and another, bigger one.

Jeremy was not only strong, but his voice was also powerful and his cry constant. (Later as he sang with the very large Wheaton Men's Glee Club, I could always pick out his voice.) My neighbor's husband could hear him through the walls of our house and offered to take him on a walk while I fed Sasha. I could hear that little voice even as he rounded the bend in the stroller. What a kindness that was.

The first few months were rough. One morning I was sitting in the lower level of our home, nursing Jeremy on the couch with Sasha leaning on my arm. When I lifted him over my shoulder, his fifty-decibel cry resumed, and Sasha went into a violent seizure. I was helpless to get up, helpless to do anything.

In just a few days, I developed a fever with a breast infection. My mom caught a plane and thankfully flew back to help.

Sasha's seizures came with a vengeance. So severe we admitted her to Wyler Chicago Children's Hospital. Jeremy wailed all night in the hotel where we stayed. Overwhelmed with desperation, I cried out once again. "Please, God, help me!" The next morning Sasha's seizures inexplicably stopped. When I asked the neurologist what I could do to save her if they came back like that again, he advised me to just let her die. When she was a baby I heard something similarly from a renowned neurologist in Beverly Hills, who dispassionately told me she wouldn't live long.

Through the years, of all the things people said to me that hurt, this was the worst. As I held Sasha in my arms, people would ask what her life expectancy was, or would she live very long as though they were asking how tall I thought she would be. I determined early on not to take offense at people's awkward comments understanding that just like me, they needed grace. But this one amazed me. Would I suggest to others their healthy babies might not live long? Sasha, in spite of her limitations was my baby—my first baby. I didn't love her less. She was not disposable. She was a gift from God.

After that stay at Wyler, God granted us a period of peace. Sasha's seizures stayed away for a while and my "rolled roast" quieted down to a normal, cuddly baby.

Make no mistake. Jeremy was a gift from the Lord. Every move he made was a miracle to me, every syllable, every accomplishment brought joy. Sasha Girl's condition broke my heart, but Jeremy was healing it.

The Move to Wheaton

Like my mom before me, I wanted to raise my kids in a better place. We moved to Wheaton, Illinois, home of Wheaton College where there were fine churches, missions, and ministries galore. Moody Radio and the teaching of God's Word were a constant companion in my home and car. It was a beautiful town and I felt so blessed to raise my children there for the next twenty years. But it wasn't easy getting there.

Wheaton was expensive. Looking for a house was discouraging. We were in another league, one we most definitely couldn't afford. After a long search, a developer friend of ours from church introduced us to a young builder named Wayne, just getting started, who was willing to build for less. We settled on a plan, and when the estimate to build it came back only a few thousand over our limit, we tightened our belts and went for it.

The hole was dug, the foundation laid, the structure formed, when in the dead of winter, our builder disappeared. We had already sold our home in Bolingbrook and moved twice and now all our money was gone. After a desperate third move, Wayne's dad, a master carpenter came in to finish what his son had left undone. He did a marvelous job. And then, with a twist of the plot, went to jail for his son. The crime? Wayne murdered the man who put in our beautiful Redwood garage door in a dispute over a copy machine. Wayne shot him while he was jogging in Wheaton. Rather than let Wayne go to prison, his dad confessed to the crime. Imagine my surprise once we had moved in, when one day the doorbell rang and there stood a smiling Wayne, with his two front teeth missing, come for a visit.

In 1980 while all of this was happening, Willie applied and was admitted into law school. Jeremy was only a few months old, the house still under construction when he began. For four years he worked days at the Public Defender's office and drove the hour to class every night. We saw him Friday nights and Sunday mornings.

But God gave me a great neighborhood. Neighbors next door had six children who loved mine and would take Jeremy home frequently to play with them. That gave me a break to get my work done in peace. Sharon, their mom and my friend, without ever being asked, would meet Sasha's school bus in the afternoons, take her off and be waiting with her in the driveway if I was running late. Some days through the window of my upstairs bedroom overlooking their yard, I would tell Sharon, how desperately lonely I was. I couldn't contain my tears.

I wanted so badly to be a good example. She was Catholic and certainly knew about and honored God, but I longed for her to have a personal faith. I cringed at the sorrow and sadness and struggle she saw in my life daily. How could she ever be drawn to a faith like that?

In an uncharacteristically candid moment, years later she told me how she watched me through the years and saw the opposite of what I feared. My struggles and response to them convinced her of the power of deep faith. It was one of the greatest gifts I ever received.

Years later, I was able to visit Sharon on her death bed to encourage and pray with her and her husband, Bob. She was such a gift to me through difficult years. I was so blessed to have been back in town just at that crucial moment and have that precious time with them.

Many nights, during those years, Sasha slept downstairs and could be heard through the heating grate having grand mal seizure. I finally had to learn I could not prevent them nor help her through each and every seizure. If I was going to sleep, I had to bear those sounds with an uncommon callousness in order to survive.

I arose each morning at 5:30 to get Sasha up, dress, and feed her and get her on the bus by 6:30. It was grueling for her and for me. If I didn't make the deadline and kept her home, I was unable to leave the house or fulfill any commitments of the day. She was often sick and unable to attend school, so the days she was being cared for were already precious to me. If God taught me anything as Sasha's mother, it was to be still.

I remember discussing this with my friend Joni Tada. A quadriplegic from a tragic diving accident at nineteen, Joni, through a determination of faith, learned to paint with her teeth, write books, record incredibly beautiful music, and begin a ministry for disabled persons known as "Joni and Friends." Because of her great intellect, she became a world-renowned author and speaker.

We became good friends who talked and sang hymns together on the phone. When sharing my difficulty coping with confinement, Joni described gently her personal routine. Awaking early in the morning, hours before attendants would arrive, she lay helpless and alone. Unable to wipe a tear or blow her own nose, she was consigned to motionless, helplessness. It was very difficult for her. She described it to me as God "holding her still." "Be still, and know that I am God," said the psalmist (Psalm 46:10).

Imagine how God silenced my complaints as I listened to her experience. God was "holding me still," teaching me patience, endurance, allowing my faith to go deep, preparing me in ways I could never have imagined.

Sasha's limitations were extensive. She was a combination of hypertonic (stiff) and hypotonic (muscles too relaxed). She could hold up her head, but not sit or stand independently. Her hands and arms moved, but not purposefully. The care she required was extensive. She wore diapers and had to be fed pureed foods. Ironically, until she was three, I had never owned a blender, and cut all her food in tiny pieces by hand. Mealtimes were long. I would prepare a meal, then eat with Willie and Jeremy. After they finished and left the table, I spent the next thirty to forty-five minutes feeding her. Sometimes she would projectile vomit everything and I would have to begin again. It was imperative to get medicine and food down her little thin body. After that, I cleaned the kitchen. Mealtimes lasted two to three hours.

Sasha had to be lifted and carried everywhere. We bought a lightweight, stroller-like wheelchair when she was small, but after Jeremy came, we purchased a unique one that worked at home and in the car. Sasha was able to recline in this chair. When I wanted to get her in the car, I pulled the front wheels up and into the well of the front floorboard, while hitting a lever that caused the back wheels to rise. I could then pivot the chair into the passenger seat without having to lift her from the chair. This was genius.

Even as a little wiggly baby, I was able to place Jeremy on her lap, fold Sasha's arms over him, and wheel them both around in a store or at church. For some reason my rambunctious baby boy knew to sit still on her lap. He never pulled her hair or poked or jabbed her in any way. How was that possible?

Despite those limitations, we took her everywhere. In church, I lifted her up the stairs and down a long corridor to the sanctuary. I couldn't stop to chat as I made my way inside and collapsed in the pew. As the organ began to play, Sasha's little face would register intent listening. But as soon as the organ stopped, she began her own, very loud rendition. "Ah . . . ah . . . ah.," she would sing. I would clamp my hand over her mouth until the organ began again. Sasha held still until it stopped then loudly sang again when it went silent. It was hilarious for most people, but others were probably annoyed. Our pastor, Dr. Ivan York, was always tender. When Sasha would break into a noisy grand mal seizure, church graciously went on, business as usual.

There was always grief. When the children's choir performed, Sasha was either lying on a palette in the pew or leaning against me, sitting up. Despite her love for music and earlier ability to match pitches, she would never be able to sing or play or participate in any of it.

My Son, Jeremy

Jeremy was one of the funniest kids anyone could have. He made us laugh constantly. When he was in pre-school, I displayed all his "artwork" on the door of the fridge. One day while cleaning, I selected one to discard and make room for the next. But Jeremy noticed it was missing and was angry. I lifted it from the garbage and placed it back on the door. A week or so later I tried again. One can't keep *every* piece of artwork magnetized to the refrigerator door. But Jeremy spotted it again and got angry again. Back to the door it went, until my third attempt.

This time I took it to the unfinished basement garbage can thinking he would never see it again.

One rainy day, I was ironing in said basement, when my three-year-old began sauntering down the wooden stairs. For some strange reason, he went right to the garbage can, and saw his discarded treasure for the third time. The veins popped out in his neck as he said to me emphatically, "I wish Sandi Patti (the number one female Christian vocalist in 1984) was my mother!"

Once, after a long hospitalization of Sasha, we brought Jeremy to the hospital and wheeled her into the lobby so he could see her. He ran to her wheelchair throwing his arms around her legs, crying, "Oh, Sasha, my Sasha!"

He was affectionate and loving. Where Sasha could not express her love, he made up for in enthusiasm. I loved taking him to the grocery story, wheeling him up and down the aisles to enjoy some time with him. Once as a small toddler, sitting in the basket, I turned my back as he emptied an entire carton of eggs into the bag. Another time when he was older, he was wandering around in an aisle as I waited in line. I heard this voice, "Mom! Oh, Mom! I love you, Mom!" The man behind me asked humorously, "What does he want?" "Nothing," I said. "That's just the way he is."

When I returned from weekends away singing, glamorously carrying sound equipment, luggage, and record album paraphernalia, he would run down the long hallway of our home to greet me shouting, "Mommy! Mommy" and throw his arms, first around my legs, then my waist as he grew taller and taller. Once, seeing my fatigue, he said, "Mommy, lay down on the floor and I'll rub your back." I lay down, still in my winter coat, as his small hands worked their way up and down my spine. Then he jumped up, and ran back down the hall, shouting, "I'm getting the brush to brush your hair!"

When he was older, we always cleaned house together with music blaring. Sometimes he would run to me and say, "Mom! Let's vacuum and listen to oldies!" On one of those days, I was cleaning the bathroom in my yellow Playtex gloves while he vacuumed the living room. On the radio came the 1963 hit by The Angels, "My Boyfriend's Back." The first line warns the hearer about the trouble coming their way with the return of her boyfriend.

Suddenly he burst through the bathroom door excitedly announcing, "Mom! I have a great idea! Christian oldies! Christian oldies! You know, 'The Lord is back and you're gonna be sorry!' he sang enthusiastically.

We were sitting on the couch one evening watching television as a family when, out of the blue, Jeremy asked, "Mom, Sasha's never going to have babies, is she?" His insight was astounding even as a child.

Our loving heavenly Father doesn't always answer our prayers, however justified we think they are, in the way and in the time we want. But He fills the voids by sending unexpected gifts to us we couldn't have imagined. Jeremy was that for me.

As the days and months and years went by with little Sasha, I felt His hand on me in miraculous ways over and over. Are those unexpected gifts and changed lives any less a miracle than physical healing? I don't think so.

Both the kids grew, but soon Jeremy became the big brother, not the little one. He loved Sasha and never complained about the difficulties of being her brother. She was a unique little person with a personality in spite of her quietness. There were always signs she understood even if she couldn't indicate it in any tangible way.

Once I was rehearsing a song as I fed her. The orchestral soundtrack was coming from a boom box on the kitchen counter. It was what was known as an accompaniment track, meaning we heard just the orchestra as I sang along, in my chair next to her. Rather than getting up, I let the tape run, which meant, the same song played again, this time with my pre-recorded voice. I was spooning the food into her little mouth, as she jerked her head toward the boom box, when my voice began. My silent little girl, who could not make eye contact, was bright enough to know her mom's voice was over there when it had just been . . . here.

This too was a gift of uncommon response from her that helped me see Sasha understood a great deal more than we would ever know.

Jeremy and his friends would come into the kitchen and ask if Sasha could come in the family room and "play" with them. It was hilarious. They would wheel her chair into the family room as silent, sweet Sasha presided over their games.

Only one time in his life did Jeremy ever express conflict over his sister. He was probably nine. We were in the grocery store. He was in his baseball uniform, and we were going to his game. Awkwardly and without explanation, he asked me if we could please leave Sasha home this time. I explained gently to him we couldn't. We were a family, not ashamed of her in any way, and she would continue to go with us everywhere. He never said another word again.

Willie graduated from law school but had difficulty passing the bar. And once he did, he decided he wanted to be in private practice and buy a building. Always the dreamer, that's the course we took, but there was hardly money to survive coming in. I took every concert and singing engagement I could to supplement our income, but it all took a terrible toll. (More on my musical life in the next chapter.)

Willie was being seriously considered for a judicial appointment in our county. I prayed for it fervently, thinking it would bring much-needed income and security. But in the spring of 1990, during a three-week concert tour in Japan I called home to hear the appointment had not come to pass. On the bamboo mat of my beautiful and compassionate Japanese hosts' upstairs bedroom, I rocked and wept before her uncontrollably, using a small dictionary to try and explain my sorrow. We were going to lose our home, and possibly our marriage.

Christmas of that year, I again took every singing engagement offered me in an effort to survive. One of those opportunities was in Oskaloosa, Iowa. If you live in Chicago and travel west, you know the hazards of Interstate 80. I left my home early in the morning, sound equipment packed in the mini-van and began the journey in mild snowfall. As the morning progressed, snowfall turned into a blinding snowstorm. I gripped the wheel tightly for hours, praying, praying. Huge semi-trucks were in the ditch, left and right. But it was too late to turn back. Barely able to make out a gas station sign, I crept my way off the highway to fill up. The attendant asked me what in the world I was doing on the interstate and recommended I try to get a room at the hotel across the street—which I could not see. As the snow blew, and by faith in his directions, I crept my way across the street, managed finally to see the hotel sign, and got the very last room. It was noon. There were no cell phones, no one to call, and as I sat on the bed in my room, I cried out once again. "Lord, no one knows where I am, and no one cares. I'm all alone. Please, help me."

In the absence of a friend or a book, I turned on the television just as *Funny Girl* with Barbra Streisand was beginning. THIS was my all-time favorite movie. I LOVED Barbra Streisand. I laughed and cried realizing God gave me this very special, personal gift to communicate to me as my loving heavenly Father that HE knew exactly where I was. And I was in His hands.

Back home a few days later, Christmas 1990 came, but I had a strange foreboding this might be our last.

Is Divorce a Sin?

After a phone call from a friend the week after Christmas, with information on my husband's behavior, I knew I could not go on. I had been seeing a great counselor named Joan for about a year. Raised on the mission field in China, Joan was a nursing instructor at Wheaton College. Dragged and hogtied by my good friend Ginger months earlier, I went to see her for the first time. I poured out my hidden story in a flood of tears to which she replied, "No wonder you're depressed, you have reason to be." It was a counseling match made in heaven. Joan was no-nonsense, bottom line. I told her things neither my parents nor my close friends knew as she gave me perspective and great counsel.

She recommended separation from Willie early on, but I didn't want that. I believed in the sanctity of marriage and did NOT want to break up my little family. But on that night after that phone call, I lay in bed awake with my husband of nearly twenty years next to me and felt God saying to me, "It's time. You can go."

The next morning, I asked him to find a place to stay for a period of separation. It was January of 1991. He left the house in a burst of anger and never came back. I thought a time apart would give him a different perspective, but that was not to be.

As the door shut behind him, my thoughts went to my ten-year-old boy. I drove to his school, brought him out of class and into the car for a talk. I told him his dad left. He asked me why, but I didn't think he needed details. Only a few years earlier, he heard us fighting in the kitchen and tried to force his little body between us, asking, "Are you fighting to split?" It was heart-rending to me that he even knew there were problems. There were other startlingly insightful comments from him along the way, but at each turn I tried to reassure him all was well. Now I couldn't hide the fact it wasn't.

In the car that morning I told him the effect of separation and divorce on children is not good. Grades can fall, bad behavior can result. "But you have a choice, Jeremy," I told him. "We can either let this destroy our lives, or with God's help overcome it." Heavy words for a small boy, but Jeremy was already an incredibly thoughtful and insightful little boy and drank my admonition in deeply.

Our church handled the divorce terribly. Joan had earlier insisted I talk to my pastor. I got up from one especially intense session, drove to the church, and poured my heart out. My pastor's response was that I should ask Willie to call him. Fat chance.

When other revelations came, I felt I could not stay any more in our beloved church of fifteen years where my children were trained and nurtured in the Word. It would have been a great lesson for them had the church dealt properly with the problem, rather than ignoring it. God has instructed us in His Word that discipline is necessary to purify and strengthen the church. We could have stayed and all been reminded the holiness God requires from His people cannot be ignored. "If you love Me," Jesus said, "keep My commandments" (John 14:15).

With Jeremy's permission, I packed up the kids and drove to Willow Creek Community Church, thirty minutes away in Barrington with Sasha in her wheelchair. Larry Shackley, Willow Creek's pianist, was a great friend who traveled with and accompanied me for years. Larry also went through a painful divorce. One day he got off the train to his suburban home to find his wife gone. She left him and their little daughter who was Jeremy's age. We became fast friends who then shared lots of musical adventures, tears, but even more laughter!

Somewhere along the line, Pastor Bill Hybels became an acquaintance too. During that first service, a soloist with the orchestra sang the beautiful hymn, "It Is Well with My Soul." Tears rolled down my face as God brought that beautiful reminder to me through music. I knew I found a new church home. Little did I know it would bring a completely new life as well.

4

I've Got the Music in Me!

Imagine what it would be like to stand on the fifty-yard line in the middle of Soldier Field, at a huge old-fashioned microphone surrounded by 60,000 fans watching you sing "The Star-Spangled Banner." Can't imagine? I can help. For three years straight, during the Chicago Bears' golden years of the late '80s, I was invited to sing for them. Pat McCaskey, grandson of Papa Bear Halas, and I met at an event where I was singing, and somewhere along the way become friends. When he called me to sing the anthem at a Bears game, I was thrilled.

My ignorance of professional sports is legion. I met and spent time with NBA Star Yao Ming in China and had no idea who he was. I did notice he was very tall, 7'6" to be exact. I mortified myself one night on *The O'Reilly Factor* by referring to "intermission" at a Major League baseball game. Years later, on radio in Chicago, I used to joke that I could talk about anything but sports and dogs. But it was no joke. When we're in person at a game of some sort that I'm obviously not watching, I'm famous for carefully critiquing players' "outfits."

It will make sense to you then when Mike Ditka first arrived in Chicago, and we appeared on the same television program, I didn't know who he was. BUT . . . those Bears! When William Perry, a.k.a.

"the Fridge," "Sweetness," #34, Walter Peyton, Jim McMahon, the "Funky QB," and "Da Coach," all came together to form that powerful team, there was enough personality to sink what was then known as "Hancock" Tower. It was impossible NOT to love those Bears.

In preparation for my first performance at a Chicago Bears game, Willie and I went to York Furriers to buy the cheapest fur possible to keep me warm. We were in process of buying a black opossum—seriously, they do make those—when Willie bragged how I was singing at the Bears game the next day. That changed everything. The salesman asked me to stay in the dressing room for a minute. He had something to show me. He came back excitedly holding a $10,000 sheered beaver coat that just happened to be in the Bears colors, bright orange and blue! It sounds gauche, but it was beautiful!

York Furriers wanted to know if I would wear that coat while singing the anthem the next day. Why not? The lucky salesman drove with us to the game where we had free parking and seats in the press gallery. I donned the coat. York Furriers must have hoped the wife of a Bear or a coach would be unable to pass up such a beauty. It caused quite a stir, but I don't know if that ever gave them a sale. Don't you think I should have been able to keep it as a memento? Ha! I actually was never paid for singing for the Bears. I'm thinking the famously cheap "Papa Bear Halas" thought it payment enough to sit silently in the press box eating hotdogs. Plenty generous—for a singer.

But back to what it was actually like . . . A rehearsal was scheduled mid-morning before the noon kick-off. It was a mic check more than anything because you had to sing the anthem a cappella. Easy enough, until you consider the half-second delay. As you stand at the giant microphone, singing your best, whatever you hear as you are singing is drowned out by the mega stadium speakers coming back at you a half-second later. Your natural inclination is to wait until a phrase or word is finished before you begin another. In this case, pausing for the end, means the stadium hears a pause, so you must sing through the song by sheer concentration. The delay also affects your sense of rhythm. The sound doesn't come back to you in the same metric rhythm it left your mouth. You have to ignore what those mega speakers are blaring at you and by sheer force of will keep the beat in spite of the out-of-sync audio.

It was never my best performance, but I sang those beautiful words with conviction, and the Chicago fans were always gracious. As I would climb the stadium steps on the long trek up to the press box, they would applaud and cheer.

One time it started raining after my rehearsal. As I descended the stairs to the field, it was like walking through the parted waters of the Red Sea to pass between those huge football players. I never felt so small. We were always on a tight schedule because of network coverage, so at noon sharp, the announcer said, "Ladies and gentlemen! To sing our national anthem, please welcome Sandy Rios, from Wheaton, Illinois!" The humongous crowd cheered, then quieted, and I began to sing . . . but just to myself. The microphone was dead. Silence in the stadium, all eyes fixed on the silent me. Standing in center field is a very long way from the sidelines. You can't make out faces or expressions much less hear anyone telling you what exactly it is you should be doing. I waited, and I waited, alone at that mic, in silence, in the middle of the field for what seemed like an eternity, not knowing where to go or what to do.

Now Chicago is a union town. That means only people designated to do certain things can do certain things. Not just anybody could come on the field and fix the microphone. No siree! It had to be the card-carrying union worker with the title, "Fixer of the Mic in the Center of Soldier Field During a Game Guy." Finally, out from between the long line of the still standing-at-attention Chicago Bears, slowly ambled a middle-aged laborer, dressed in baggy work pants, his large ring of keys jangling from his belt. He was in no hurry as he made his way toward me and began to jiggle the mic, adjust the stand, and whatever else people with his special expertise were supposed to do. It didn't work.

I was instructed to do a solo walk down the fifty yards to the end-zone and climb up into the band box to finish my one-minute-thirty-five-second assignment. Once, a *Time* magazine sports reporter asked me if I would be willing to sing it as fast as I could to break the record. The funny thing is the allotted time for the anthem was always given to the networks for advertising, it was not broadcast on the network. But this time, because of the delay, I was on national television. We had a good time when tons of friends and family called from around the country surprised to see me singing at the Bears game!

Mike Ditka and I were together for several events after that. He made a commitment to Christ while in Dallas under the influence of Dallas Cowboy coach, Tom Landry. The Christian community in Chicago was more than thrilled, and unwisely overwhelmed the gifted coach with invitations to speak. Mike was a powerful personality, but he was only a baby in his Christian faith. He was not ready to be a Christian leader. It was unwise and harmful to rush him. When later he was arrested for drunk driving, the Christian community dropped him like a hot potato. That was wrong on so many levels. I remember trying to talk to Mike the few moments I had with him about his faith. Always honest, he expressed his doubts. And then he fell off the Christian radar completely. I wonder if he thought—like I did about myself once—God could never forgive him.

Years later, I tried to persuade him to run for Senate to oppose Barack Obama. He thought about it, and it was a great loss to all of us that he declined.

Bears linebacker Mike Singletary and his wife, Kim, attended Willow Creek Church. Leslie Frazier and "Big Al" Harris, of the famous "46 Defense," later became friends at my radio station. The delightful Connie Peyton, "Mrs. Sweetness," used to listen to and call into my show. Bob Thomas, kicker for the Bears and a strong Christian, later became a good friend. Bob eventually became chief justice of the Illinois Supreme Court. What a blessing it was to have been part of those wonderful Bears championship years!

Singing the anthem for the Chicago Bears, however, was not my highest musical achievement. My version of "Windmills of Your Mind" went up in Skylab 4, the third and final manned visit to the Skylab orbital workshop in 1974. Astronaut William R. Pogue, pilot of that mission, was a graduate of my alma mater, Oklahoma Baptist University. He carried the Bison Glee Club album that included my rendition of "Windmills of Your Mind" so it could be played during what turned out to be the longest manned flight (eighty-four days, 1 hour and fifteen minutes), in the history of manned space exploration to date.

Those are two of my musical achievements people seem to enjoy hearing about most. But becoming a musician had lots of exciting and entertaining moments along the way!

The Budding Musician

I didn't just dance on my tiptoes at age three to Tchaikovsky's *Nutcracker Suite* because of the rhythm. The music captivated me. From the beautiful bouncing flutes of "Dance of the Sugar Plum Fairies," to the haunting, understated beauty of "Arabian Dance," my little body was all in to express it.

I made my solo debut at four when my father lifted me onto the stage at church to sing "Zacchaeus Was a Wee Little Man" followed by, "I've Got the Joy, Joy, Joy, Joy Down in My Heart!" I still remember standing on that stage, wearing a pleated skirt with suspenders my mom made and a crisp, white blouse, hair permed and parted in the middle.

When my big sister began piano lessons, I begged Mother to let me take them too. I was only four, but already LOVED music. It's amazing how the gifts God gives us often show up in us even as toddlers.

At nine, Donald Peel, the Washington grade school band director in Carmi, began his crusade to recruit members. Once again, I begged my parents to let me join, and once again, they acquiesced.

As I practiced away on my B-flat Bundy clarinet in the bedroom, squeaking profusely, I understood why they hesitated. But soon proficiency came, followed by music contests on clarinet and piano and lovely blue ribbons won by hard practice.

At our church, First Baptist in Carmi, beautiful Pat Stinnette was our most gifted soloist. Her voice was absolutely stunning, and I listened in rapt attention each and every time she sang. It was Pat who sang "My Lord Is Near Me All the Time" in a way that imprinted on my heart. So strongly did it impact me, it was the song I sang when labor with Sasha began. Pat was my singing role model. I wanted to sing like her when I grew up.

When I was little, I accompanied my parents to choir practice every Wednesday night. Wearing pajamas and carrying my doll and pillow, I made my nest on the pew behind the basses. As I grew older and learned music, I would stand behind my dad, and sing the bass line in his ear. And as I became more proficient at piano, I was assigned to turn pages for community performances of great works like Handel's *Messiah* or Dubois's *Seven Last Words of Christ*. Carol Peel, the accompanist, was the wife of Donald Peel, my band director. Greatly talented, she took me on as a piano pupil, and much more, as a friend. Our families became close, and I eventually became the trusted babysitter for their children, Leah and Gary.

I learned great musical literature from that little choir in that little town. Contemporary Christian thought on music in the church now insists music be "dumbed down" and made simpler for smaller churches. I reject that notion. Carmi had a population of 6,000—First Baptist Church, a whopping 200 people. Yet we sang beautifully intricate music and performed it well.

What a loss to the church to consign the people of God to three or four chords, unremarkable melodies, and repetitive lyrics.

It was a cold, winter Sunday night when my sister and her best friend, Carol, took me to church for a special concert. Mother and Daddy were laboring to complete the inside of our new home, but they agreed to let us go alone if we rolled our blue jeans up and kept on our long winter coats. Girls didn't wear pants to church then. It was 1959. That's how old I am.

That night a group known as the "Bison Glee Club" from OBU gave a ninety-minute, rapturous performance. Patterned after the famous Fred Waring and the Pennsylvanians, it was a men's glee club, but with nine, beautifully dressed girls who stood in front and sang with the men. I was spellbound. Never in my wildest dreams did I guess that ten years later this little girl from Illinois would be one of them.

My singing "career" in grade school consisted of Miss Beulah Huber, the fourth-grade teacher, plucking me out of the line on our way into the gym assembly, insisting I sing impromptu for the whole school. Next was a Christmas performance on stage of "All I Want for Christmas Is My Two Front Teeth," with Black-Jack gum hiding my own two front teeth.

We lived in rich farm country. There were huge cornfields directly behind my house. At harvest time each year we celebrated with a festival for the City of Carmi, known strangely enough as, Corn Day. There was a parade in the morning where the band marched and played, firetrucks blew their horns and wailed their sirens, and politicians and business owners displayed their endeavors on colorful floats. Convertibles with beautiful queens of this and that waved and smiled followed by Color Guards carrying the American flag. We decorated our bikes with confetti and clothes-pinned cards to flap in the spokes of our wheels for fun noise. Carmi was the county seat, so people came from all around to cheer and celebrate. Main Street was blocked off where vendors sold cotton candy, taffy, and corn dogs. And there was a big stage in the middle of the town featuring entertainment all day long.

One particular year, the twelve-year-old version of me sang a song on that stage from the blockbuster hit musical, *Oklahoma!* Dressed in a cowboy hat, with hands on my hips, I belted out, "I Cain't Say No," as sung by the character, Ado Annie. In the movie, the song is sung by a caricatured Western-girl, hilariously describing her response to seduction. I had no idea what I was singing about.

It was small-town America at its finest. And I will be forever grateful for the simple pleasures it brought. Simple pleasures, I eventually learned, are the best. They are the pleasures you miss most when times get difficult.

I have never forgotten my roots in Carmi or the people who formed my character, honed my skills, and shaped my life. What a wonderful foundation from which to launch into a very big world.

Before television, people often entertained friends in their home. This wasn't necessarily fun for me because my otherwise wise mom insisted I perform for EVERYONE. I had to play piano or clarinet or sing on demand. I was mortified. Remember, I was that girl who, in spite of the gifts God gave me, didn't actually think much of myself. It wasn't until I was in my thirties I was able to perform without debilitating nervousness.

In junior high band, Mr. Peel implemented the challenge system. You were seated in order of ability and if you thought you could play better than the person next to you with a higher rank, you were allowed to "challenge" them for their seat. Judy was first chair clarinet, and I was in the second seat. I was younger, but better, so I challenged her. Judy and I were ushered into a room while Mr. Peel stood outside the door and instructed us to each play a passage while he listened. He selected me, and Judy was devastated. So devastated, I couldn't bear to take her chair away from her.

It was a noble thing for a twelve-year-old to do, don't you think? But when we do a good thing, help people, give money or time, the Bible tells us it is to be done in secret. No boasting or preening, just an act of worship by helping others. I only tell you this story because I failed that test miserably. Years later in Chicago, I unexpectedly met Judy in a friend's home. It was great fun seeing her, but in my careless foolishness, I made a clumsy joke about that incident in junior high.

I embarrassed her when I brought up a painful memory, but most of all, I embarrassed myself.

Band director Mike Croghan took Carmi by storm. A fresh graduate from Murray State University and a native son from Carmi, he came into Carmi High School with a bang. The first year we had over 100 members in our marching band, wearing white spats and doing intricate turns and bows.

We performed at the University of Illinois and then at a Purdue football game, with their giant marching drum. The fellowship and fun of band and the thrill of playing a single part that fits into dozens of other single parts to make an incredible, musical whole is an experience every musical kid needs to experience.

But band wasn't all Mr. Croghan brought to Carmi. There was the "One-Niter." An inauspicious name, I know, but we were too innocent to realize it at the time. It was a no-holds-barred variety show that was great fun for school and community, and it brought out so much never-before-discovered talent in students of every age.

There were the faux Tijuana Brass, a hilarious sketch of the old-time radio show, *The Bickersons* about a couple who bickered incessantly. There were homegrown comedians and magicians. What fun we had.

But if not for my mother, I would never have been a part of it. Once again, my always-present low self-esteem issues were paralyzing me. I hadn't sung publicly since Corn Day and convinced myself I lost my ability to sing. I did sing constantly with the radio, in the car where no one but my mother could hear. When it came time to audition, she encouraged me to try out, but I was afraid. "You think I can sing because you're my mother. Please don't tell me I can sing if it's not true!" I pleaded. "Sandra Kaye. I wouldn't say you could sing if it weren't true!" Mother replied.

With that bit of encouragement, I found myself on stage for the first time, now at fourteen, singing "The Boy from New York City," while three boys sang backup and danced behind me. I practiced over and over for weeks watching the reflection of myself in our large "picture window" at night to perfect my moves.

We were a great hit, and overnight I was launched into high school stardom. Vance was an incredibly gifted pianist who accompanied me on piano everywhere from then on. Mr. Croghan sent us out all over the community to perform and raise money for the music program.

One night when Vance wasn't available, my friend Teresa went with me to perform for a ladies' bridge club. There was just one problem. When we arrived, the women were playing cards in the basement while the big, old-fashioned piano was on the main floor. In a dash of genius, Teresa and I formulated a plan. She sat down at the formidable looking high-back piano, adjusted her music, and waited. I climbed down the basement stairs and the woman in charge introduced me. "Tonight we have special music from Sandra Duckworth of Carmi High and her friend, Teresa Schumacher." I nodded my thanks, took a long broom handle, and banged loudly on the ceiling. Above me, right on cue, Teresa began to play the long, familiar doo-wap intro to "To Know Him Is to Love Him." The sound came wafting down through the heating vents, as I belted out the song,

> "And I do (bah, bah, bah [Teresa banged out the
> triplets]),
> And I do (bah, bah, bah), "yes, I do!"

Smashing, although hilarious, performance!

Carmi prepared me musically in so many ways. Between Mr. Peel's meticulous ear and Mr. Croghan's panache, I learned to perform with precision and flare. My mother's insistence on making me sing for everyone no doubt helped me overcome my paralyzing self-consciousness. When I chose Oklahoma Baptist University to be my college, it was the perfect steppingstone for a small-town girl entering the big world.

OBU, All Hail Thy Name!

During my junior year at Carmi High, three boys came for the summer, selling Bibles and Bible commentaries. It was common then for college students to do that all over the country. Mother was over the moon one Sunday morning when they were sitting in the balcony at church. Not one boy, but three—all of them Christians. I think she thought she found my future husband.

One of the boys was a music major at Oklahoma Baptist University. We became friends for sure as he spoke glowingly of the music program. I wasn't especially interested, but it was a seed planted. When a year later it was time to choose a college, for reasons I've already mentioned and because my sweet mother was so excited at the thought of me going to college in her home state, I settled on OBU.

As a freshman I wanted to sing in a musical group but had no idea which one I should audition for. Modestly, I chose the all-female Bisonette Glee Club, hoping I would be selected. The director was a phenomenal conductor/musician named James Woodward. I have never in my life even to this day sat under a more marvelous conductor. Through the combination of skill in his execution and his expressive face we mimicked musically, we made beautiful music. His choice of songs was exquisite, and I greatly benefited from my year with the group.

But once a new year started, it seemed clear to me "Tune Clippers," also led by Mr. Woodward, was a much better fit. They sang pop, wore great clothing, and were incredibly talented. They travelled on USO tours, entertaining troops and others abroad. I wondered, *Could I make such a group?* I was determined to try. I selected what I thought was the perfect audition number and for most of the summer after my freshman year, spent hours transcribing orchestra to a piano score by listening to the cassette recording.

When fall of 1968 began, I was ready, but nervous beyond measure. I walked into the rehearsal room for the audition to sing for

Mr. Woodward and some of his hand-picked Tune Clippers. With a trembling hand, I gave the pianist my self-drafted piano score. And nervous I should have been. She was a weak sight-reader and botched the accompaniment badly, so I barely executed the song. Still, hope springs eternal.

OBU always posted grades and audition results on large bulletin boards in the hallway. After waiting a few days, I heard the results of auditions for Tune Clippers were posted. I ran to Shawnee Hall, the music building, as crowds of kids gathered around, craning to see their names. I joined in the craning, but quickly realized, my name was not there.

I was devastated. I went back to my dorm room and cried uncontrollably. I didn't want to go back to the Bisonettes. Mr. Woodward would no longer be the conductor and besides, I wanted a bigger challenge. I wasn't chosen! That was a blow to me. I had always been musically chosen—always been first clarinet, soloist, the blue-ribbon winner, the high school musical star. And to make matters worse, two pretty girls were chosen who were only average singers. I watched them flirt with Mr. Woodward on the bus on tour with Bisonettes. How could this be?

The singers currently in Tune Clippers were phenomenal. I hadn't forgotten my place in the musical pecking order or that I might not ever measure up to them, but these girls? They could never sing at the level required, or so I thought. (Remember, these were the four "lost" years.)

It took me weeks to get over the pain of that loss, and I tried my best to be content with the Bisonette Glee Club. But a month or so into the semester I got an unexpected visit. There was another prestigious group on campus known as the Bison Glee Club. It was a men's glee club joined by a handful of women known as "Little Sisters." They were pretty girls, beautifully dressed, poised, and talented. This was the group I saw perform in Carmi when I was a girl.

The director was Dr. Warren M. Angell, a New Yorker in the middle of the Oklahoma plains.

Dr. Angell was the dean of the School of Music at OBU. He was a world-class pianist and singer who was a top tenor with "Fred Waring's Pennsylvanians," and arranger and soloist with the Robert Shaw Chorale. He wore a blue satin brocade coat for concerts and led us as much by his dancing feet as by the baton waving in his hand.

A few "Little Sisters" came to my room to ask me if I would consider joining the glee club. I was flabbergasted. No audition? Just an invitation? Unheard of. But that's what God did for me when my heart was cold to Him. He gave an incredible gift of mercy and grace to a broken-hearted girl who felt once again like a great failure.

The Bison Glee Club (BGC) had long traditions. One of them was to audition freshman, and make those selected, pledge for an entire year. During that time, they were to memorize the music and learn the choreography so they could begin their sophomore year with full preparation. This was fall of my sophomore year, so I had to move quickly to catch up.

I loved singing with the Glee Club. We sang an incredible variety of music from the classics to hymn arrangements to pop, show tunes, and classics of Dean Angell's era, the thirties and forties. The men sang beautiful arrangements of Welsh hymns penned by Charles Wesley, sung by coalminers in the eighteenth century. "O for a thousand tongues to sing!" their rich male voices would proclaim.

We sang the haunting melody of "September Song," recorded by Frank Sinatra. The Little Sisters sang tenor on many songs, complimentary embellishments on others. We were patterned after the Fred Waring Singers. We wore flapper dresses to sing songs from *The Unflappable Mollie Brown*. We danced and moved on stage, performing in large groups. Changing clothes countless times, we had incredible fun. It was actually the perfect place for me, and through God's never-wavering love and care for me, He got me there.

Mr. Woodward, my musical idol, never seemed to have much respect for me. He addressed me coldly, as, "Duckworth"—never by my first name. Isn't that strange? The man I respected the very most musically had no respect for me.

By God's great undeserved mercy again, Dean Angell became my mentor. When the bus would pull out for a concert, I often rode in the car with him, listening to great stories of his days in New York. He had such a sense of humor and in his sixties, was still full of life. He taught me that some sins were "regional." We had both found ourselves in a very conservative place where dancing, drinking, smoking, and cards were anathema to the Christian life. Without ever undermining anyone on anything, he planted the seed that the things we must be concerned about are the deep truths of Scripture and the sins clearly laid out there. Not the questionable activities that became culturally forbidden over the course of time for reasons other than scriptural ones.

I became a soloist for the BGC. My junior year, the dean asked me to sing "Windmills of Your Mind," from the 1968 movie hit, *The Thomas Crown Affair*. The guys sang back up as I executed the intricate words that never repeated.

The first hour of our concerts consisted of beautiful sacred music. The second, pop music and just plain fun! One night we opened in the church sanctuary, then moved to the basement for the second half. But the church basement had no microphone and the low ceiling muted whatever volume we could manage. As I was trying my best to project the sultry sounds of "Windmills," I got distracted and lost my place. Since the lyrics NEVER repeated and there is no chorus, it was impossible to find my place. I sang the entire rest of the song saying "La, la, la-la, la, la la-la." Out of the corner of my eye, I could see the shoulders of the guys heaving as they fought back laughter. But I continued to perform with great bravado those meaningless syllables, as Dean Angell conducted with great enthusiasm.

My second year in glee club, I suggested to Dean Angell he give someone else a chance to sing that solo. I had, after all, sung it for a full year and others would love the chance. But he wasn't having it. "Sandy!" he said. "You light up that stage when you sing!" That was the most wonderful musical affirmation anyone ever gave me.

There are so many great memories with Glee Club. There is the time I snuck my pet rabbit, "Fru-Fru" onto the bus for the ten-day spring tour.

There was the time we sang the great Glee Club tradition, an a cappella version of "Dry Bones." But this time the pitch pipe guy who always gave us the first note, forgot the pitch pipe. The arrangement called for a series of random percussive, pitchless sounds, including banging a saucepan. And by some miraculous intervention, when the triangle was struck, we all belted out the first phrase "E-E-E- Zekiel cried!" on the exact same note. And Thomas Jefferson said there were no miracles . . .

And then there was my first business meeting with the club. A question was posed and clueless me on the front row with the other "Little Sisters" raised my hand to offer an opinion. I felt a chill in the room as I offered it and was later informed that Little Sisters don't participate in business meetings. That's men's work. Imagine student council–me hearing that. But it wasn't worth fighting over. The guys treated us like princesses. They carried our luggage, opened our doors. It really was lovely, in spite of what the feminists might think.

Harold, Darold, and Gerald Ware were identical triplets in the club. You can imagine the confusion of audience members as they identified one—two—then three guys who looked just alike.

There's the time my parents and sister came to hear us sing in Chattanooga and my sometimes verbally harsh father, over dinner, decided to choose me as the recipient. My stomach was churning, hands shaking as my big sis leaned over and offered me a Valium before the concert. I took half a tablet and barely made it through the performance. I had never had a drop of alcohol, much less a sedative, and was dangerously wasted for hours.

Once, a fierce storm hit Shawnee during Bison Glee Club rehearsal. We were on the top floor of Shawnee Hall, singing away as we watched sheets of rain press against the windowpanes. We were performing a classical work, singing the amazingly apropos phrase, "And there was thunder and lightning!" when, as Dean Angell dramatically executed the percussive cut off, all the lights went out. We made our way out of the building in the dark to a quiet cafeteria where no dinner could be served. Strange sirens wailed in the distance as we realized a tornado at that exact moment hit and three people were killed.

It rained for days afterward. So much so I put up a picture of the Mona Lisa with a cutout of an umbrella over her head on our apartment door.

The handsome Paul Purifoy played piano for me as I sang one of my favorite songs, "Spooky." Paul and I had great fun. He was younger and very much in love with his future wife, Margaret. He was the strongest believer in Christ I came across at OBU. He worked with Navigators, memorizing Scripture and applying it to life, and he was concerned about me. One long road trip on the bus, he sat next to me sharing Scripture and pleading me to come alive again. But I couldn't. Not yet.

Certainly, the Bison Glee Club was the center of my OBU musical life, but there were other life-changing musical experiences.

Time to Grow Up and Get Serious

I mentioned in chapter 2 how I learned to play cards my freshman year and generally do lots of dorm shenanigans that kept me up late at night. I had no self-discipline. I had roaringly good fun, but then couldn't get up in the mornings for my 8:00 a.m. music theory class with Mr. Wolfe. Music theory was an entirely new discipline to me. And Mr. Wolfe was a terribly droll professor. Theory was a five-day-a-week class that added up to LOTS of credits. Bottom line, because I never made it to class to actually learn theory, I made an F in that section. In the other section—sight-singing and ear training, which came naturally to me and required no study—I made an A. So I ended up with a C, forever blighting my final GPA.

Well, that and Old Testament. My freshman year I rarely attended that very large class and only showed up for exams. Always multiple choice and true or false, I was a good guesser. I made a C there too. I thought I was very clever.

During my freshman year, I became a piano major. Miss Merrill, prim and proper, with long skirts down to her ankles and the short, straight haircut of a spinster, was nevertheless an excellent teacher. She announced to me that if I wanted even a C in piano, I would have to practice a minimum of two hours a day. Piano majors in those days faced "juries" at the end of each semester who determined their grades.

When I went to my last lesson before Christmas, I couldn't play any of my pieces by memory, or even well with music for Miss Merrill. The week we were to return from break in January, I was to perform all of them for said jury. It was a sad hour, that last piano lesson.

I went back home to Carmi, embarrassed by my laziness, determined to do my best to make up for lost time.

I'll never forget entering the jury room that January day in 1968. Miss Merrill and the other piano professors were seated on the risers next to each other. I saw Miss Merrill hang her head as I sat down at the piano. I played a Beethoven sonata, a Chopin waltz, a Bach invention, and all my scales and arpeggios, major and minor, with proficiency. Miss Merrill wrote on her critique of my performance, "You could be a fine pianist if you wanted to be." That blew me away. I had never had that kind of accolade. Would I have been a better student if I had? I'll never know.

It took my entire freshman year to grow up and apply myself. I was ashamed of my grades when the year ended. I retook theory and made the highest grade in the class on the five-hour final. In that same class, I was asked to write an original piano piece. My teacher, the very stern Miss Higgenbotham, actually suggested I have it published.

I entered OBU at seventeen, self-conscious and uncertain of my abilities. God gave me a wonderful mentor, healthy failure to help me grow up, and as my mother would say, and the apostle Paul would echo, an "accurate view" of my abilities (see Romans 12:3).

Back to Carmi

When Willie took on the role of youth director at First Baptist Church in Carmi the summer we were married in 1971, I decided to organize a youth event. It was the era of Christian contemporary musicals. It was a new concept. Great words and themes set to very hip music made available with soundtracks you could perform with.

Life was one of those musicals. I heard it and thought it would be perfect for the teenagers of Carmi. I ordered the materials, organized rehearsals, and beat the bushes for willing teens. We ended up with fifty of them. Not bad for a subset of Christian teens in a small town who were also musical. I was going to be the organizer, and recruited Mr. Croghan, our band director, to lead. He came to one rehearsal and decided he didn't want to do it. I was crestfallen. I worked so hard, and we had come so far—too far to quit. So, in spite of my trepidation, I decided to take it on myself.

I took conducting at OBU, but never actually conducted a group. I had to learn quickly to apply the theory to the practical. We worked hard and rehearsed endlessly. When the night of the performance came, the kids, some of whom never had a musical experience, did an incredible job and they were rewarded by a standing ovation from the community.

It was yet another skill for me as I realized I loved to conduct!

Berlin brought the opportunity to sing with the U.S. Army Band but more than that, clarity on what I actually wanted out of life. Sasha's birth, by God's design, I know now, held me still to go deeper. California nearly broke me, but returning to Chicago was a new beginning musically.

5

Sweet Home Chicago

During those last few months in California, in the summer of 1977, I was offered a job to conduct a large chorus in South Pasadena. The contract was in my pocket as we drove back to Chicago for that summer visit with my family. I also auditioned for the world-renowned Roger Wagner Chorale.

Now, that was funny. I followed the address to a large building with a long corridor, where dozens of singers were lined up in the hallway. People were vocalizing up and down the hallway, preparing themselves to enter the audition room, one at a time, and meet their fate.

When my turn came, I entered the room, probably in that same polyester pants suit, having absolutely no idea what to expect. It was a choral room with chairs placed on graduated levels in a semi-circle. There were four people in the room, three looking down at the pianist sitting on the bench on the main floor. None of them were friendly. I should have brought a cherry pie.

I was handed a large page that was obviously the score for a major work of some kind. The staves filled the page, and each page only contained about four measures. (Sorry, non-musicians. You can skip this part.) The piece, whatever it was, was in Latin, and I was asked to sing second soprano a cappella, one of the hardest lines to read. The pianist refused to establish the key, and instead just gave me one note. The meter was in 4/4 but often felt like 3/4. It never locked into something that made sense, so I began conducting myself in order not to lose the beat. Sweating profusely, I stopped to ask if, since I took two years of Latin, could I please drop singing in Latin, and concentrate on notes and rhythm. I heard a grunt of sorts that must have meant yes, so I continued.

When I departed from these unfriendly folks, I had no idea what to think.

Weeks later I was invited to come back for a second audition.

When Willie accepted the job as dean of students for Downers Grove North High School, those two job opportunities for me were lost. But God, as always, had other plans.

I was still living with my parents in Carmi in the fall of 1978 waiting to move to Bolingbrook to join Willie, when one Sunday night the phone rang. The Jandrises were having an after-church college social in their home and Willie was calling to introduce me to someone. Anita White Pancratz was a beautiful woman who, with jet black hair, porcelain skin, and beautifully natural, heart-shaped lips, reminded me of Snow White. She was so beautiful she was crowned Miss Illinois in 1971. Married to Bruce Bickel, former quarterback for Navy, they were the special guests in Tom and Lois's home that night.

Anita told me she and Bruce were moving to Kansas City where he was to be head of Fellowship of Christian Athletes. She was leaving behind a place in a recording group known as the John Wilson Singers, and wondered if I would be interested in auditioning to take her place. I had just left behind in LA a potential slot in the Roger Wagner Chorale and a chance to conduct a large chorus in South Pasadena. Before I even moved to Chicago, God was at work.

We had just moved into our Bolingbrook home when the phone rang, and it was John Wilson, editor of Hope Publishing, composer and arranger. Anita made good on her word to recommend me.

John and I hit it off immediately. At first, we discussed my musical experience, but then discovered we were both parents of disabled kids. John's only son, Johnny, had severe autism, and functioned like an eighteen-month-old baby. John and his wife, June, kept Johnny in their home, lovingly caring for him, much the same as I did for Sasha.

In his enthusiasm, John asked me to come sing alto with the John Wilson Singers at the next session in January. I hung up flattered, but flummoxed. What kind of a conductor worth his salt invites you to sing in studio without ever hearing you? John must have had second thoughts too because a few weeks later he asked if he could drive out to Bolingbrook for a visit. He sat at my new Yamaha high-back grand as I sang for him, and both of us, I'm sure, were relieved.

Universal Studios

That first session was at Universal Studios on Rush Street in downtown Chicago in January of 1978. It was an intimidating place, where famous groups of the past and present came to lay down famous music tracks. The finest Christian artists and musicians in Chicago were part of the twelve-member John Wilson Singers. Myrna White, of "Day of Discovery" fame, was top soprano. In all the years I sang with Myrna, I NEVER heard her make a mistake or deliver less than a perfect sound. It was a high bar, and I was intimidated but excited to be able to sing with her and the other fabulous musicians.

We recorded choral demos for Hope Publishing Company and other miscellaneous choral music distributors. We recorded anthems, musicals, swing-choir music, and more. George Beverly Shea came to narrate one of our Christmas musicals. John Innes, organist/pianist for the Billy Graham crusades was often our pianist. John was so talented, he could transpose Bach. (Sorry again, non-musicians. That means he was phenomenal.)

I'll never forget my first solo. It was from a show choir piece written by Marge Roedig and it went like this:

Schubert had a horse named Sarah.
He took her to the big parade.
And all the while the band was playin','

Schubert's Sarah . . . Schubert's Sarah . . . neighed.[1]
(Cue horse neighing . . . THAT was me!)

We sang together and became like family for about twelve years. John became another wonderful mentor. He also conducted a group affiliated with Wheaton College known as the West Suburban College of Nursing Choir. They made record albums and traveled all over the country. The girls loved him and when he left them after thirteen years, he asked me to take his place.

A Concert of Just Me?

This good Baptist girl found another church home at First Baptist Church of Bolingbrook. Not long after we started attending, a group of ladies asked me if I would prepare a solo concert. I was incredulous. Just me? For an hour? They insisted and I went to work choosing music and inviting Vivian, a professional accompanist to play for me, whom I met through the John Wilson Singers. She offered to bring her son, Randy, to play violin and I busied myself writing charts for him.

The night came and inexplicably the place was filled to capacity. We poured our hearts into those beautiful songs and at the end received a standing ovation. When God pours out His blessings, He fills the cup to overflowing.

He was setting another new course for me I never saw coming.

Me, the Feminist

Perhaps my only real bruising brush with the role of women in the church was at FBC Bolingbrook. Growing up, Ann Horton was the choir director of my church in Carmi. It was Ann who led rehearsals, conducted the choir, planned the music. But she did not lead congregational worship. I was music director at FBC South Pasadena in California before coming to Bolingbrook, with the same configuration. But I was not and never have been a feminist. I respected God's Word enough that I was never interested in pushing the limits of my own role in the church. If God said men were to be the leaders of the home and the leaders in the church, I trusted Him and I trusted His Word. It is He who designed and fashioned us and understands more than we do how we best function.

I was the pianist at FBC Bolingbrook in 1978, but soon the pastor, whom I greatly admired, asked me to take over the choirs and plan all the music with a caveat. An insurance salesman named Oscar, who could not read music, would get the title and the authority of "Music Director," while I would do the work. This would cover the male leadership requirement, our pastor thought. I listened but declined. I pointed out to him respectfully how this was simply "straining at a gnat and swallowing a camel." A female choral conductor gives orders, makes demands constantly. And further, this would set up an impossible situation that made no sense functionally. Very politely, I said "no." And was quite content to continue as pianist.

But "no" was not what my pastor wanted to hear. In the ensuing months, his anger with me took some terrible turns. He viewed my refusal as pride and looked for every opportunity to humiliate me. It got so bad he actually called me out in a service, accusing me of pride.

Sasha was only three, and although my strong opinion may have caused him to diagnosis pride, the reality was very different. And his public humiliations hurt deeply.

I think feminism has done terrible destruction in the church and in the world. But I did see male dominance in church life interpreted in unhealthy ways. And this was one of them. Women have gifts and talents that should be used as much as possible. When in China, many years later, I met several young Chinese women from Western China who were placed in charge of hundreds of thousands of Christians in the underground church. Missionary history is filled with single women who went into unknown parts and literally changed the world with their teaching. There were prophetesses in the Old Testament, so we can be sure God uses women. I can't explain the finer points. I can't. But I never fought for a larger role in the church than what was asked of me. God gave me other outlets in His own way and in His own time that I would never have thought to ask for.

Beautiful Wheaton

In early 1979 we left FBC Bolingbrook and the Southern Baptist Convention altogether to join Wheaton Evangelical Free Church near what would be our future new home. The Free Church denomination originated in the Nordic countries, so there were tons of fun Swedes vs. Norwegians jokes in that crowd. "Free Church" was a term used for a church in Europe not state-controlled.

Free Church doctrine was nearly identical to the SBC although their system of governance was not. They were committed to deep Bible teaching from primary through adults, and warmly embraced AWANA Clubs and Bible memory for children. It was a perfect place to be.

Jack Schrader, also a new friend from the John Wilson Singers, was the music director and welcomed me warmly. It was almost a seamless transition to make our home in that new church.

I loved singing in the choir under Jack's leadership. On occasion I led for him and, eventually, he asked me to conduct a smaller chorus of twelve from within the choir. Because of their skill level, we were able to execute some beautiful music and perform at Free Church conventions.

Ironically, after nearly fifteen years, my pastor at the Free Church, who was also very traditional in assigning women's roles in the church, incredulously asked me to be the music director. That meant conducting the choir, planning all the music, and yes, leading Sunday morning worship. My final night as music director, I conducted DuBois's

Seven Last Words of Christ with orchestra and chorus. It was a wonderful experience!

And later, after I was long gone from that church, and on radio in Chicago, imagine my surprise when the men's ministry at Wheaton Free asked me to come be the main speaker at their men's retreat. The non-feminist was breaking new barriers. Ha! Honestly, I view it as an exception, not the rule.

In addition to the talented Jack Schrader from the Wilson Singers, Wheaton Free Church had some wonderful, professional musicians. John Innes, organist for the Billy Graham Crusades was one of them. On those occasions when I was to sing, if I saw John in the audience, my stomach gripped and most of the time, my voice expressed my nervousness in an embarrassing glitch. Remember I told you I couldn't perform without paralyzing nerves until well into my thirties.

As invitations to sing around Chicago came in, I put together a great band to go out and perform with me. There was Duncan Mathieson on bass, Doc Dalrymple on guitar, Dave Zsycki on drums, and lots of greatly talented keyboard guys on synth and piano. Their names alone were enough to make you laugh, but besides their crazy names, each had a great sense of humor. We called them the "Four Beards." Between the five of us, trust me, none of us did it for the money. But these were professional players who loved to play, and we became such fast friends, it was a joy. And most of all, God worked through our music. For the first several years of concertizing this way, I never performed the same concert twice. I was forever finding new music, writing guitar and bass and piano charts, and rehearsing them with the band a few hours before the performance. It was insanity. No smart musician I know does this, but for whatever reason, I loved the pressure and the freshness of each new challenge.

My Choir Girls

The West Suburban College of Nursing was an affiliate of Wheaton College. Located just west of Chicago proper in the beautiful Frank

Lloyd Wright–famous suburb of Oak Park, my friend and mentor John Wilson was director for thirteen years. During that time, the choir toured and made countless recordings which were played around the country on Christian radio. When John stepped down, he recommended me to take his place as director.

The girls absolutely loved "Papa John," so taking over after him was a bit like how Truman must have felt after Roosevelt.

It was actually a wonderful new phase of my musical life. We rehearsed twice weekly in the upstairs auditorium of West Suburban Hospital. Because of the constraints on me with Sasha and Jeremy, I arranged our twice monthly concert commitments to be on one Sunday a month—a morning concert followed by an evening concert in another location. Often I would sleep in my car in some random parking lot in the afternoon, then freshen up and tackle the evening.

Another gift God brought me as a result of leaving FBC Bolingbrook was a nurse named Joyce Coon. She graduated from the West Suburban College of Nursing Choir, had served in the Navy in San Diego, and was a much sought after geriatric nurse. With endless amounts of patience and love, Joyce loved working with the elderly.

Almost as soon as we met at Wheaton Evangelical Free Church, she offered to babysit for Sasha. She would drive the fifteen miles to Bolingbrook initially and soon became a part of our family. While maintaining her full-time job, Joyce lovingly cared for Sasha from the time she was three until I placed Sasha at Marklund seventeen years later. When Jeremy was born in 1980, she folded him right in. Once when he was a baby, I returned home from a trip and heard him call her "Mama." I was crushed, but that's the kind of care she gave them both.

Joyce and I were the same age, but she had never been married. Imagine her joy when she met and married Bob Coon. Sasha was fourteen by then and Joyce wanted her to be a bridesmaid. Dressed in the identical royal blue dress as the other bridesmaids, she was pushed down the aisle in her wheelchair by Bob's young son, Andy, in a tux.

Other than my mother, no one knew the circumstances of my home, better than Joyce. When she died of a horrible, unrelenting cancer in November of 2014, I flew from Washington back to Wheaton to say a final farewell. Losing her left an irreplaceable hole in my heart.

The West Sub girls were absolutely delightful. The nursing program was vigorous, and at that time the students who chose Wheaton had foreign missions or service of some kind in their mind for their future. They were a unique breed of dedicated, serious-minded girls.

But we had SO much fun. I could always tell what kind of nurse they were going to be by their personality. The take-charge gals went into emergency or surgical medicine—and they were always our choir presidents. The sweet, soft girls loved pediatrics.

Much like the Bison Glee Club, our concerts were in two parts. For the first part, the girls wore their beautifully starched uniforms, complete with white-trimmed nursing caps. But for the second half, they wore their own, individual long gowns. Sounds like a mess, but they looked wonderful.

We toured every spring to the East Coast or to Florida for ten days. These were absolutely wonderful getaways for me as an exhausted mom. The first day generally began with a long drive, always leaving me in a trance-like, sleeping stupor. After a few days of rest, my personality and humor returned, and I had more fun on tour than any of the girls could possibly have had.

While touring Washington, DC, I insisted we see everything. We hired a tour guide and sprinted from site to site all day long following her red umbrella. When we got to our host church that evening, we agreed to do a concert—just for the families. So, after that long day, we dutifully set up the risers in the church basement and began the rigor of a concert.

I was conducting a very difficult a cappella number. Mid-song, I looked at the girls, bedraggled, slumped, and tired—dressed in their street clothes, singing this very reverent song, and an internal thing welled up in me I could not control . . . laughter. I began laughing at the ridiculousness of it all, and as they gazed at my face in concentration, one by one they became overcome with stifled laughter themselves. Slowly each section became softer and softer until the piece fell apart completely. At this grand fizzle, I turned around to our audience and offered profuse apologies, but it was impossible to describe what just happened.

We sang in Disputanta, Virginia, on one tour where Reverend Brian Hobden was the new vicar. It was an old Episcopal Church, built in the 1700s. When we pulled into the parking lot of the beautiful, old stone building, it was packed, with people excitedly making their way in. The place was full and we were warmly received. Brian relocated from England where he served as vicar in the Church of England. But he found renewed, personal faith in Christ through watching *The 700 Club* and was filled with the love and joy of Christ.

The church suffered a split because, prior to Brian, it atrophied into several little old ladies, who even at this point in their lives only ever read the *Common Book of Prayer*. Brian came preaching the gospel, alive and living, and many were offended and left. So new people came from all around whose lives were being transformed. I will never forget Brian and his wife, Mary, and our wonderful conversations around the table in their large rectory where I stayed. When God is at work, He is not concerned with our labels. A staid and proper British vicar found a personal relationship with Christ through a charismatic television program. And the world in that part of Virginia was transformed.

So many funny things happened with the choir over the course of the seven years I led them. Once my watch chain caught on the button of my sleeve on my right arm and I had to finish the concert with one arm. I often wore that white suit with buttons to lead them, and sometimes people mistook me for a doctor conducting these nurses.

One Easter "my choir girls" (as little Jeremy used to call them) and I were doing a concert in a small town called Perry, Michigan. The girls were in their uniforms as the ushers began passing around a program that on the back was soliciting for the PMS Emergency Relief Fund (the Perry-Morrice-Shaftsburg Area Ambulance Service). Once again, hilarity spread like wildfire as each girl read their program. It was Easter Sunday morning, for heaven's sake, but I could barely control my laughter! I was thirty years old when I took the choir. Not much older than the girls and, as I said, always mischievous.

The Bus Driver Who Couldn't Read a Map

On a tour out east, we boarded the Trailways bus for the first day of travel, expecting a seven-hour drive, followed by a concert. As we drove and drove—and drove—we realized our bus driver was lost. And when he was lost day after day and we were late for every performance, we realized Trailways assigned a driver who had never left Chicago and could not read a map. In addition, he was surly and rude. What else could go wrong? Plenty, I would learn.

I called Trailways and demanded a replacement. Our driver was a very tall basketball-player-sized man. As he towered over me, he accused me of wanting to replace him because he was black. I summoned my full 5'7" frame, and looking up at him, pointing my finger, shouted, "I don't care if you're purple! You will treat my girls with respect, and you will get us to our concerts on time!"

Could I just insert here, there are white racists . . . and there are black racists. There are white people who can't read a map, and there are black people who can't read a map. Incompetence comes in all shapes and colors, and it is not acceptable for any of those shapes or colors.

I assigned someone each day to sit next to the driver and read the map for him. As we moved on in our journey, he burned out the brakes of our bus in the mountains and ran into a car on a ferry in New York State. Then he got lost in NYC, so our expected "tour" of two hours was reduced to thirty minutes. It was nerve-wracking and upsetting and, above all, I felt responsible for the safety of those girls.

I asked Trailways to give us another driver and they refused. I wrote them a scathing letter when we returned. Had anything happened to those students, there would have been hell to pay.

I am completely direction-challenged myself. I can read and follow a map, but cannot, for the life of me "feel" where I am or remember where I just was. So, when the choir traveled by car occasionally, I would take the lead, BUT would always assign one of the girls to ride shotgun to guide me. This wasn't just a matter of direction; it was a matter of story-telling. I would be telling my passengers some hilarious story, get totally distracted, and end up in the wrong state.

On one of our weekend tours of Indiana and Michigan, we drove in a caravan of vehicles. I led as usual with the help of my student guide. This time, a few hours in, we were met by a barrier warning: "Do Not Pass" with arrows to a detour. But we had a concert to make and fancying I knew better about such signs, I reckoned it couldn't be all that bad, so I proceeded to drive around it. Soon we were in trouble. Construction rendered the road nearly impassable and as I soldiered on, I looked back on the ten or so cars behind me, careening, and bouncing up and down wildly, students jostled out of their seats—and guess what I did? I got tickled. I always laugh when it isn't appropriate. I can't seem to help it. I do it to this day on radio. I will tell a terrible story and something about it will just seem hilarious, and I start laughing.

Once I was singing a dramatic song in the middle of a concert, on a stage with a spotlight fixed on me, when looking at the audience, all I could see was a sea of glasses. It looked like an audience of racoons gazing back at me, and you guessed it, I could barely finish the song for the laughter welling up in me. How could I explain that?

My First Visit to a Bar

We had a bus breakdown once in Wisconsin. Out in the country, there was no one around. Only a lone bar with a neon sign was in walking distance. I had never been in a bar. I had never had a drink.

Sunday school girl that I was, I felt strange and guilty entering that dark place to ask to use the phone. It's funny, isn't it? And really so silly how people who love God hold to so many labels, put up so many barriers God doesn't erect. I made my phone call and got out quickly lest sanctified-me be contaminated by such a place. What sanctimonious hogwash. Still—it's funny, don't you think?

A Major Ouch in Oostburg

Once our choir president, Terry, brought us to her hometown, Oostburg, in upstate Wisconsin where we all went tobogganing and most of us promptly bruised our tailbones. Their director—me—spent the night in excruciating pain, next day rising slowly and miserably from the front pew to conduct her wounded choir.

The hard seats of the school bus taking us back to Chicago made the return home another unforgettable adventure. Our young male driver, who had also joined in the toboggan fun, winced with pain each and every time he lifted his foot from accelerator to brake. I lost my sense of humor on that one.

Where the Boys Are

As the years went on, the college changed affiliations to Concordia at River Forest. And as that changed, at last a male student came into our midst. That was a challenge, but it too was fun.

Ray was fun and talented. We also brought Sam into the fold to handle the sound equipment. The two of them roomed together on tours. I laid down the law to them about having relationships with the girls. It was forbidden—unworkable—unwise—period. But as my last year with them progressed, I realized Sam had fallen in love with one of them, a beautiful girl named Kristin. They entered a secret engagement. But neither of them knew I knew.

At our last concert, we always had extra amounts of fun. One year the girls wore black garbage bags with tights and dressed like raisins, surrounding the audience as they sang Marvin Gaye's, "Heard

It Through the Grapevine." At the end of that concert, I brought Sam up to the front and proceeded to thank him profusely for his dedication and excellence in the many years he traveled with us. And then, I told him, as a way of saying "thanks," we had a gift for him.

Sam turned to see Kristin decorated with a huge ribbon as I brought her to his side.

Perspective

I almost said "no" when John Wilson asked me to take the West Sub Choir. How could I manage another responsibility with Sasha and a new baby? Since my parents lived 300 miles away, having twice-weekly rehearsals required intentional planning on my part for childcare. But God gave me another unexpected gift in the love of those West Sub girls to me. I poured my heart and mind into nurturing them, and in return I was the one most blessed. I had the time to pray and read my Bible on tours like I never got at home. I had time to think, and God gave me time to laugh and remember the joys of life.

My "Choir Girls" turned out to be one of the greatest blessings of my life.

One more thing. Occasionally, when Jeremy was little, I brought him to rehearsals with me. He charmed them all. But one day he was not so charming to his mother. I led rehearsals from the grand piano so all my attention was focused on the music. Toddlers aren't crazy about sharing Mom's attention, so as I was leading the girls, they watched as Jeremy dug into my purse, found a pack of matches and struck and lit one on the piano. I didn't laugh that time either.

From Concerts to Recordings

Meanwhile, back home, after those long four years of law school, Willie took the bar for the second time and, devastatingly, did not pass. Our good friend, Tom Johnson, had just lost a bruising campaign for U.S. Congress by less than one vote per precinct. His opponent had terminal cancer during the campaign, but Tom, out of honor would not use his knowledge of it in the campaign. The Republican powers at that time supported this ill candidate with the idea that if he did indeed die in office, they would appoint their hand-picked candidate, Denny Hastert. That's exactly what happened. Denny was elected to Congress and became Speaker of the House from 1999 to 2007.

Tom and his wife, Ginger, poured their hearts into that campaign, chicanery ensued, and they were terribly discouraged by the defeat. They asked us out for dinner to "celebrate" our mutual defeats.

I will never forget that discussion as we explored what it meant to be a "failure." Were losers always failures, or were losers often the ones who won? Were, in fact, winners sometimes losers? Deep and challenging stuff. We discussed next steps for all of us. Then Tom turned to me and surprised me by asking what I wanted to do next. Quietly I told him I always wanted to record a solo album, but with our finances, it would just never happen.

He told me to call his law office Monday morning to make an appointment. We would set up a limited partnership and I would have my album. And we did just that. People in my church and outside of it who enjoyed my music ministry bought shares until we had enough money to produce it. How humbling and exciting it all was.

John Innes, who had by now become a friend (even if I was still nervous to sing in front of him), agreed to produce it and we began to collect songs. Ten were needed and we chose carefully. One day John came to my house to present a song he had just written for my consideration. He sat at the piano and in another moment of complete irony, self-consciously sang for me, "Whenever I Praise Him." It was a beautiful song and became a radio play favorite.

We recorded in Anderson, Indiana, with the Indiana Philharmonic Orchestra. Sandi Patti, who was the number one female Christian recording artist at that time, sat in on one of the sessions as her two brothers provided back-up vocals.

Dr. Ivan York, my pastor, led a private dedication ceremony for the investors. We worshiped together as we listened to the title song,

"Sasha's Song." That project more than any other reflected the depth of my sorrow and my struggle to be faithful.

Getting More Back Than You Gave

When you record something like this, it doesn't just inspire the listeners, it blesses you in ways you never have imagined. Years later, after a sleepless night of worry, my alarm, set to radio, woke me up to . . . me, singing Jon Mohr's "He Is Able"!

And just like that time during the snowstorm in Iowa when God gave me *Funny Girl*, I knew He was speaking to me—this difficult morning through my own voice, reminding me of His loving, caring presence.

In ways yet to be told, the timing of "Sasha's Song" was such that my concert life exploded. The phone began ringing off the hook as I began to travel the country sharing about Sasha and singing of God's faithfulness.

Even in All This There Was Humor

We were so poor when I recorded *Sasha's Song*, I had to borrow clothes for the photo shoot to use on the cover. My first concert tour was in Ohio. On a Sunday night in Elyria, the pastor announced there was only one flight back to Chicago that night. He asked if the audience would please allow me to exit down the aisles after the concert. We were to say farewell at the outer doors so I could make that flight.

After I sang the last note, I waved to and thanked everyone, as I hurried up the aisle to the back. The audience politely followed me out to peer through the floor-to-ceiling glass doors protecting them from the cold. As the car pulled into the covered circular drive, I opened the door, and as I was waving furiously at the audience on the other side of the windows, while looking back, my worn-out half-slip fell to my ankles. I quickly stepped out of it and jumped into the car as it drove away.

Lord, I Believe

I confess, my second album began with less altruistic motives. Did people come to my concerts and buy my recordings only because of my story, or was it my voice? Was I good enough to be enjoyed only as a singer? It was important to me next to be accepted by a record company as a sort of Blue-Ribbon Seal of Approval.

In 1987 I signed with Diadem Records and recorded *Lord, I Believe*. This time I wanted to make a strong statement about my faith in Christ rather than sing of my struggles. I wanted to title it *Credo*, the Latin term for Creed, since the title song was based on the words of the Apostles' Creed. In part and paraphrased it says this:

> Lord, I believe in God, the Father Almighty, creator of
> heaven and earth.
> I believe in Jesus Christ, his only Son, our Lord, who
> was born of a virgin, crucified, died and was buried.
> I believe that he rose again from the dead on the third
> day and is seated at the right hand of God the Father
> Almighty.
> I believe He will come again to judge the living and the
> dead and that I will live forever more, just like he
> said.

My producer, Don Hart, had just produced an album for the Brooklyn Tabernacle Choir when he flew to meet me in Chicago. He presented one of their powerful songs, "I'm Goin' Home," as a potential duet. It was a no-brainer. Don's arrangement was gorgeous and so was Michael English's voice as he joined me unexpectedly at the last minute in studio the morning we recorded it. Mark Baldwin, well-known soloist, composer, and song writer was scheduled to join me, but woke up with laryngitis. He reached out to Michael and assured the concerned-me that Michael had a great voice. It was the most successful song of the ten, reaching #4 on the CCM Music Charts in 1987. (Michael was the new guy in Nashville then who later became a multiple Dove Award–winning artist and soloist with the Gaither Vocal Band.)

We premiered that album at the Odeum in Chicago. Greg Brown, who later became a dear friend, was a well-known Top-40 DJ in Chicago and he hosted the event in his dapper tux. We had a large band this time with background singers. Manny Mendelson, the Chicago pianist famous for his rendition of "Rhapsody in Blue" on all the United Airlines commercials, came to play along with my long-time musical partner and accompanist, Larry Moore. It was a great night.

I met Larry at Stuart and Jill Briscoe's church in Waukesha, Wisconsin. He was the keyboardist for Elmbrook Church and accompanied me the week I was part of their spring musical. I needed a new accompanist, but neither of us could have imagined the three-hour drive time separating us would prove not to be an obstacle. For the next many years, Larry and I traveled all over the country to perform.

There were such hilarious moments. Like the time Larry needed a new suit for performances and hired my good Chicago friend, Odie, who owned a very large fashion house for custom men's wear. Odie and his beautiful wife, Sharon, a fashion designer who made dresses for me, drove a Rolls Royce and lived in a beautiful home decorated in white complete with a white baby grand. Odie had panache. Larry on the other hand was a no-nonsense upstate New Yorker—and he was color blind. So, when the suit he chose arrived at his home in Wisconsin, his wife, Carol, pointed out to him, as she pulled it out of the box, he had chosen bright purple.

One more Larry story. Don't play poker with Larry. He often has an expressionless face that disguises his wicked sense of humor. We were performing a Christmas concert one year, I in red glam and Larry in his tux, when the next tune in the line-up required a full orchestra. The only way I could perform it was to have someone play the orchestral track by holding a mic next to a boom box. I was all into this great tune, when I glanced behind me to see it was Larry standing erectly in his tux, holding the boom box to the mic, looking straight ahead with his famously deadpan expression. Once again, inappropriate hilarity ensued.

We had such great times and great fellowship. Larry and Carol are like family to Bruce and me still today.

The Sacrifice of My Parents

How did I manage that travel with a new baby and a disabled daughter? Amazingly and unequivocally, it was my selfless mom and dad. As opportunities began to flood in, my parents drove 300 miles to my Chicago home to stay with the children. But as these occasions became more frequent, I sat down with my parents and explained clearly that I did not have to do any of those concerts. I stressed to them I did not expect them to drop their lives to serve my needs.

Twice we had this conversation, and twice they affirmed their willingness to come whenever, however long I needed them. And so it began. They had their own bedroom. They took over the feeding, bathing, and lifting of Sasha and the care of my little boy, Jeremy, whenever I called.

When I was asked in 1990 to come to Japan for a three-week concert tour, they lovingly, willingly, came. And in addition to the regular responsibilities, Sasha had spinal surgery just before I was to leave. My mom and dad took on all of that—for me. Whatever criticisms I might deign to make of them are silenced by that act of love. We were a team. And I was thrilled to bring them so much joy and pride in the music and ministry God gave me.

Japan, Sin, and Shame

In Japan I sang nineteen concerts in twenty-one days. We moved from place to place on the bullet train to each of the five cities we visited. Song-Rise Ministries was my sponsor. Since learning English was all the rage in Japan at the time, they invited Christian artists to come sing for secular audiences as a gateway to presenting them the gospel of Jesus Christ. I spent years doing concerts in the United States, sharing about my experiences with Sasha, my faith struggles, and God's goodness. What in the world would I say to a Japanese audience who knew nothing of Jesus?

As I prayed, the idea of the Eastern notion of "shame" struck me as the way to approach the issue of sin. Without acknowledgment of our sin, we can't ever really know God. He is holy, and the gulf between us and a holy God requires that. We can only come humbly before Him, if we understand our need.

I began to speak of the shame they clearly understood. Japanese are known for suicides if they disappoint family, their culture, or in any way bring shame. And there is no remedy for this in their culture. I tried to explain how God sent His Son to take away their shame. I discovered that in Japanese culture it was a shame to have a disabled child. They hid their broken children away for the fear of it.

I was then able to share about Sasha and how she enriched my life in unexpected ways and gave me a clearer understanding of everything. They began to bring their disabled children to my concerts. One night a large group came along with a neurologist. They asked to meet with me after the concert. I felt so totally humbled to be asked such open questions, to encourage and comfort them from my own broken heart. It was a wonderful thing God did during those three weeks.

But of course, there's always the funny stuff. After a very long day of travel, we arrived at a large Japanese home to spend the night. I quickly changed for the evening concert without time to bathe. When I got home, the elderly wife stayed up late to prepare a bath for me. I was utterly exhausted, but had to avail myself of her kindness nonetheless. Japanese bathrooms are large. The entire room is tiled. A stool with soap and a scrub brush sat next to the big, heated tub called the *ofuro*. You were to clean yourself thoroughly on the stool, then step into the tub to rinse off. It was about 55 degrees in the house that night as I shivered sitting on that stool, hurriedly scrubbing my tired body. I couldn't wait to get into the warm *ofuro*, but as I lifted the lid, the water was literally boiling. My sweet, thoughtful landlady had set the temperature too high. I was unable to rinse off, and my body temperature had come down so low, I was unable to sleep for shivering with cold all night. It made a funnier story much later.

I always jogged on overseas trips. It was a wonderful way to see the country and the people. We were staying in a very large Japanese home. It was early morning as I walked to the front entryway to slip on my shoes and go out. Suddenly the wife appeared and in a flurry of Japanese, bowed and backed out of the room. She managed to communicate to me to "please wait!" Soon, her husband appeared and as I watched, proceeded to put on his shoes also. Motioning to the door, he was going with me on my run.

We had only gone a few yards when my host began to breathe heavily, then heave. I stopped running and took his arm to stop him. He recovered for a minute, then led me on a circuitous route to an unknown destination—a track! I hated running on a track, but dutifully, that's what I did as he watched.

Later, when we had an interpreter, I discovered my dear, most gracious host was seventy-seven years old and had never run a day in his life! He just didn't want me to get lost.

The year 1990 would be the last year of my touring life.

Willie and I separated in January of 1991.

Once again, I resolved in prayer I would do anything God asked of me. I had no need to be well known—just obedient. I had never even imagined the wonderful musical opportunities He brought into my life, but I was grateful for them.

So, with open hands, I let them go. I would teach a neighborhood Bible study.

6

Radio Moscow

It was the spring of 1991. "Glasnost" or "openness" had come to the Soviet Union. After nearly sixty years of oppression, propaganda, poverty, and harsh punishment of dissent, the Iron Curtain was sagging. From intellectuals like Russian author Alexandr Solzhenitsyn who was banished to the Gulag, to just ordinary believing Christians, beaten and jailed—the grip of Communism was in a free fall.

Oligarchs were plundering their own country, selling minerals and other important natural resources to enrich themselves. The Russian people, uncertain at first, were carefully, gingerly stepping out to speak up. Some were becoming cautious capitalists, beginning businesses, insisting on payment in "hard currency" (i.e., American dollars). It was a time of national confusion and uncertainty.

Americans of all stripes were descending upon Russia to take advantage of this "window of time" when opportunities were endless. Christian ministries did the same. The gospel, or "Good News" of a Savior for all men could be openly proclaimed! Time could not be lost to proclaim it.

It was into that mix I was hired by the Bible League to spend two weeks in Moscow, gathering stories and testimonies of the Russian people that would culminate in a radio special broadcast back to the States called *Seven Days of Hope*.

In the spring of 1991, I co-anchored the first American broadcast from Radio Moscow with Scott Hatch of CBN. While Pravda masterfully exported the powerful Soviet Communist delusions in print, Radio Moscow was the sister propagandist on radio. Broadcast in over seventy languages, and focused primarily on Russian/American tensions, it was a world-wide propaganda powerhouse to be reckoned with. If you can remember from the '80s the awe of metaphorically stepping over the wall dividing West and East Berlin to peek inside the Communist East for the first time in decades, you can get a glimpse of the awe we felt at being allowed inside this formidable tool of our enemy, the Soviets.

We were each given code names, using American screen stars. Mine was Raquel Welch. It probably should have been Carol Burnett. We entered the building, signed in with our celebrity names, then climbed to the top floor studio where our consistently drunken engineer Sasha, greeted us. ("Sasha" in Russia, is the short name for any man named Alexander. It was Dr. Zhivago's pet name for his son in the movie from which I got my daughter's name.)

Seven Days of Hope was miraculously transmitted back to the States to tell the story of what was happening inside the Soviet Union. And to urge Americans to send money in order to produce and distribute Bibles during this incredible window of time.

How Did This Happen?

How in the world did I get an assignment like this? A Christian musician conducting serious interviews about world affairs? It makes no sense to me either, except for God's hand on my life. Here's how it happened:

Do you remember the first solo concert I was asked to do when we moved to Chicago from California? I walked away from an opportunity in Berlin to go to New York to "become famous." I let go of musical opportunities in California to move to Chicago, and before I even moved there, was linked miraculously to John Wilson. It was at a recording session with the John Wilson Singers where I met Vivian, who then accompanied me at my first concert.

Vivian, in turn, asked me to come and sing on a Sunday night at Christ Church Oak Brook, her home church. Christ Church is a beautiful place. I sang in the chapel that night, designed with a wall of greenery and a cascading water fountain. Nervous, as always, I chose to sing a song based on Psalm 91, "He Shall Give His Angels Charge over Thee." It was a psalm of hope that reminded me of my precious Sasha, so I poured my heart into telling her story and delivering that song. Vivian's son, Randy, once again joined me with his violin.

When I finished, there was no response, no expression from the audience. I felt sad that I had failed somehow to communicate. I learned later, Christ Church was part of the Christian Reformed Denomination, famously stoic during church services. The Dutch just don't show expression in church. It's part of their culture. For many years after that, I was a frequent guest at Christian Reformed retreats, churches. I did a two-week tour of Christian Reformed Schools in Iowa, Nebraska, and South Dakota, and spent years thereafter being the voice of the Bible League radio specials. But more on that later.

On that night, God did something miraculous. In the midst of my discouragement at the lack of response, a man and his wife and three kids surrounded me with superlatives. Jim Warren was vivacious, effusive, and moved by my story and the song. He was a music director for Calvary Church in Oak Park, on vacation that Sunday evening. He and the family went to another church first, but when they realized the service was going to feature missionary slides, quickly left and came last-minute to Christ Church. He was not supposed to be there that evening.

Jim was the host of *Prime Time America* for Moody Radio, heard nationally each weekday during drivetime. Right there on the spot Jim asked me do an interview to tell my story. Little did we both know that would be the beginning of a decades-long friendship. Later when Jim's co-host left to get married, he asked me to join him.

I thought he was crazy. I'd never done radio, and I had a Southern Illinois twang from my upbringing. Who would want to listen to me? But he insisted. I sat next to him responding to news stories, music, or whatever came across and began to get compliments on my great abilities as a broadcaster. It seemed so wrong to me. I was just talking. *You mean they pay people to do this?*, I asked myself.

Jim was a master teacher. He covered the news, played beautiful music, interviewed great guests, and taught me the basics of radio that of course laid the groundwork for a future I could not have imagined.

Music was still my life. I continued to sing, conduct, and travel, but would carve out two weeks at a time to co-host on *Prime Time America*. For at least ten years we did this. Together we hosted a live show from Urbana 84, a huge missions conference held at the University of Illinois every three years where thousands of college students dedicated their lives to foreign missions.

One of the highlights for me was interviewing Billy Graham in the locker room at U of I where we set up our studio. I grew up listening to Dr. Graham as often as possible. My mother loved his preaching and so did I. I loved how he merged current events with the gospel and how the Holy Spirit moved so powerfully through his words. That merger of news and gospel laid the groundwork for what became my own attempt to do the same in the various mediums God opened to me.

Because of my admiration for Dr. Graham, it was all I could do to maintain my composure to ask him questions. I was NOT a seasoned broadcaster by any means. There was a steep learning curve. Once, Jim asked if I wanted to take the lead in an interview with Senator Strom Thurmond. I had a great question, but after summoning my very best announcer voice to introduce him, I just froze. Nothing would come out of my mouth. Jim graciously jumped in, saying "Did you forget your question?" Mortified, I could only nod a silent, "yes."

When I recorded *Sasha's Song*, Jim insisted on featuring all ten songs. I must admit the album had the anointing of the Holy Spirit all over it. It was a work of love and submission to the sovereignty of God and to this day, the songs still move me.

The day Jim interviewed me about those songs, then played each and every one of them, was the day my phone began to ring off the hook for concert work. No one can tell me God wasn't in each of those miraculous meetings, leading me each step of the way to serve Him in new and different ways.

A Divorced Christian Musician

Christian musicians or church leaders who went through a divorce at that time were no longer permitted to be in official ministry. I knew when my husband and I were officially divorced on what would have been our twentieth wedding anniversary, June 5, 1991, it would be the end of my Christian music career. Divorced women, it seems to me, often take the course of widely berating their former husbands, sometimes, I think to justify the divorce, or perhaps other times, out of their great pain. I was determined NOT to do that to my children or my former husband. People would have to think what they wanted to think, and God would justify me in His own time and in His own way. I remember attending a large church in Wheaton one Sunday where I had sung many times. I could feel the stares of people in the congregation, but while reading Scripture, God gave me 1 Corinthians 4:2–5 (NIV, emphasis added):

> *Now it is required that those who have been given a trust must prove faithful. I care very little if I am judged by you or by any human court; indeed, I do not even judge myself. My conscience is clear, but that does not make me innocent. It is the Lord who judges me. Therefore judge nothing before the appointed time: wait until the Lord comes. HE will bring to light what is hidden in darkness and will expose the motives of the heart. At that time each will receive their praise from God.*

To be clear, I absolutely hold the biblical view that divorce should not take place without biblical reasons. Marriage remains a sacred vow that should not be broken. But I was not going to share the details of mine in order to save my own reputation. God would take care of that and He would take care of me and my ten-year-old boy and sixteen-year-old girl with severe disabilities. I trusted Him. My fervent prayer was I would honor Him in the way I conducted myself as a single woman. If not as a Christian musician, I would serve Him in new ways.

And that's when the phone rang.

It was Domain Communications calling to ask if I wanted to go to Moscow for two weeks and gather interviews for a radio special. You can't understand how miraculous that was until I tell you about my love for Russian history. My fascination began when I was a girl growing up during the Cold War, then increased when I lived in Berlin where Russian/American tensions were felt and heard at their most intense. I read *Nicholas and Alexandra*, the story of the last Czar of Russia and his wife and family being brutally murdered by the Communists. I learned of Rasputin, read *Peter the Great*, and learned of the bloody history and great conquests of the Russian leaders. I watched *Dr. Zhivago*, and named my daughter Sasha, but for last-minute insistence from my husband, would have named my son, Nicholas Michel.

When that call came, while I was still separated, not divorced, the uncertainty palpable, I knew once again God was showing me His great love and in addition making provision for me and my small family.

Even with the experience with Jim through *Prime Time America*, I conducted precious few serious interviews, and certainly not by myself. This was a big leap of faith for Domain, and for me, but we took it!

Back to Russia with Love

Off to Russia I went to meet up with the chief engineer of the project, Jimmy Leonovich. Jimmy was a fluent Russian-speaker whose family were refugees from Russia. Thank God for that, because when we got there, the promise of an interpreter and a list of already scheduled interviews vaporized. Through Jimmy's Slavic gospel contacts, we managed to secure a former ballerina, Tanya, to be my guide and help find great people to interview.

I've already described the final broadcast, but in the days leading up to it, there were so many incredible experiences and interviews, an entire chapter could be written on that alone.

The KGB Agent with a Heart

Yuri Miniyev was the head of English Language Programming at Radio Moscow. He walked me through the huge open room where broadcasters sitting in glassed-in booths could be seen reading and transmitting, up on risers, like an elegant gymnasium, in several languages. Yuri let me listen in on the absolutely beautiful Russian woman with the captivating voice, reading Russian propaganda to English-speaking people around the globe. It was not hard to guess the effect on the listeners.

We proceeded to an upper floor and moved to a large wooden table with equally large, heavy wooden chairs that made loud noises when adjusted on the parquet floor. I set up the equipment and began, without notes to conduct the interview. Yuri, the KGB Agent, head of English language broadcasting, was amazingly candid with me. He told me he had a grandmother who was a Christian who told him about God. Everyone I interviewed told me they had a grandmother who told them about God. As America has now moved to a time in which our children and grandchildren don't have the respect they once had for their grandparents, I have never forgotten what the Russian people I interviewed told me about the power of their grandmothers to plant the seed of God they never forget, in spite of sixty years of atheism. Yuri showed me a box he opened to reveal a cross his grandmother gave him.

Later in the conversation he shared how up until recently the KGB went into underground church meetings, beating and arresting people. I looked at him and said, "But, Yuri, your grandmother was part of the underground church. Didn't that bother you to do that?" He paused, moving his very loud wooden chair as he adjusted his seat and said dramatically in a low, emotional voice, "It affected me . . . very much."

The Ballerina and Her Sorrow

Tanya was a wonderful interpreter. We traveled all over Moscow and the suburbs together, interacting with everyone from a drunk in a public park who shared with me, "We have no hope," to a professor at Moscow University, living in the run-down, urine-drenched, high-rise government apartment like everyone else in Moscow. Everyone lived the same in Communism, you see, all in the same horrible, run-down squalid conditions.

As women do, I shared with Tanya about my family—Jeremy, Sasha and her disability. It was then I realized as in Japan, it was a shameful thing in Russia to have a disabled child. Reluctantly at first, Tanya told me about her son, Alex, who suffered from autism. It was yet another gift from God to allow me to encourage her from experience and to give her, no doubt the first time in her atheist life, a glimpse at God's view of such a thing and His power to help us through it.

That led us to the next incredible interview. Tanya wanted me to meet the doctor who was a specialist in autism, who treated Alex in her "clinic" in Moscow. The clinic was yet another apartment in a run-down high-rise Dr. Clara Labidinsky converted into a place to treat autistic children and their beleaguered families.

Dr. Labidinsky was a beautiful woman with incredibly blue eyes and lines on her face to demonstrate her years of devotion to such a sad, thankless task. As we began the interview, she demonstrated her brilliance by describing to me the history of autism, the medical indications, the theories on root causes, as though I was attending a lecture from a distinguished professor. But then her voice changed. I watched as her thoughts drifted and she gazed off to the side and upward and said quietly, "but we are beginning to think . . . that MAYBE . . . there is a God."

I will never forget that moment. I can still hear her voice, her inflection, and chills still move over my skin to recall it. It was a holy moment—just like the one I experienced with Yuri. A moment when the realization of the reality and presence of God came to each of them. And I had a front-row seat. It changed me as I saw God change them.

Hand-Copied Bibles

Because of "glasnost," we were able to attend a large open gathering of members of the underground church in a Communist Meeting Hall. The world was strange during that window of time. The room was filled in no small part with babushkas, older women in scarves, clutching hand-copied books of the Bible, hand-copied hymnals. They had weather-beaten faces, making them all seem old when they were likely not.

I watched from the audience as Christians from various ministries came up on the platform to speak to those beleaguered saints who had long suffered oppression. The Americans had on beautiful clothes, new shoes, complete with perfect hair as they preached from their leather-bound Bibles. Something came over me I didn't expect. It was shame. When I got up to speak, I felt God prompting me to apologize and say it is we Americans who should be sitting at their feet, learning from them. I thanked them for the example they were to the world of faithfulness and steadfast endurance. And then I shut up. What could I teach them?

Socialized Medicine Is Great

Perhaps the most challenging interview I conducted was at a large hospital in Moscow. At the table was a Russian doctor in a traditional, Western-style white coat. Next to him was a Russian Orthodox priest who looked like he stepped out of the fourteenth century. If you can imagine photos of the famous mystic Rasputin, advisor to Czarina Alexandra, just before the Russian Revolution—with long black hair and beard, a black cap, a long black robe with a cross—this was the priest.

I was not prepared for what they told me. In Russian hospitals, there was so much corruption, families had to bribe people to clean the room or bathe their loved ones. Nothing was safe from theft, and no one could be trusted to administer whatever medicines were available.

Abortion was used as birth control. I asked the doctor and the priest if, after sixty years of atheistic communism, there was any guilt expressed by women aborting their babies. They told me that at least in some, there was. Imagine that. They didn't believe in God yet they felt inherently bad about the process of eliminating their babies. Romans 1 tells us that from the beginning of time God has revealed Himself to man through nature. God-consciousness seemed to have broken through atheism in that situation.

And then they asked me something completely stunning. They sincerely wanted to know what it was like to have churches involved with hospitals. As an American, I couldn't think of a hospital that wasn't affiliated with a denomination or church. Good Samaritan, Christ Hospital, Lutheran General, Our Lady of Mercy. The Christian beginnings of the Red Cross, the concept of the Great Physician—all were unknown to them, and medical care without those foundations was incomprehensible to me. How could I answer that?

They were brainstorming trying to merge the two concepts because they speculated that compassionate care and integrity was what was missing in their system.

How could I have ever believed in 1991 that America in a few decades would begin moving to the Moscow model—a Godless system devoid of mercy, driven by money and profit?

Meeting Tanya's Sasha

On my last day in Moscow, Tanya wanted me to meet her little boy and her husband. My Russian-speaking travel partner and radio engineer, Jimmy, took me to the subway with copious notes on how to transfer more than once so I could make it safely to the outskirts of Moscow.

Tanya was waiting for me when I arrived at the station, and we walked to her single-family home a few blocks away. Alexander was an adorable little seven-year-old, and her husband, who also looked like Rasputin, was fascinating. An illustrator for science textbooks, he created those incredibly detailed black and white renderings of insects and other intricate creatures. At that time food was not easy to get for Muscovites, but Tanya made a full, wonderful meal of roast chicken and peas with potatoes.

Her husband somehow maintained his Russian Orthodox beliefs. After we sat at the table, I asked Tanya if it was okay if I prayed. She interpreted that request to her husband who immediately jumped from the table, turned toward the East, and began to bow in repetitive fashion, speaking chant-like phrases in Russian. I jumped up to join him as best I could and then prayed in English. It sounds amusing, but it showed me once again how big our God really is and how He manifests Himself in different ways around the world. People have their particular ways of worship and practice, but He is the same, almighty, all-powerful Creator of the universe who makes this world make sense.

God was so good to me to break me out of how small I made Him out to be, not only in the rigid traditions I was raised in, but in the lost joy of rejecting other cultural reflections of Him because they are different from mine.

Mahatma Gandhi once said, "I'd be a Christian if it were not for the Christians." Albert Einstein, an agnostic not an atheist, reportedly observed that the vastly incomprehensible, but incredibly orderly universe made him believe in a "lawgiver." But, whatever power it was, Christians had made "him" too small. I understand in part what he meant.

And thus, the seeds were planted for an expansion of my own heart and mind as He took me out into the world to learn from others and share what God taught me with them.

I came back to the States a changed person, waiting for my next unknown assignment.

And then the phone rang again.

Great-Grandpa Towery, center,
Grandmother Minnie (my mom's mother)
5th adult from the left

Lorene, Lois, Lucille, Lillian & Charlie Wilson
1926

Picking fruit in California 1926,
Lois second from left

Pioneer Family — L to R,
Earl, Grandma Fannie
Bland, Ida, Grandpa
Bennie, Dovie

Grandpa Duckworth, a neighbor & his work horses

My beautiful mom in the rose-colored dress
she designed & made

Cpl Wallace Duckworth — on the
ship to England and World War II, 1943
Look out, Hitler!

Kindergarten — I wouldn't smile,
because my front tooth had been
knocked out. See a pattern here?

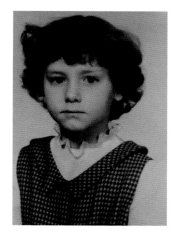

"Close that book, and bathe that baby!"

My little ones, fresh from a bath

Sandy, Sasha, Jeremy

Sasha, happy & innocent at two

Sasha when she could still smile — age three

Sasha & G'pa Duckworth summer '77

Sasha with my mom & dad at our home in Carmi

Singing "Sasha's Song" at Joni Tada's Conference on the Church and the Disabled — 1988

Celebrating Sasha's 16th birthday with friends who loved and cared for her. Joyce is behind me, L to R, Christopher Verbel, Joyce's husband, Bob, Jeremy, Judy Everswick, Seth, then Ruth Verbel, my mom, Sarah Verbel, and my dad

A tender moment, 1994

Congressman Henry Hyde escorts Sasha

Easter with my grownup girl

Sasha's Marklund family

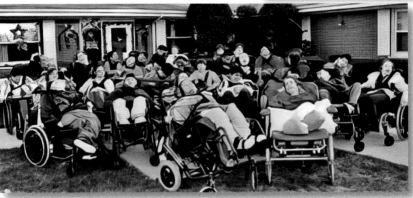

The first time Sasha met baby Moses — little did we know it was our last time to see her alive

Jeremy preaches at Sasha's funeral

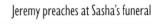

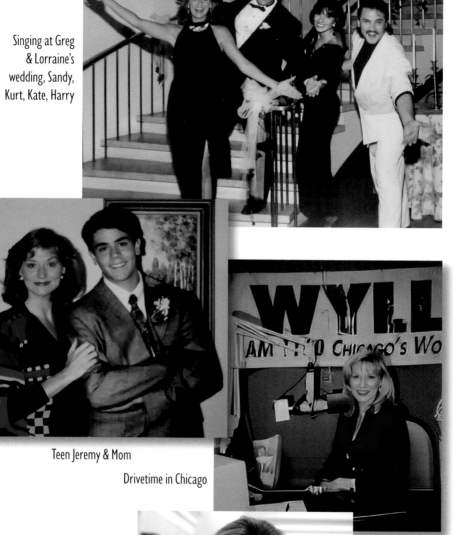

Singing at Greg & Lorraine's wedding, Sandy, Kurt, Kate, Harry

Teen Jeremy & Mom

Drivetime in Chicago

Can't talk about dogs or sports!

Ask me about my dog.

Radio Moscow

Comrade Rios

Smiling for Mao

"I'm standing
on the Great Wall
of China!"

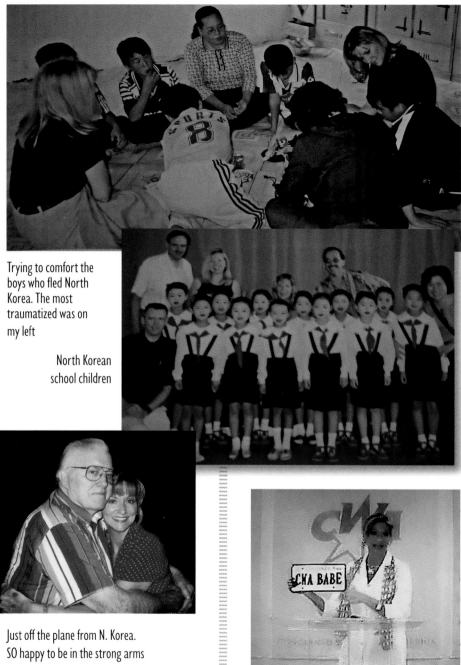

Trying to comfort the boys who fled North Korea. The most traumatized was on my left

North Korean school children

Just off the plane from N. Korea. SO happy to be in the strong arms of my dad!

The CWA Babe — having some fun with my staff

Barry Lynn, Sandy, Michael Newdow, Jerry Falwell & Phil Donahue

Chuck Colson, Joni Tada, Ken Tada, Sandy, Andrea Lafferty, signing the Manifesto on Biotechnology & Human Dignity

FBI Graduation 1989 — Bruce with his mom and dad

Not a bad date! Spectacular night at the White House

Best night ever! January 31, 2009

Dr. Lutzer tying a good knot!

Who laughs like this at their wedding?

Bruce & his college
buddies — trouble

My dear friends!

Great way to start a marriage! Colonoscopy for two at Mayo

Beautiful Mt. Rushmore, July 3, 2020

President Trump's best speech ever!
July 3, 2020 Mt. Rushmore

Comforting a Gold Star mom with my friend,
Ginni Thomas, at the annual "Wreaths Across
America" at Arlington National Cemetery

Happy Mothers' Day, 2016!
Biking accident in front of the
White House

It was a great
twenty-four years! !

Gordon Chang & me sharing
a moment of laughter

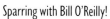

Sparring with Bill O'Reilly!

Sometimes we actually have fun!

My dear friend and mentor, Phyllis Schlafly

Going after the SPLC!

A moment with my friend, one of
America's champions, Tom Fitton

Infamous meeting with President Trump
at the White House

"The Return" September 2020

Home from
Scotland!

Which beard is real? Jeremy & Asa

Grandma in her glory!

Sweet Cates, healing my heart

Let's go, Cubbies!

The day before Bruce jousted
with Angus — and lost

Buried in love

Bruce loves this photo.
Black Hills of South Dakota

Me and my "Big Sister"

Sweethearts forever!

Worshipping at my home church

7

Another Phone Call?

It was the summer of 1991. It was up to me to support my family now. Concert work and choral conducting brought in decent money, but not enough to sustain a home and two children in the beautiful town of Wheaton.

"Chapel of the Air," at that time a well-known broadcast ministry founded by David and Karen Mains, graciously reached out and gave me a job organizing meetings in major cities focused on spiritual renewal. As a singer, I was often greeted at my destination with flowers and snacks in my room. In this new role, I deplaned anonymously in jeans without makeup and went to work sorting boxes of books, setting tables, and juggling rosters. I enjoyed it immensely. Organizing was something I loved to do, and anonymity was a precious gift. I didn't want to be the center of anyone's attention as I processed what this new life was going to be.

My parents were more than generous. They paid off the mortgage on my home and the loan on my car. All I had to do was earn enough to supply the rest of our needs. John Wilson hired me to write piano arrangements which were published by Hope Publishing. I knew how much I needed to make ends meet, and for the first time in my adult life, I didn't toss and turn with anxiety over money. Jeremy, Sasha, and I had just enough to cover our needs. I never liked depending on my parents for money and once they freed me from debt, I never had to ask for another penny. I can't tell you how gratifying that was.

But it didn't happen apart from God's provision.

One day, in that same house in that same kitchen, just as the phone rang before, another call came that would transform my life again.

It was the anchorman for Moody Broadcasting, Ted Seelye. In his deep, resonant, voice, he told me there was a new radio station in Chicago with a fresh-on-the-scene new afternoon host named Dick Staub who had become very successful. They were looking for a woman to do an early afternoon show to build audience leading up to Dick's show. "Would you be interested?" Ted asked me. "Is a blue bird blue? Is the Pope Catholic?" I shouted at the other end.

Soon thereafter I found myself in the office of WYLL Station Manager Phil Bandy. Phil was such a nice guy. Personable and fun, I liked him immediately. The interview process was slow, and in the interim, I was offered the chance to move to Orlando, Florida, and co-host a new show with Vonette Bright, wife of the founder of Campus Crusade for Christ, Bill Bright.

I relayed that information to Phil, hoping he would move ahead with the process. Transferring to Orlando with Sasha, leaving our support system, would have been daunting. Thankfully, Phil brought me in for another interview and offered me the job that day. Then he added, "We're looking for a show on women's issues."

Everything in me recoiled and with unmitigated hubris, and without hesitation, I answered, "If you're looking for a show about breast-feeding and menopause, I'm not your man!" Oh, brother. Who does that? Me, a single mom with a young son and a disabled daughter and no real job, could afford to be so brash, right?

Rather than putting me in my place, Phil simply asked, "Well, what would you want to do?" I told him I wanted to talk about the world, the news, music, fashion, movies, all of it with NONE of it relating specifically to men or women. Just a good talk radio show where I could talk about interesting things that interested me.

To be fair to myself, I already had an aversion to feminism and women's rights. And from the time I was a girl, I preferred the conversation of men. I don't know why. I certainly love being a woman, and I had great women friends, but I always worked with men. It just happened that way.

There were very few women, if any, who did serious talk radio then. The thought was men wouldn't want to listen to women talk about news and politics as they didn't prefer women doing sports announcing. I did not set out to change that. It just happened.

After I was on the air and established my own audience, women, men, teens, and grandmas were regular listeners. So were black and Hispanic Chicagoans, suburbanites, and city dwellers, Christians and non-Christians. But all of that developed over time.

Let me tell how it really happened.

Embarrassing Myself

The first time I hit the airwaves on WYLL, Phil Bandy thought it would be good for me to fill in for Dick Staub. Remember I had NEVER done a radio show by myself. Never managed the controls, never watched the breaks, never delivered the news and weather, never learned how to do a proper interview, tease a segment. I was a musician—period.

So that first outing was a lot like throwing a minnow in a shark tank. I was to do two hours. The first hour was on the topic of gambling because Illinois was in the midst of expanding its casino licenses. I knew nothing about gambling. I spent the morning reading everything I could find and talking to people who might know something.

Heart pounding, I placed colorful "stickums" on the controls so I could remember what was what. There were a lot of "whats." I identified myself in my best announcer voice then proceeded to lay the groundwork for the gambling dilemma. Next, I opened the phone lines. THE PHONE LINES? What if no one called? What would I say for an hour by myself about gambling?

Oh, Lord. I went to a break and prayed the ten lines would light up. And guess what? They did. As the minutes proceeded, I felt myself relaxing as I got the hang of answering the phones, placing people on hold, or dropping the rude ones altogether.

The next hour would be a piece of cake. Two of my Willow Creek friends from the Vocal Team of which I was a part were commercial jingle singers. Renee and Greg came into the studio and sat across from me, watching with humor as I tried to navigate the logistics. Renee was the famous voice from the Miller Beer Commercials, and Greg was the voice of the McDonald's "You Deserve a Break Today" campaign, among many, many other credits between them. We played sample commercials and talked about the jingle industry which was at that time booming in Chicago. It was great fun. I loved it. Until . . .

It was time for the third hour of the show, which the regular host Dick Staub pre-recorded. It was my job to set up that last hour properly at the top of the final hour. I had sixty seconds to welcome people back, introduce myself, and set up the pre-recorded segment. When the music began, I watched the producer through the window carefully as she pointed at me to begin. In my best announcer voice, I welcomed them back, introduced myself and proceeded to say with confidence and verve, "Stay tuned, ladies and gentlemen. Because in the next hour it will be your favorite Dick. And he's mine too!"

With that fine pronouncement, my minute was gone. I felt the hot rush of blood run up my face while an equal force of absolute hilarity welled up in my stomach. What had I done?! This was Christian radio. I ran down the hall to Phil Bandy's office and breathlessly confessed what I said before anyone else darkened his door. Phil just laughed, and in my mortification, I did too. Greg and Renee told me later they nearly ran off the road listening!

And that's how my career in radio began.

Chicago—1:00–3:00 Chicago One to Three

At the last minute, Phil decided to give me a co-host. I didn't blame him. Ken Smith was a local media personality who did a dead-ringer imitation of Johnny Carson. With dry wit, he was a funny guy. But he was a free-wheeling dude who could NOT follow a radio clock. I would be waving frantically that it was time to break, but he was just enjoying his story too much to stop. He was a sweetheart, but it just wasn't working. Eventually, Phil gave him another assignment, and I was left on my own to figure out how in the world to do talk radio.

In time, Phil let me hire a producer. Steve Bynum was a towering, former football player from Notre Dame. He looked like a black terrorist, intimidating with his bald head, single earring, and scary demeanor. But he was a pussycat. So smart and so sweet, we became fast friends.

Later, as things became complicated at work, Steve was my rock. For some reason Dick got it in his head I wanted to take his drive-time show—which I never did—but his paranoia led him to say and do some very bad things. He was making my life miserable with threats, canceling my guests because they were "A" List and should only be on his show. I knew he was unhinged when one day, during a live show, he went into the control room and began shouting and threatening Steve, while Steve was operating the board. Had Steve chosen to respond, Dick would have gotten the short end of the altercation stick. It was crazy. And one of the complicating factors was Phil was so nice, he was letting it all happen.

One really bad day, my very good friend, Joe Scheidler, founder of Pro-life Action League, known as the "Green Beret" of the pro-life movement, was in studio with me. When I told him I was afraid I was going to be fired after the show for wearing perfume, he surprised and delighted me with a story about a day in Boston when a host was about to be fired because of the discussion they were having on abortion. Joe and the host locked the studio doors and continued to broadcast to the end, as the station manager pounded on the door. He had me laughing so hard, my nerves settled down. And thank goodness, Phil didn't do Dick's bidding on that day.

The war raged between us, or from him to me, I should say, and every day became misery. One day it all stopped. I came to the studio just before noon, to find Phil Bandy had been fired. So had Dick Staub.

In a quick turn of events, the new station manager offered me Dick's 3:00–6:00 time slot, gave me two weeks to hire my own staff, and an altogether new chapter began. And how ironic. I NEVER wanted Dick's spot. In fact, when it was offered, I dreaded it, because I understood the responsibility I was taking on. We lost a great talent in Dick and just an altogether great guy in Phil.

The Sandy Rios Show

In 1997, the new station manager, John Timm, and I flew to Colorado to meet with the regional Salem VP to plan the new show. I was taken aback by the confidence they had in me. They told me I could be the best host on the Salem Radio Network. I didn't really believe that. But they put their money on my abilities, and gave me free rein to hire not one, but two producers.

I knew by then how radio worked and what I wanted to do. I wanted to do a top-notch radio show offering the highest quality content. I wanted to create a show that appealed to Christians and non-Christians, male and female, black and white, and anything in-between. But I did NOT want to hide the truth of the gospel, the Good News that there IS a Savior for all people. I was NEVER ashamed of my faith in Christ nor did I ever shrink from sharing it. But how would the show work?

I hired a great young talent who graduated from Moody Bible Institute and had great radio production talent. He was hired by one of the top morning DJs in Chicago, Fred Winston. Dave Senes was in his early twenties and was tasked with producing great openings, bumpers, fun drop-ins, and great pieces telling the news of the day in clever ways.

Dave recommended another Moody grad who had just gone through a divorce to be our content producer. I was happy to help a talented brother out, so Kevin McCullough was tasked with booking guests, and researching segments.

As it turned out, Kevin was also good at production. Both were good at voices and Roger, one of our morning show guys, did a dead-ringer imitation of Jesse Jackson.

The combination was dynamite. We used secular, not sacred music for bumpers, outros, and intros. We were careful not to include offensive language, but the effect was to draw listeners across the board as I had hoped.

During the Bush vs. Gore "hanging chad" fiasco, we had a recurring bit with Al Gore counting ballots in the back of a semi-truck. "One thousand one, one thousand two . . ." droned the perfect Al Gore impersonator. In another, "Jesse Jackson" read *Green Eggs and Ham.*

When the Democrat Party was killing stray dogs on the street in Los Angeles in preparation for the 2000 Democratic Convention, listeners were treated to, "Who Let the Dogs Out!?" superimposed over with gunshots and yelping dogs that drove dog lovers crazy. We had to explain every single time that was exactly what the Dems were doing—shooting dogs. Every time listeners called to complain, I played it again to make the point. Controversial, but effective.

When Elian Gonzales was wrested from his mother's Cuban/American sister's arms by federal agents and sent back to Castro in Cuba, Dave produced a haunting piece we used repeatedly to illustrate the tragedy of it all.

When Bill Clinton was being impeached, we pulled the fiery House floor speeches of Congressman Henry Hyde, Chairman of the House Impeachment committee, quoting Shakespeare, superimposing his dramatic voice over music with famous phrases like the one from *Macbeth*, "Full of sound and fury, signifying nothing!"

We won seven Tesla Awards for production and an Angel Award for best interview. Bill Curtis was the host for that award, but the gripping story had nothing to do with my talents.

The Willises

One afternoon Scott and Jan Willis decided to hop in their mini-van with their six younger kids and drive to Wisconsin to visit their three, already married, adult children. Scott was a Chicago public school teacher and pastor of an inner-city church. Traveling north on I-294 behind a large truck, a piece suddenly fell from that truck, rolled beneath their van, and struck the gas tank which then burst into flames. As the flames from underneath the car licked up through the console, Jan and Scott unfastened their seatbelts through the fire, both suffering severe burns on their hands.

As they frantically moved around the car and slid open the back door, to their horror the van was engulfed with flames. They watched helplessly as five of their six children, including a six-week-old infant, burned alive before their eyes.

Jan was starting to collapse, when Scott grabbed her by the shoulders and declared with only the supernatural power and perspective God can give, "Janet! It is for this moment God has prepared us." And then, "I will bless the Lord at all times. Forever shall His praise be upon my lips," he quoted King David from Psalm 34. Who could do that in a moment like that?

Somehow Benny, their twelve-year-old son, managed to get out of the van, only to perish in the hospital that night.

Chicago media went wild. On every channel in every news report, Scott and Jan Willis were telling their story and proclaiming the gospel to a normally spiritually disinterested world. They got the attention of even the hardest hearts with their response to that tragedy and preached Christ's redemption in the process. It was powerful. I had the privilege of doing two long form interviews with them during which I was gripped as we cried and laughed together. It was that powerful interview that resulted in the Angel Award.

Years later, we learned the truck driver was an illegal immigrant by the name of Guzman. We exposed the fact that Illinois Governor George Ryan had, as Secretary of State, been selling drivers' licenses to illegal immigrants for his campaign coffers. And Guzman was one of them. He couldn't speak English and thus couldn't understand warnings from others as he barreled down the interstate. After that revelation, I went after Ryan on the air with a vengeance.

At a governor's prayer breakfast where I was speaking, Scott Willis courageously came for the express purpose of privately offering forgiveness to Governor Ryan face-to-face. But when Scott identified himself and tried to speak, Governor Ryan lost his temper, cursed at, and berated Scott.

Ryan was a terrible governor and a terrible man who later joined a long line of Illinois governors imprisoned for corruption. There is sometimes justice in this world.

John Wayne Gacy

The serial killer John Wayne Gacy raped, tortured, and murdered at least thirty-three young boys from the Chicago area before he was caught. Gacy was affiliated with the Democrat Party, high enough up in the chain to boast a photo with First Lady Rosalyn Carter. He performed at children's hospitals as a clown, painted creepy portraits of clowns, all the while hiding all those bodies in the basement of his suburban home.

Parents everywhere were worried sick about their children. If not for the doggedness of Des Plaines Chief of Police Joseph Kozenczak, Gacy might never have been caught. Lt. Kozenczak had a son the same age as Gacy's victims and would not give up the search until the killer was identified and convicted. But it wasn't easy. Detectives had been surveilling Gacy for some time but were unable to catch him.

Three detectives were assigned to spend time with him, befriend, go to bars with him, and watch every move. Finally, Gacy was arrested in December of 1978, sentenced to death on March 13, 1980.

On May 10, 1994, the day he was executed by lethal injection, I invited detectives Michael Albrecht and David Hachmeister to be my guests in the studio. Tough, hardened Chicago detectives, I asked them this simple question: "Was Gacy mentally ill or was he evil? One by one they weighed in: "evil" . . . "evil." Lt. Kozenczak was so traumatized by the experience, he left the force after Gacy was executed and wrote a book about the ordeal.

At his execution, Gacy refused to admit or show remorse for anything he did.

Jeffrey Dahmer

In the case of Jeffrey Dahmer, known as the Milwaukee Cannibal, who killed and dismembered seventeen men and boys, the story came in an unexpected way. After he was convicted and serving time in a Wisconsin prison, a Christian woman began corresponding with Dahmer. She contacted a pastor nearby to report that Dahmer had become a Christian, asking him to go into the prison to do Bible study with him. We did an interview with that pastor to get his story.

He did not want to go into the prison to minister to a monster like Dahmer. His whole body recoiled at the thought of being in the same room with him. But out of obedience to God and nothing else, he complied. It was his opinion that Dahmer was sincere in his conversion and growing in his faith. It wasn't long after that, Jeffrey was murdered in the shower by fellow inmates. Only God knows if his repentance was real.

The Shy Nurse

One day I got a call from a pastor advising me that one of his congregants—a nurse working at Christ Hospital in Oak Lawn—had come to him in great distress. The hospital was placing infants, born alive after failed abortions, in a closet and leaving them to die. No food, no water, no care. I persuaded him to ask the nurse to join us on air to tell the story.

It was a tough request. She was still working at the hospital and to speak out on Chicago radio was an incredibly brave move. During the first interview, Jill Stanek did not identify herself initially. She was shy, quiet, and reticent. But in subsequent interviews she became bold, fearless, and determined to stop this horrible practice no matter what the personal risk.

The story of live birth abortions was told first on *The Sandy Rios Show* in Chicago. From there, over the course of time, it evolved into major legislation passed by both houses of the U.S. Congress in 2002. By the time that happened I was working as president of CWA in DC and wonderfully was present the day George W. Bush signed the Born-Alive Infants Protection Act into law.

After much derision and harassment, Jill left her position at Christ Hospital and became a nationally known warrior for the cause of life.

Congressman Henry Hyde and the Impeachment of Bill Clinton

> *"What we are telling you today are not the ravings of some vast right-wing conspiracy, but a reaffirmation of a set of values that are tarnished and dim these days, but it is given to us to restore them so our Founding Fathers would be proud. It's your country—the President is our flag bearer, out in front of our people. The flag is falling, my friends—I ask you to catch the falling flag as we keep our appointment with history."*
> —Chief House Manager, Congressman Henry Hyde, delivering the "Resolution of Impeachment" for President Bill Clinton in January of 1998

America was in shock. Not only did Bill Clinton have a sexual relationship with a young White House intern, Monica Lewinsky, he did so in the Oval Office during times of national crisis. He denied what he did under oath while at the same time trying to destroy young Monica with the help of his wife, Hillary, through her brainchild, the "Bimbo Brigade," a group of people formed to destroy each and every woman who accused Bill Clinton of sexual misdeeds. Another "bimbo," Monica was "mentally ill . . . delusional," they said. Until Monica's blue dress with Bill Clinton's semen on it appeared.

Suddenly newsmen and anchors were openly discussing oral sex. Children in school were asking questions. It was a degradation of cultural norms that sent us spinning into the moral abyss. But it wasn't just the sex act that coarsened public conversations, it was the redefinition of what lying is. "It depends on what 'is' is," Clinton famously said during a deposition. He lied under oath. Suddenly we were saturated with discussions and news articles suggesting "everybody lies," and of course successfully inferring, the long-held, biblical standard of truth no longer applied.

Of this situation, Congressman Henry Hyde said,

> "A failure to convict will make the statement that lying under oath, while unpleasant and to be avoided, is not all that serious. . . . We have reduced lying under oath to a breach of etiquette, but only if you are the President. . . . And now let us all take our place in history on the side of honor, and, oh, yes, let right be done."[2]

These were the terrible twin blows delivered to American values and culture by President Bill Clinton.

Congressman Henry Hyde granted me his first interview after the impeachment trial of President Bill Clinton concluded. We kept in touch during that trial, so I had privileged access to the House managers. The young Lindsey Graham, Asa Hutchison, Bob Barr, were all courageous heroes in the impeachment battle despite whatever bad choices they made later in their political lives.

Dave Schippers, a colorful and street-smart attorney who happened to be a Democrat from Chicago, was appointed by Congressman Hyde to be counsel for the House Impeachment Committee. Dave also became a frequent guest and later a friend. I think it might be possible we had the best coverage of that event of any radio show in the country.

When Henry came into the station lobby that day for his first interview after the impeachment, separated by the glass behind which I was seated in the studio, I saw him arrive with not one, not two but three bodyguards. There were threats against his life during the proceeding—threats from Alec Baldwin on television to burn down his house, destroy his family. It was bad.

Henry sat across from me and told me things never reported publicly during those news-saturated days. He told me the file on Bill Clinton reached back to his days at Oxford where he had also been accused of rape. He told me Bill Clinton raped Juanita Broderick, a Democrat operative in Arkansas, not once, as was reported, but twice. The vault where they placed this evidence was sealed throughout the trial, only to be visited by members of Congress. After impeachment was successfully completed in the House, it moved to the Senate for deliberation. Think of the House as the grand jury who found evidence to indict, and the Senate, the jury before which that evidence was to be presented.

Chief Justice of the Supreme Court William Rehnquist came into the Senate Chamber to preside. Henry told me not a single Senator darkened the door of the evidence room. I watched as each Senator cast their vote in what I now understood was complete ignorance or apathy. There was so much corruption even then, no one seemed to have the moral fiber to be offended by the president's actions. It was a show trial at best.

When Senator Trent Lott glibly banged his gavel with a big smile and declared the matter concluded, I felt I was watching some game show, not a serious deliberation in the country's most esteemed chamber.

Congressman Hyde was perhaps the last old school statesman to grace the floor of the House of Representatives. Passionate about the value of human life, he penned the Hyde Amendment which prohibited taxpayer funding of abortion and still stands as tribute to him today. Congressman Hyde and I became friends through the pro-life movement. I will always treasure a photo of him pushing my Sasha in her wheelchair at Marklund Children's Home, later called the Marklund Hyde Center, where Sasha lived the last fourteen years of her life.

Bill Hybels and Willow Creek in 2000

Of all the things God has asked me to do through the years, this one was one of the hardest and most painful.

After leaving my church in Wheaton and finding a new place to worship at Willow Creek, I found a refuge where I could be anonymous and heal from the loss of my marriage. Bill Hybels became a friend as did the members of the drama and vocal team on which I served for ten years. Bill would come into the studio as my guest on occasion. Willow Creek was the center of my friendships, worship, and social life.

One Friday afternoon I got a call from a Willow Creek insider concerned about Bill inviting President Bill Clinton to address the Willow Creek Association conference the following Thursday. It was an election year and the race between George W. Bush and Clinton's vice president, Al Gore, was tight. Bill Hybels's influence at that time was so great in the evangelical world, an implied endorsement from him before thousands of pastors from all over the country would be powerful. But it would be wrong on many levels.

Bill was invited by Clinton to be his spiritual mentor when he was first elected in 1992 and they developed a friendship. Despite

Clinton's reputation and behavior, none of us felt criticism of Bill for agreeing to be his spiritual guide. We thought it could only help, but what happened next foreshadowed what I would later see in Washington again and again and again.

Almost every strong Christian leader I have known and worked beside eventually has his head turned by access to power. So, rather than the prophet speaking truth to the king, the king begins to pull the strings of the prophet. The privileges are too great, the fame, the proximity, and access too hard to resist.

Why did someone contact me from Willow Creek? Because my show was centered on politics and on God's truth in the culture. With 20,000 attendees every weekend, Willow Creek was the largest and most influential church in the United States at that time and Pastor Bill Hybels was spearheading it all. Bill Clinton was the most powerful leader of the free world, and now the prophet seemed to be allowing the king to use him to sway an election. Worse than that, to excuse his personal behavior.

I spent the weekend praying and asking God what I should do. Early Monday morning I drove the forty minutes to Willow Creek, sat in the lobby in front of Bill's office, and waited for him to arrive. After waiting for some time, I left a note for Bill. He returned my call early that afternoon. I begged him not to have Bill Clinton speak. I reasoned with him about why it was not only inappropriate because of the upcoming election but also inappropriate because Bill Clinton did not have the moral qualifications to stand on a stage in our church and speak to thousands of pastors as though his not-so-private sins did not matter. He argued that the Willow Creek Association's Leadership Conference invited all kinds of people to speak. I argued that Bill Clinton wasn't just a president or a world leader, he claimed to be a brother in Christ and the standards for him were different as an alleged member of the body of Christ.

The pastor told me Bill Clinton confessed his sins with women, and I countered even if that were true, he had not confessed his radical abortion stand. It was Bill Clinton who vetoed not once, but twice the ban on the brutal procedure known as Partial Birth Abortion, and there was no repentance for that. He could NOT be given a place of prominence on that stage. Bill Hybels asked me not to talk about it on the show. I told him I couldn't NOT talk about it. It would be a dereliction of my calling to avoid such a situation, even if it was my church. I asked him to join me on air to explain his position, but he wasn't willing.

We said "good-bye" and I drove to the radio station in deep thought.

I called Dave and Kevin into my office and shared privately with them what was happening and my angst over what to do next. I made them swear to keep it to themselves until I had time to think about. This was private information in every way. Later I heard it on the news and discovered Kevin, in order to curry favor with a news anchor, leaked it to CBS News. I was furious.

The next day I drove to the parking lot of the station and sat there praying, begging God not to make me take this on. Just then my cell phone rang. It was Lee Strobel, now a famous author, but at that time a pastor at Willow. Lee had a dogged determination to tell the truth as a *Chicago Tribune* reporter, but his powerful conversion from atheism to the God of all Truth fueled his passion even more. I expressed my ambivalence and my dread, but Lee admonished me that I MUST in fact take it on. I knew and admired Lee, but he had never called me before. I knew it was God speaking. And until the penning of this book, I have never told anyone about his call.

I went up to my office, sat at my computer, and began to write. As I wrote, the tears ran down on the keyboard as I asked God to give me the exact words He wanted me to say.

When the show began, I told the story of what was planned at Willow Creek in three days, and why it was wrong. I confronted my own pastor publicly and challenged others to do the same.

Thursday morning, I went to the conference. I wasn't allowed in the sanctuary but was sent instead to the basement to sit alone in a room and watch remotely. I saw Bill Hybels in a completely new and disappointing way as he skillfully manipulated those pastors into giving Bill Clinton a standing ovation, casting it as an issue of judging like the Pharisees if they didn't.

I was disinvited from the Vocal Team retreat and threatened with church discipline by the elders. The shocking thing to me was the Willow Creek elders didn't have the biblical knowledge to even understand church discipline. A young Vocal Team leader called me to her home to rebuke and discipline me. Not a pastor or an elder, but a young girl singer. My friends Bob Neff, who was vice president of Moody Broadcasting at the time, and his wife, well-known author and radio host, Miriam Neff, insisted on coming with me. You would think I would have the strength to defend myself, but I was too sad about it all to raise a syllable in defense.

It wasn't that I thought I was wrong, I was just astounded by the twisted, sad nature of it and the underbelly of shallowness and doctrinal vapidness of the church I loved so much. After listening to the sharp rebuke by this young girl, Miriam jumped to my defense asking her, "Do you have any idea who this woman is that you are rebuking? Do you have any idea what she has done and how God has called her?" I was taken by surprise and overwhelmed by the support of someone of Miriam's character. My young friend was silenced and the meeting ended.

A business meeting was convened where a large group of members attended. A heated discussion ensued, and hundreds if not thousands consequently left the church. Anyone who would get joy from that just doesn't understand. This is not a war of people and personalities, but of dark forces working against the body of Christ. There was no joy in any of it. But the only way Christians can stay the course during these wicked days is to purify ourselves personally and corporately. It's painful but necessary.

In the middle of this episode, I reached out to Dr. Erwin Lutzer, who was senior pastor of Moody Church in Chicago, to be my spiritual mentor as I walked through the events. I had known Dr. Lutzer for years as a friend and he had, in fact, been a wonderful encourager when I was going through my divorce, but this incident bonded us in a new way. His wisdom and insight were a lifeline to me, and when I was to move on to the next big challenge, he and his beautiful wife, Rebecca, became a refuge of a different kind.

The Countess de Romanones

My daughter-in-law, Liesel, is a voracious reader. On one of my visits to Vancouver, she gave me a series of books to read about a beautiful American girl, recruited to model, who became one of the first female spies for the Office of Strategic Services, the precursor to the CIA. *The Spy Wore Red* was the first in the series, written by Aline Griffith of her adventures of being dropped behind enemy lines in Spain during World War II. It was absolutely fascinating. I devoured the other two books in the series in short order.

Back in Chicago in 2008, I got a call from a friend with a tip about the Countess De Romanones returning to the States to receive an award for her work with the OSS during World War II. He had her contact information. Did I want to interview her? I fairly screamed with delight as I realized this was Aline Griffith, the author of the books Liesel and I so loved.

Graduating with degrees in literature, history, and journalism, Aline was a brilliant woman. I was enthralled as, in her beautiful aristocratic lilt, she shared stories of learning to decipher code, fight, and even kill, which she once was forced to do. Part of her cover in Spain was as a fashion model. As she carried out her clandestine work, the life she lived was the stuff of—yes—novels. She married the Count of Quintanilla and bore him three sons. She was good friends with Audrey Hepburn, The Duchess of Windsor, and later as countess, entertained historical icons like Jacqueline Kennedy, Grace Kelly, Salvador Dali, and the list goes on.

The thing about Aline was she was at heart, a down-to-earth, all-American girl. When our paths crossed, she still maintained an apartment in New York City, but lived primarily in her villas in Spain. She still loved and cared for her native country. We spoke privately of politics and presidential candidates. We disagreed and debated. I felt privileged with every moment I had to spend with her. I tried to help get her a new publisher for those great books which were by then out of print. She invited me to visit one of her villas in Spain and later sent me an unpublished book she wrote, filled with photos and the story of her labored restoration of one of those ancient villas.

For me, it was a brush with history and even though short-lived—for Aline was well into her eighties when we met—I have never forgotten the joy of knowing her.

Winston Churchill

Celia Sandys, Winston Churchill's niece, joined me one day to talk about her memories of the great British statesman. I always admired Churchill's speeches and wondered to myself where he got his strong values and courage. I watched an old video of a secret meeting he had on a ship in the Atlantic with President Franklin Delano Roosevelt. I saw them singing beautiful hymns together along with a military band in the midst of a worship service on deck. Churchill was not known for his spiritual leadership. He was, in fact, a rascal. Where did this come from, I wondered? So I asked his niece.

Amazingly, she told me that in the long and frequent absences of his beautiful American mother, Jenny, he was raised by a "Free Church" Nanny. The Free Church in England and elsewhere in Europe was the name for churches not affiliated with the state church, in this case, the Church of England. Free Churches believed in personal faith and a powerful God. This nanny taught Winston Scripture and about that personal faith in Christ. Whether or not he ever made that commitment, I don't know, but it answered the question of how he was exposed to the power and strength only God can inspire. And that story was not in her book.

Important Relationships

As a radio host, not just contacts are built, but friends are made with guests through discussions over through the years. Andy McCarthy, prosecutor of the Blind Sheikh after the first World Trade Center bombing; Barbara Olson, wife of Solicitor General Ted Olson, who died tragically on 9/11 when United Airlines Flight 93 went down near Shanksville, Pennsylvania; the vibrant and controversial Ann Coulter; writers like Byron York and foreign affairs correspondents like Bill Gertz; national security experts like Frank Gaffney and many more became more than guests to me.

And that was important for the next step in my journey.

You guessed it. Another phone call.

But you'll have to read a few more chapters before I can tell you about that one!

8

Me, the Swinging Single

My divorce finalized on June 5, 1991, my twentieth wedding anniversary. I was married at twenty-one, two weeks after graduation from college. From the time I was twenty-four, I was the mother of a severely disabled child, and the wife of a restless husband. I was old when I was young. I was laden with worry and stress, but believe me, I never in my life longed to be single again. I wanted Sasha to be well and my marriage to be whole, I did NOT want to be single.

Soon after my separation, a good friend came to see me to pour out her heart about her unhappiness with her husband. She told me she envied me. I was "lucky" I had a reason to divorce. I was flabbergasted. I looked her in the eye and told her if she wanted to trade places with me, she would have to take everything about my life: all the years of sorrow, the uncertainty of finances, and yes, a disabled child along with it.

And she was not the only married woman to express the desire to be free and single again. I could write another entire book on the sadness of the unhealthy imaginations some women seem to indulge themselves with, and the sense of entitlement that too often keeps them from serving not only their husbands but their children as well. What pornography is to men, romance and fantasy is for women.

It creates dissatisfaction, discontent, and bitterness with its comparisons. The Bible teaches us that husbands and wives are to love and serve each other—mutual submission. It's a winning formula.

In the years after my divorce, I became very close to two couples who exemplified that kind of love to me in incredible ways. I had never experienced it, but it gave me hope.

There are two ways to tell my single-life story. The serious and the funny. I'm going to tell you the funny stories because you won't believe them. I hardly do.

Willow Creek was a church of 20,000 with a drama team including many equity actors and a music team full of professional singers and players. They came from all walks of life.

Renee, the jingle king, was dramatically converted just a few years before I met him. Lots of the instrumentalists, also new believers, played in clubs in the city. Many of the actors found a place of refuge at Willow from a theater scene that had become base and immoral. So it was a great landing place for a wobbly, new single woman who loved music.

I auditioned for the spring musical and landed the part of "woman carrying the pot." It was a hilarious assignment, second only to my debut neighing like a horse in the studio back in 1978. But it gave me a chance to just be anonymous and enjoy the fellowship with great talent in a great production. Harry Newman was one of the lead soloists at Willow and we became fast friends. We became such fast friends, that while we were speaking with great animation backstage one night, he missed his cue on stage for his solo.

Harry had a beautiful voice but an even more beautiful heart. From that spring he became my best friend for the next ten years. He listened as I poured my heart out endlessly and later navigated the dating world. He loved God and held me to a high standard in every way. We made music together as singers, and later I helped him produce a solo album. God was good to bring me a friend so kind and faithful as Harry.

Harry introduced me to the incredibly powerful lead in the Easter drama, Kathy Sanford. Her portrayal of Mary, the mother of Jesus, for me should be the industry standard. Kathy and Fred Sanford—yes, FRED SANFORD!—were graduates of Northwestern University and were new to a personal relationship with Christ. Fred was a songwriter who famously took Michael Jackson to court in the '80s for stealing one of Fred's songs, which Michael named, "The Girl Is Mine!" The trial made national news as the defense brought in Quincy Jones and other stars to testify who had absolutely nothing to do with the song, but everything to do with the headlines. The judge in the case brought Michael Jackson into his chambers to give autographs to his kids. Shockingly, Fred lost the case.

We spent countless hours and days together, laughing and sharing. Fred and Kathy loved each other so unselfishly, they gradually helped rebuild my view of what marriage should be. We began to add others to our motley, seemingly unmatched group until we built a family that shared sorrows and hilarious times together. My home was once again a place of joy but in a whole new way. I entertained these dear friends and many more as God allowed Jeremy, Sasha, and me not to feel so lonely and strange.

Each New Years' Eve I hosted a big party. It went like this. Early in the evening I invited ten or twelve to a sit-down dinner of steak or crown pork by candlelight. At around ten o'clock, others began arriving until the house was full. We talked, played games, watched movies until we couldn't stay awake. The couples got the two spare bedrooms, the single girls all slept in my room, and the single guys went to the basement. Next morning Kurt Leafblad would fix a big breakfast which we enjoyed immensely as we sat around the table to talk and talk. We never ran out of words.

Later we convened in the living room to share what we were thankful for, sing and make music or just entertain each other until once again it was dark. It was a twenty-four-hour party that brought joy and bonding to all of us.

Jeremy was entering the fun as well. But when he turned fourteen, he was invited to his first New Years' Eve party. I wasn't crazy about that, but it was going to be at his best friend's house, supervised by his single mom, so what could go wrong? When nearly midnight, it suddenly occurred to me how funny it would be if all of us crashed Jeremy's party. We grabbed our pillows and drove over in a caravan. Fred and Kathy's daughter, Brooke, rode with Jeremy earlier to the party. We rang the doorbell vigorously as Brad's startled mom opened the door. "Happy New Year!" we all shouted as we marched through the living room clutching our pillows. Descending into a very dark basement, we observed young people doing things young people do in the dark, looking up like deer in the headlights as we passed through shouting, "Happy New Year!"

Jeremy and Brooke were back home with us in about fifteen minutes. Can you imagine having a mother like me?

It wasn't easy being Jeremy's mom either. He was one of those boys who became a man at fourteen. Strikingly handsome, it was all I could do to discourage adult women not to ogle him. A female student teacher began to call him at home. I turned her into her supervisor. Girls would call and I would answer and ask if their mothers knew they were calling a boy and then dismiss them. I realize this sounds archaic, but I knew if I didn't protect him, no one else would. I wanted to preserve his innocence as long as possible.

Meanwhile I had my own singleness to navigate. As soon as I was separated, my phone began to ring with interested suitors. What in the world? I wasn't even divorced yet. I doubled down on my prayers for God's protection, but after many years of neglect and rejection, the sudden attention made me smile at this affirmation of my womanhood which I believed was also a gift from God.

Of all the mistakes I made as a newly single Christian woman, it was that I began dating too soon. It was unwise and very hard on my son, as I realize looking back. I had been virtually alone for years, though married, but no one, not even my little boy understood that.

Willow Creek held dances for their singles' group, and with trepidation I went. The first time I attended, I stood against a wall as far back in the room as I could get. You can't imagine how strange it is to spend twenty years of your life NOT looking or giving any kind of encouragement to men who aren't your husband. And now? Suddenly it's alright?? It was a huge barrier. And rightfully so. God did not intend for the marriage bond to be broken for a reason.

I will never forget as I went out on the floor to dance, looking over my partner's shoulder to see my friend, Karen, also a recent divorcee, having her arm stiffly pumped up and down like the spout of a tea pot by an awkward dancer. It's like we were back in Junior High! I caught her eye as the two of us stifled our laughter at the ridiculousness of it all.

The first time I brought a man to our home, Jeremy, age eleven, came into the family room, and said out of the blue, "Excuse me, Sir Bob. But what IS your occupation?" He was rightfully guarding his mom, and funny as it was, I wish I never put him in that situation.

What a Story!

And speaking of situations, I got myself into an incredible one, all on my own. In the early months of my divorce, I was invited to sing at a women's event in a Chicago suburb. The woman who arranged it, I will call Marjorie. The event went well enough, but when Marjorie found out I was single, she decided to take me on as a project.

She lived in a wealthy northern suburb and was the heir to a famous Chicago business fortune. Her husband was a former federal agent and they lived in a large home close to the North Shore. Making good on her word, Marjorie invited me to their home for a party. Marjorie was a challenge, but she was certainly not boring, nor were her friends. I met a beautiful Lithuanian woman who designed nuclear power plants. I met an Australian novelist, representatives from various Chicago consulates, business leaders, and society mavens. It was fascinating. But Marjorie's real mission was to set me up with an eligible bachelor.

She fixed me up with a manic-depressive former Secret Service agent, and then tried to match me with a successful real estate mogul. But by then I realized Marjorie wasn't who or what I thought she was. I met her in a church setting thinking one thing, but found out, she was quite another. But she was determined and persistent. I told her clearly I didn't want to get involved with anyone physically. She responded by telling me Middle Easterners made better lovers. I repeated I wasn't interested in anything like that. She countered by giving me a book whose title I can't repeat.

She asked me to dinner with some of her friends. As we sat at the table having dinner, I was the center of attention, the project. The Sears executive next to me slipped me his business card, asking me to meet him for lunch someday. It was bizarre to me. I was truly a sheep among wolves. All the time I was praying God would give me the right responses that were clear and unequivocal about my faith in Christ, who Jesus was, and what He required from those who follow Him. Marjorie seemingly ignored those things and pressed on.

All the while she was on her mission, I was on mine. I wanted to make sure Marjorie understood what it really meant to follow Christ once and for all. I invited her to church countless times because I felt the style of Willow Creek could reach her. At last, she committed to a Saturday night service. I was elated.

At about four o'clock that afternoon, she called to inform me she arranged for all of us, her husband included, to go to her Middle Eastern friend's home for dinner. Earlier, Marjorie shared with me that she slept with the man I will call, Ahmed. Now she committed me to come to his home to meet his wife and several of his Middle Eastern buddies. Oh, Lord. What had I gotten myself into?

Once again, I prayed then got on the phone and begged Harry to come to church with me, then afterward to the dreaded event. Ever my friend, he came, bringing our buddy Curt along as well—strength in numbers.

As only God can do, a miracle occurred. First of all, no Middle Eastern friends came. I did catch Ahmed taking random pictures of me all evening. Ahmed's wife—whom I'll call, Sabrina—a beautiful American girl was not only a great conversationalist, she was also a musician. Between Harry, me, and Kurt, we listened to Sabrina sing, shared stories of musical experiences, and in the process shared our faith in Christ to the likely startled and uncomfortable Marjorie. "What man meant for evil God meant for good."

But the story didn't end there. Sabrina and I became friends. Even though she was raised in the south, as far as I could tell, she had no religious background. One Saturday morning I got a jolting phone call from Marjorie that Ahmed and his son had disappeared on Lake Michigan the day before and police were giving up the search. Sabrina hired a small, private plane. Would I be able to go up in the plane with her to search for him. Paula asked? I drove to Pal Waukee Airport as fast as I could and boarded the plane with my new friend Sabrina. I sat on one side of the plane with binoculars to search the vast waters of that ocean-like lake, while she did the same on the other side. But Ahmed and his son were nowhere to be found. Eventually their lifejackets floated to shore and the remains of one of them washed up further north days later, but they were otherwise never seen again.

Since Sabrina had no church background, I interceded for her at Willow Creek with Dr. Gilbert Bilezikian, one of the pastors who was Middle Eastern. The chapel was approved for their service where Dr. Bilezikian delivered the message of redemption.

There is no doubt that God allowed me to spin way out of my comfort zone. But honestly, I'm not sure how Christians can be salt and light in any meaningful way if they stay behind the walls of a church and limit their relationships to only their brand of believers. God was stretching me in ways I could not imagine. Testing me, strengthening me for more rigors ahead.

Eighteen Years

During my eighteen years of being single, I had some of the most hilarious, meaningful, and bizarre dates you can imagine.

Honestly, I didn't like "dating." Most of the stories I have are of one-time events. Like, for instance the dentist who took me to dinner, insisting I have a full Maine lobster. I am nearly 5'7" and then only weighed about 126 pounds, so it wasn't five minutes into the meal when the richness of the flavor along with the butter, caused me to reach for the bread. "You're going to eat bread when you have a whole Maine Lobster!" he barked. Wow! First AND last date. Period.

I had a wonderful evening with a CBS executive in charge of artist development. As we launched into an animated conversation, he told me about how difficult it was to prepare Mariah Carey for the public because of her rough upbringing in the "hood." He wasn't a handsome guy, but I loved his personality and would have gone out with him again. Until we discovered he was thirteen years younger than I . . HA! That happened way too often.

One night at a Willow Creek dance, I met a delightful guy named Manny, with whom I danced all evening. We were dancing to a song he loved. It was released the year he was born, he shared as we moved across the floor . . . the year John Kennedy was assassinated. Another night of robbing the cradle.

At yet another Willow Creek dance, I struck up a conversation with a waiter who told me he was an opera singer from New York and was hoping to return there soon. I listened and encouraged him and then, spur of the moment asked if he would like to join me and my musician friends at my house the next night to make some music. He agreed. As we sat around the piano, singing separately and together, I introduced him to my friends, explaining his extraordinary background and talent at which time he stood up to sing. Out of his mouth came the loudest, most horribly unbearable sound I ever heard. Yet he continued. I glanced around the room at my friends, all of whom were caught between horror and hilarity. I never lived that one down.

And then there was "William the Widower." (Some of the names have been changed to protect the innocent.)

I was still in bed one morning when the phone rang. I answered to a man identifying himself as though I knew him. The name sounded slightly familiar, so I listened as he carried on. He owned some radio stations, he said, to which I relaxed, thinking he was calling to offer me some kind of work. But then he got right to the point. "I don't know if you have heard what has happened to me" (I didn't remember who he was much less had I heard what happened to him.) "But my wife died recently," he continued. "I'm coming to Chicago, and I wondered if you would be willing to have dinner with me." As he talked I vaguely remembered our connection. I knew from that affiliation he was a Christian but remembered nothing about him. What was the harm? I agreed to the dinner.

He called me a few times in the ensuing week, getting ever bolder, telling me he had been thinking a lot about me. Oh, brother. He then asked if I would please keep the date to myself because his wife had only been dead a few months. OH, BROTHER!

The night came. I was up in my bathroom getting ready when the doorbell rang. Jeremy answered. I heard pounding feet as he ran up the stairs. Jeremy looked at me and whispered loudly, "Mom! William's old!!" I went downstairs to greet the older gentleman as graciously as possible.

He took me to a restaurant and, before we had a chance to order, told me he figured we could be friends for six months and then get married. I nearly fell out of my seat! Quietly I explained to him I had a very busy and fulfilling life and was quite content being single. What I didn't say was what I was really thinking: *GET ME OUT OF HERE!*

It was the shortest date in history. I got home within an hour of departure, jumped out of the car, and headed for the door.

Poor William. I understand in retrospect how he must have been terribly lonely, enough so he was desperate to replace his wife. I wasn't as patient or kind as I could have been. It was fight or flight for me.

I think I really found peace the minute I stopped dating. Who needs that? It's so artificial and time-consuming and I was content with my great friends.

Speaking of Great Friends . . .

You might remember Greg Brown who was a top-forty Chicago DJ and hosted the premiere of my *Lord, I Believe* album at the Odeum in Chicago. Greg became a great friend. During that first spring musical at Willow Creek, Greg and I traded punchlines. As the "woman carrying the pot," I told him I was carrying the ashes of my late husband. There was no end to the fun. It was such a joy to laugh.

Later Greg began a love relationship with the beautiful former Honey Bear, Lorraine Orr, founder of "Luvabulls," (cheerleaders for the Chicago Bulls) at a New Years' Eve party in my home. When Lorraine and Greg got married, Harry, Kurt, Kate (another wonderful friend), and I sang at their wedding at the Chicago Historical Society. Dr. Lutzer performed the ceremony. Here's the funny part. In spite of the fact it was held outside a church, the crowd was Moody Church all the way. So when, at the end of the ceremony, as Greg and Lorraine were joyfully exiting, we began to belt out, the Michael Bolton hit, "Love Is a Wonderful Thing!" The crowd, much more accustomed to hymns and organ, sat frozen and horrified. But there was no turning back. For Greg and Lorraine's sake, we sang with even more enthusiasm.

At that wedding I met a couple who would eventually be two of my very best friends.

Val Mazzenga was raised in an Italian-Catholic family in the area of Chicago known as Little Italy. Val always said he had two choices: become a ditch digger like his father or a robber like his friends. When he was fourteen, he walked into the *Chicago Tribune* and asked if he could have a job. They made him a copy boy, working with writers and photographers. One day, Marilyn Monroe visited the *Tribune* for a photo shoot. The young Val stood in the back as she posed for the camera seductively, fan blowing strategically. You can imagine the effect. But greater than that awakening, was the discovery that he had a great eye for photography.

Val grew up to become a Pulitzer-nominated, world-renowned photographer. His famous aerial photo of the Jonestown Massacre was seen all over the world.

Val met Shelly Lawler when she was a student/waitress at a Chicago hangout he frequented. Miss Chicago in 1984, Shelly was a singer, model, actress, and writer who studied at Oxford and had great ambitions for her future. Val was much older so what began as a friendship slowly became a long-lasting, incredible marriage. Shelly and Val were couple number two who demonstrated what it was like to really love and be loved in marriage.

Our conversations were exhilarating. Val's stories were legendary. Mother Theresa—Bengal tigers—Richard Nixon—Yvette Mimieux on a floating ice cap at the North Pole. I persuaded Val to do his first radio interview with me to tell those stories. He was old school Italian, a tough, former Marine who didn't consider himself a public speaker. It was with great trepidation that he agreed. He was a sensation. And from that interview, Shelly created a slide presentation enabling him to go out to other audiences and tell his stories.

Just before the last hour of my radio show, I would often call Shelly and Val and ask them to join me at the movies. It was always a weeknight, but I can't remember them ever refusing. We met at the theater, and armed with large bags of popcorn, enjoyed whatever was playing. In truth, Val confessed later that going to the movies with me was a pain. Because? More often than not, I would walk out when things got rough and wait for them in the lobby. We laughed and laughed, cried, and prayed. Val began as a man who believed in

God but grew further into a man who read Scripture and prayed constantly. It was a wonderful thing to behold. He was like my brother, Shelly like a sister.

While writing this book in December 2022, we got the call that Val had left us. We dropped everything and flew back to Chicago to attend his funeral. Jeremy came from Vancouver to bring the sermon, and Shelly gave me the awesome privilege of telling the audience about his incredible life. Writers and photographers from all over the country came to pay their respects. I have never been to a funeral where people came earlier and stayed later, lingering to talk and take in Val's incredible work displayed in the atrium.

Ten years earlier Val suffered a debilitating stroke, and for a decade Shelly poured her life into caring for him. Selfless devotion is what they lived before all of us, for each other. He died in her arms in their home, leaving Shelly and all of us who knew and loved him with a gaping hole in our lives.

Harry, Fred and Kathy, Val and Shelly, and many others are the relationships that sustained my life for the eighteen years I was single.

Jeremy and I

A single mom can never take the place of a father. Jeremy and I were close as he was growing up. We enjoyed good conversations, popcorn, chocolate, and quirky movies. His friends were always in our home. We took road trips together while Sasha stayed with my parents. Those were lonely times, but God provided.

Once, at Disneyworld, the two of us were standing in line watching families all around us, feeling the loss of ours. It was a sad day. Suddenly I looked up to see a familiar face, a familiar family, in fact! Paul Hayes was the worship leader at my childhood church in Carmi. He and his wife and three kids just happened to be at Disneyworld on the same day in the same place! We hugged in tearful reunion, and as natural as breathing they invited us to join them for the day. It was another loving gift from God.

I was a strict mom as Jeremy was growing up. I adored him but I believed in discipline. As he grew into manhood, it was not always easy to exercise parental authority as a stand-alone mom.

Once when I told him "no" in response to something he wanted to do, he became very angry. Towering over me, I felt that anger and half expected him to hit me, but he didn't. Nevertheless, his words were hurtful, and I began to cry, while adding, "Don't mistake these tears for weakness!" I highly recommend that to all single moms.

Later I thanked God for a good son who could have easily overpowered and ignored his mom but chose instead to obey. God's rules for the nurture and admonition of our children are sure and true.

For three years Jeremy helped me lift and care for Sasha. When I went on the air at WYLL, he started grocery shopping and cooking dinner. When I got home, we ate together, and I cleaned up.

When he played Fagan in *Oliver*, I went to the performance, not having any idea what to expect. I sat next to a mom/friend of the talented girl star as the musical began. I was blown away by my son's talent. Speechless, in fact. My friend leaned over and asked, "Who is that kid playing Fagan?" He was so in character, he was unrecognizable.

My friends-like-family all came to see him perform. They bowed and teased him chanting, "We're not worthy . . . we're not worthy."

We had the cast party at our home. I turned on the radio to some rock station, thinking that would please them, but the kids turned it off so they could sing and play in the living room. His Wheaton North friends were such polite and talented kids, there was only good behavior, and absolutely no spills all night.

God was blessing me once again through my son.

With another phone call, our lives were to change dramatically again.

The Agony and the Ecstasy

I bought a cell phone early on so Jeremy could reach me at any time. As I was driving to WYLL one late morning in 1994, my cell phone rang. It was Marklund Children's Home, a place for severely disabled children whose administrator, Pat, I had known for many years.

She said in a quiet voice, "Sandy, we have a place for Sasha if you're interested." "How soon?" I managed to ask. "In two weeks" she replied. I couldn't speak. A wave of grief came over me like an avalanche. My voice broke as I promised to get back to her. I began to wail in grief in the car. From the depths of my soul, I felt the sorrow of such a decision. I drove on to the station and went immediately to then–Station Manager Phil Bandy. Phil had a severely disabled son, much the same as Sasha who lived at home with him and his wife. No one in my life could have understood my grief but Phil on that day and at that time. I cried and cried, wept and wept as Phil listened. When it was time to do the show, I dried my eyes, washed my face, and carried on.

Only a year earlier, my dad was diagnosed with cancer. It was sudden and unexpected. Not only did it throw me into grief because I dearly loved my dad, it removed his protection and care of me and my children. No longer could I count on my parents to come to my rescue in any capacity. It hit hard and for the first time, I really felt alone. Although my dad lived for many more years (he died in October of 2008), the chemo and radiation affected his legs, and in addition, he began to have a series of mini strokes. He just wasn't able to take care of his little girl anymore. Instead, my sweet mother had to take care of him. She faithfully did that until one unexpected September day in 2000, she suffered a massive brain aneurism and died two weeks later. She was my best friend . . . my sister in Christ. On the night she died, I awakened from sleep to the power of the Holy Spirit surging through my body manifesting in out-loud laughter. Alone in the same bed where I had surrendered my life to God in 1958, my sister called from the hospital a few minutes later to tell me she had just passed.

Pat's call from Marklund was uncannily timely. Once again God miraculously provided. I accepted Pat's generous offer—the offer of a friend who understood the burden and reached out to help. Sasha was twenty years old by then and it was only getting harder to lift and care for her. Jeremy also needed me. He was in his teen years, busy with activities, and it was time to be more available to him. In moments of sorrow, I reminded myself that if Sasha had been a normal child, she would have already left our home. Two weeks went by quickly. With a heavy heart, I packed her clothes and stuffed animals in her room of so many years. We had a party with our neighbors and her caregivers the night before. I dressed her like the beautiful little baby doll she was with earrings and hair ribbons as we celebrated her life.

The next day Harry went with me to take her to Marklund. I have never experienced anything like the equal parts of agony and ecstasy I felt that day. Agony to send my little girl away—forever from her home. Part of me will never forgive myself for doing that. The ecstasy because I was exhausted from twenty years of her care. How does one reconcile that?

So within just a few years, I was no longer a married woman or the loving, caregiver of Sasha Richelle Rios. The void was unbearable, but soon filled by God's assignments in my life.

Swinging single indeed.

9

Lost in India, and Other Overseas Adventures

I have a notoriously bad sense of direction, so it was risky to jog in distant corners of the world. It was September of 2000. My mother's funeral took place only a few days before I was scheduled to travel once again—this time to India. Although India is sadly poor and unclean, the hotels were the gorgeous opposite. We began our trip in central India in Madras. In Hyderabad we heard what Barack Obama famously called the "most beautiful sound in the world," the Muslim call to prayer. Day and night, it wailed on, grating at our nerves, not so beautifully. Just before we arrived, a Christian pastor and his son were burned alive in their car by radical Hindus. We met pastors who told us of the dangers, but also of the miraculous way Evangelicals and Catholics dropped their barriers and begun to work together.

I rode in the back, crunched in the jump seat of a Jeep as we traveled up the winding highway 400 miles from central India to New Delhi. The "highway" was filled with bicycles laden with baskets, quirky little trucks, motorcycles, buses, semis, and strange-looking cars. As I watched from the back window, I saw monkeys jumping from tall tree to tall tree. It was fascinating.

The morning after we arrived in New Delhi, I went for my usual run. I could see the world better on foot, smell the smells, see the faces. I loved jogging this way and for this purpose.

Not far from the city buildings, were small open dwellings, people cooking outside in crude pots, squatting to stir them. It was early morning, and the sights and sounds were intriguing. I completed my run and headed back to the hotel only to realize I had no idea where I was. I didn't even remember the name of the hotel, and with over 400 languages in India, could not possibly explain who or what to look for to anyone. None of the team knew I left or where I went. I was the lone woman rooming by myself. Panicking, I paused on a very busy city street, cars whirring by and prayed, "Oh, Lord. Please help me!" Just then I looked to my right, across the many lanes of traffic to see what I thought was the hotel. And it was.

The twelve of us, talk show hosts from all over the country, loaded on to a small bus for a short tour of the city. The driver took us to a park where a snake charmer could be seen plying his trade. I jumped off the bus first to make my way quickly for a closer look. What I didn't take into account was the fact that unlike the United States, where we have safety regulations, there was no such consideration in India. The snake charmer proceeded to place a very large boa constrictor around my neck. That very large, scaly, cold snake, decided to get friendly. As his head arched and came toward my face, I moved toward the charmer, suggesting strongly he remove the unwanted snake from around my neck.

By then the guys arrived and were standing back at a distance to watch their sister talk show host try to get out of this predicament. As I moved toward the charmer, there was a collective gasp from those brave men, as they warned me—from a distance—that I was passing too close to a venomous cobra residing in a basket I couldn't see because of the very large boa around my neck. I moved slowly back to my place, but two minutes later was freaked out again by the wandering head of my new, slithery friend. Once again, I moved toward the charmer, imploring him to remove the snake, once again accompanied by gasps from my distant brothers. It wasn't lost on me there were no heroes in that bunch.

It's good they were radio hosts, not a search and rescue team, don't you think?—nor photographers, because no one thought to take a photo. But it really did make a great story!

Me and the Dutch

Remember those stoic Dutch worshippers at Christ Church in Oak Brook? That fateful night was just the beginning of a long partnership with the Christian Reformed Church and the Dutch people. Their culture, the food and immaculate cleanliness, their intellect and warmth, and finally their great history of industriousness were all fascinating to me.

In the early '80s I met the new president of the Bible League at a CR event in Wisconsin where I was singing. Denny Mulder was a passionate communicator, filled with the power of God. His vision to raise money to send Bibles all over the world was captivating to me.

It was the Bible League that in 1991 sent me to Russia to help present *Seven Days of Hope* from Radio Moscow.

And it was the Bible League that, after that first major radio project, sent me all over the world to interview persecuted Christians, bring their stories to life through radio, and help raise money to send Bibles translated into indigenous languages. Thus began some of the greatest adventures of my life!

China and Its Wonderful People

My first trip with the Bible League as their spokesperson was one of many we took to China. It began in Hong Kong.

On my first morning on that first trip in 1994 I took an early morning jog. Winding around the streets and into a park, I saw dozens of people moving in graceful sync performing Tai Chi. The mist was still on the water as I heard the low, resonant sound of foghorns from ships, moored in the harbor. If God ever groaned, I think it might have sounded like that. The sound was deep, larger than life, like a sleeping giant awakening and stretching. Wonderful, unforgettable sounds.

Hong Kong at that time was still controlled by the British. Free and democratic in governance, it was one of the most powerful centers of wealth on the globe. Banking, commerce, Christian worship, vibrancy, were all synonymous with Hong Kong. It was separated only by that narrow harbor from the Communist mainland. Like East and West Berlin, the contrast was stark.

The crowded but exciting city of Hong Kong operated in both English and Cantonese. Amusingly, there was a morning show I loved to listen to with an English DJ, interacting with a Cantonese one—each in their own language—without translation. They were hilarious as they interacted, and it was great fun.

It was devastating to watch the British hand back control of Hong Kong to the Chinese in 1997, and later to see the Chinese Communists impose their tyranny on those poor people who fought so valiantly to stay free. In 2019–2020 countless young people took to the streets in non-violent resistance. Many held candlelight vigils, singing worship songs, and praying. Many were beaten and others disappeared. Their courage was no surprise to me because I saw it up close and personal in China so many times before.

The Smuggler

On a later trip to China, we visited many cities and met with countless Christians in the underground church. We met clandestinely to hear their dramatic stories of beatings, of fear, and of courage.

In Shanghai I met a Bible smuggler we called "Jonathan." He was a handsome, muscular man with a larger-than-life personality. His conversation was sprinkled with Bible verses, and the joy only God can give was evident on his face. His was a very dangerous task. He lived off the grid, running Bibles to various provinces at great risk to his life.

After a long conversation, it was time to say "good-bye," so we stood in a circle, holding hands to pray. I asked Jonathan if he knew the famous American song written by Michael W. Smith and Amy Grant, "Thy Word Is a Lamp unto My Feet." Based on Scripture, it speaks of the power of God's Word to guide us in every situation. My Bible-smuggling friend wanted to learn every verse.

I sang the song and then, slowly, verse by verse, taught it to him. Those lyrics expressed the essence of the dangerous work he was doing.

Jonathan made a huge impression on me in that encounter. But nothing like the one to come.

The Great Wall

The Great Wall of China is one of the Wonders of the World for a reason.

The endless expanse of stone fortress and walkway winds from mountain to mountain and can be seen from space.

The first time I visited it, Bill Blount, owner of several New England radio stations, was on the trip and became a great friend. Without the responsibilities of work and home, we were like two mischievous kids. Seriousness about the mission perhaps made the funny moments funnier.

By that time, I was the host of the Bible League radio specials. On this particular day, in September of 1998 it was rainy, wet, and blowing. It was my job to read a serious script that would introduce a soon-to-be-produced radio special.

Bill and I made our way up the steep incline, rain drizzling, wind howling, bodies bent by its force. The umbrella waved wildly as Bill tried to maintain control. Once we made our way to the top of the ridge, holding the microphone as Bill struggled with the umbrella, I pulled out my script to begin.

As my paper rattled noisily in the gale, and the rain dripped down my face, I mustered up my best announcer voice to begin, "I'm standing on the Great . . ." But then I looked at Bill, struggling with the umbrella, hair flying in the wind, water dripping down his face, and burst out laughing. I tried again, "I'm standing on the Great Wall . . ." My voice broke again into hilarious laughter. In spite of such a serious a task, undertaken by two serious-minded adults, neither of us could control our laughter. Finally, after several takes, I successfully and with great panache, managed to say dramatically, "I'm standing on the Great Wall of China!"

Kentucky Fried Chicken and the Great Wall of China

The next year in September of 1999, we returned to China and our friends immediately reported how our Bible-smuggling friend Jonathan was arrested and spent most of the year in a prison camp. Newly released, it was too risky for him to meet with us even in private.

A few days later, while standing at the base of the wall, Winter, one of our Chinese friends, took me by the hand and led me into a Kentucky Fried Chicken store. Yes—Kentucky Fried Chicken! I was standing in the midst of the crowded dining room, when a man suddenly stepped in front of me and began to sing, "Thy Word is a lamp unto my feet, and a light unto my path." Tears overcame me as I recognized Jonathan. We hugged in joyful reunion and later, courageous man that he was, he took the chance to meet the entire team of twelve in a private room. We all crowded around the table, with me by his side as he relayed the story. He was placed in a labor camp at a diamond mine. He pulled out his handkerchief to display the handful of stunning stones he managed to keep. The workdays were long and unbearable. He was forced to stand in putrid water up to his waist for hours on end. Hungry and cold and trying to survive, it was difficult to find time alone to pray. One day a guard pulled him aside to beat him.

As the guard delivered the blows, Jonathan said the power of the Holy Spirit came over him. As he looked up at the guard's face, seeing the sweat dripping from his body onto Jonathan's, with inexplicable compassion, he said, "I'm sorry that you are having to work so hard to beat me." Stunned, the guard stopped immediately and released him.

I heard similar stories of Chinese Christians witnessing to their jail and prison guards and the guards becoming Christians. The Chinese Christians were so bold, despite the danger, they witnessed to everyone constantly. Often, one of our special friends came late to a meeting, face glowing, with an apology and a story about how he won his cab driver to Christ. The more they were persecuted, the more joyful they became.

Several shared with me their initial fear and reticence to speak out. But one by one, they told me how once they abandoned their fear, they felt inexplicable joy and peace. They explained how the power and presence of God became so precious, they had no desire to return to what once was. They begged us not to go back to the States and intercede in the name of human rights. God was at work in China, and millions were giving their lives to Christ.

I have thought about and shared this story many times since. And I am grateful God allowed me a front-row seat to persecution. I believe, for Christians in the West, this is our future. And because of the example of my Chinese friends, I am confident the same Holy Spirit and presence of the Living God will sustain us too.

Communism by Another Name

Back in April 17, 1975, the Khmer Rouge, or Communist Cambodians led by Pol Pot, marched into the capital city of Phnom Penh. The locals were elated because they believed the Khmers were coming to liberate them from the long war in Indochina.

The Americans abruptly left Vietnam, and many Cambodians believed all would be well and peace would come. In a very short time, a horrible reality set in. Pol Pot and his band of Khmer Rouge were murderous totalitarians in the exact mold of Stalin and Mao Zedong.

They began rounding people up in droves. Anyone suspected of not having the correct attitude toward the new regime was brutally murdered. *The Killing Fields* became a well-known movie, but no Hollywood embellishment was necessary to make it more shocking. They shot people and threw them into large pits. But there were so many to kill, it took too many bullets. So they started hitting them in the head with their shovels and throwing them in the pits to bury them alive.

Like the Nazis, they sat people in chairs, took measurements of their heads and photos of their face, front, left and right. Their photos are still on display in a crude museum. The skulls of many of their victims are stacked in a glass pavilion on display today. You can still see fragments of clothing in the soil where thousands were brutally murdered, worked to death, or starved.

The Khmer Rouge rounded up intellectuals, writers, doctors, teachers, and religious leaders for special treatment. Converting a school into their special prison, they tied them to metal beds, tortured and killed them slowly. When I was in Cambodia, the S-21 Prison was open to the public, but probably not as you might think. These displays were not cleaned up and sanitized for public consumption. The metal frame bed and mattress were in the place and condition they were left. Blood stains were on the filthy floor, and in each room on the wall was a large picture of the tortured prisoner who once occupied that bed.

In the center of the town on the top floor of a colonial-styled building was a large restaurant/bar where correspondents from all over the world met to talk during the Vietnam War, where they wrote and submitted their stories back home. It was from the balcony of what was then called the Foreign Correspondent's Club, where famous photos were memorialized of the Khmer Rouge marching into the city.

I sat on that balcony, with my own recent memories of the Vietnam War. Such a sad and tragic life the people of Cambodia lived through. There was a palpable sadness. Christian ministry there, if not large, was strong. It was in conversation with one of our Cambodian brothers when I learned a profound truth.

Unlike the Nuremburg Trials where Nazi criminals were brought to justice and hung before the whole world, there was no such reckoning in Cambodia.

For decades people lived next door to former Red Cambodians who slaughtered their families and loved ones. No leader took the blame, no one was ever punished, except for one man.

This story I cannot verify, but my Cambodian friends told me one leader in the Khmer Rouge became a Christian and publicly confessed his crimes against his fellow Cambodians, asking their forgiveness. That was the only instance they knew of anything resembling a reckoning. (In an interview with Morse Tan, Dean of Liberty School of Law, in January of 2023, I learned that the man's name was Kang Kek Iew. Known as "Duch," he was sentenced to thirty years, later to life imprisonment. But Kang admitted what he done, asked for forgiveness, and yes, became a Christian. During his trial, he provided detailed accounts of the atrocities of the S-21 Prison and inside the Khmer Rouge regime.) The result, it was explained to me by a Cambodian, was people were lost and confused. A great pall seemed to hang over the country. People by their very nature require justice, and there had been none. It was then I understood more fully the importance of punishment, not only for criminals, but for society. Clear punishment and justice bring sanity. Lawlessness brings the opposite, in children and in societies.[3]

"Look Betta in Picture"

One last story. Our host in Cambodia was one of the most charismatic, godly pastors I have ever met. His testimony of coming to faith in Christ from Buddhism was gripping, but it's a less lofty story about his wife I want to share.

She was Cambodian royalty of some type. Beautiful and arrogant, she was an unlikely match for this humble man. We were sharing pictures of our families back home, when she saw a picture of me. She stared at my face, then looked up at me directly in the face and said emphatically, "Look betta in picture!" I didn't laugh then, but Bruce and I repeat it often now, laughing every time.

Tragically, the beautiful Cambodian "princess" was so disliked by others, not long after we left, some of the women threw acid in her face. It was harsh retribution used frequently in that pagan culture.

My Birthday

Our trips always took place in September. I spent more than one birthday tucked away in some remote corner of the world, barely giving thought to my age.

On the trip on 1998, in a secluded area of China, we flew in for the explicit purpose of smuggling Bibles. We didn't often do that, but this time it was important. We each carried a generic suitcase packed to the brim. There were probably ten checkpoint areas. As we tried to exit the airport, we had to pass through those checkpoints first. We spread out and chose different screening desks, acting like we didn't know each other. Hilariously, when we learned later this was part of China that rarely saw Westerners. We stood out like twelve sore thumbs.

I carried a special suitcase filled with Bible commentaries, priceless to the recipients. I wanted to be the one to carry that case. As I was going through my line, I glanced about three checkpoints down, to see one of our guys get stopped. Guards began yelling, and in the confusion, while my screener was distracted, I grabbed my suitcase and headed for the exit.

That's when new screaming began. This time at me. But I was determined. I prayed and set my sights on that door. It was my birthday, and I was going to get those commentaries through.

As soon as I exited the door, a sea of people surrounded me. Someone grabbed me by the arm and led me quickly out to a bus which I boarded promptly then ducked down in the aisle. My heart was pounding, but I was happy! Happy birthday to me! Best present ever! Thank You, Lord![4]

Don't Get a Massage in Thailand

On another of my birthdays, we found ourselves in Bangkok, Thailand in 1997, in an absolutely gorgeous hotel. Before we went out one day, I went up to the top floor to make an appointment for a late-night solo birthday celebration. Here's what happened:

Thailand was and perhaps still is the sex capital of the world. It's a pagan culture with none of the barriers we are accustomed to in Western civilization. With that in mind, I knew I needed to be very careful about that appointment. I leaned over to get closer to the girl at the desk and said slowly, "I would like to have a massage by a woman—no sex." Okay, a little weird, but I wanted to be clear. Seeming to understand, in her broken English she agreed.

When evening came, I spent time on the treadmill, then moved into the adjoining suites for the appointment. When the door to the massage room opened, a man appeared. I turned to the attendant and said anxiously, "I would like a woman." "You no like man?" she asked. "He velly, velly good!" "No!" I responded emphatically.

A few minutes later the door opened, and out came a very tiny woman. She led me back through a long corridor with large wooden doors on either side. I followed her through one of those doors to discover a large room surrounded by bleacher-like wooden risers, where masseuses were busily working on a host of mostly men.

I glanced over to see one of our guys who we nicknamed "The Emperor." "You want next to him?" she asked. "No!" I declared nervously.

Each mat was separated by a flimsy curtain. I laid down on a mat across the room as this tiny person began awkwardly to pull on my arms and my legs. With the strength and stature of a tiny hummingbird, I'm guessing she had never given a massage in her life. It was miserable, but SO funny, I relished each moment for the story it would someday make.

Probably the worst interpreter we ever had was Chuchart in Thailand, but he was very sweet and funny. One night we all had dinner at the opulent buffet in the main dining room in the hotel. Delicacies were everywhere at multiple stations. As we waited in line there was a group of three Thai women, dressed in colorful, traditional dress complete with elegant, pointed hats.

Sitting cross-legged playing a stringed instrument spread across the three of them, at first it was enjoyable, but since Asian music isn't based on the Western scale, pitches are inexact to our ears. Twangy and piercing, it began to grate on my musical nerves. I was standing in line with Chuchart just behind me, wincing at the sound, when he leaned close to my ear and whispered, "I just LOVE this song!" My irritation melted as laugher welled up inside—laughter I could not share with Chuchart!

Blessed Is the Nation Whose God Is the Lord

We traveled for hours by multiple planes, then by bus and foot to get into a jungle area on the border dividing Thailand and Myanmar (Burma). We were headed to a refugee camp populated by a people known as the Karen. A tribal group, they were not considered Thai. Some of them lived on the Thai side of the river and others on the Burmese side.

As we entered the camp, we began to see neat wooden houses raised on stilts. A beautiful red cloth, woven in distinctive style graced homes and people. We made our way through the muddy path to hear, coming from a nearby tent, the sounds of a man, speaking English with a Thai accent, lecturing on the "Philosophy of Feminism." We moved further into the camp to see Thai children sitting on wooden stumps learning English grammar. What was this place?

We climbed up the crude steps of one of the wooden structures to meet the pastor. As it turns out, the Karen people were a Christian tribe. During recent violence in Myanmar, the pastor proceeded to tell us of his family's sudden forced exit from their home. As they struggled to carry his mother-in-law, he lacked the strength to manage his treasured theology books as well. It was a great sorrow for this brilliant man to have to leave those books behind. We sat on the large bamboo mat, listening to his stories in rapt attention.

We later convened in another place, under a thatched canopy to meet the children. We were placed in "chairs" on the stage. The headmaster introduced himself, telling us a bit about the children. We heard their happy voices as they flooded the "room," taking their place on roughhewn logs. They were dressed in that lovely red fabric, a hallmark of the Karen.

When the headmaster turned to speak quietly to the children, the hush was immediate. The students were respectful, obedient, and happy, but that was not all. On cue, they stood in unison and began to sing with power and conviction, "Blessed is the nation whose God is the Lord!" I was brought to my knees in my heart by those people. Humbled once again to be reminded how all the wealth and power in the world cannot bring greatness. Greatness is something flowing from the character and selflessness that develops in people who serve the one true, great and mighty God.

We were then led to a shelter where a large spread of special foods were prepared just for us. None of the Karen ate with us. We later learned they sacrificed their ration for that day to feed us.

How incredibly humbling and revealing about our own hearts and attitudes. I will never forget that day or its lessons of humility and servanthood.

One Last Jogging Story

While jogging early morning in Hong Kong and India delivered wonderful sights and sounds, Thailand offered something quite different: Black Crabs. Not just an occasional crab, but herds of them ambling sideways across the street continually while I was jogging. It felt like I was dodging tarantulas. I tried not to think about it.

And speaking of tarantulas, at rest stops in Cambodia, big black ones, deep fried were offered up on a giant platter for all to see and purchase.

Vietnamese Soldiers

Often in these faraway countries, we could join Christians to sing American hymns and worship together. That happened all over the globe, as a matter of fact. It has been a great loss to see American churches move almost completely away from those old hymns, if for no other reason than missionaries of old provided a common musical language now mostly lost.

I could sing "Amazing Grace" in English on the back of a bus along with a Vietnamese soldier singing in Vietnamese and we could understand each other. And as a matter of fact, I did.

When the U.S. pulled out of Vietnam, the North Vietnamese Communists poured into the south and the united country became one, big oppressive, communist country. Christians were arrested and fined and became the outcasts of society.

We bribed a bus driver in order to meet with and interview some of these soldiers. In the back of the bus, we asked them questions, as we drove around ostensibly on a "tour." The soldiers spoke fondly of their camaraderie with American soldiers and the sadness they felt when we left. Some Christian G.I.s had taught them a hymn and so we began to sing it together:

"Amazing Grace! How sweet the sound, that saved a wretch like me. I once was lost, but now am found. Was blind but now I see."

They sang with such enthusiasm it was pure joy to share that moment. I taught them the last verse:

"When we've been there ten thousand years, bright
    shining as the sun.
We've no less days to sing God's praise, than when we
    first begun!"

I think we touched heaven with our rendition.

Prelude to North Korea

Northern Manchuria, separated by the Tumen River from North Korea, was our destination on the last trip I was ever to take with the Bible League. It was September of 2001. Chinese Christians were hiding North Korean refugees at great risk, and we were to meet with them and gather their stories.

Some of our group traveled to Mongolia, and the six of us left separated into two groups. This time there was another woman named Rita from KKLA in Los Angeles. The men were sent to caves where refugees from North Korea were hiding, while Rita and I were sent on our own adventure.

Our first destination was a house in a remote area of Northern Manchuria. The owner was a plump, huggable woman with the radiant smile of your favorite aunt. As we got out of the car, we saw neighbors staring and we worried our soon-to-be new friend might be reported.

Just as this single Chinese sister exuded warmth and love, so did her house. She had pots cooking on the stove as she led us into a large area, something like a living room. We sat on the floor in a circle with three young boys she was hiding who had escaped. Actually, these boys were not so young, they were simply malnourished. They were young men of about seventeen.

One of them was chatty and engaging. He talked about the fact that when his mother ran out of food he jumped in the Tumen River to swim across and try to find rice. We asked about their school. Teachers taught them the reason there was no food was because Americans sunk all the ships bringing in rice. The Americans were responsible for every bad thing according to North Korean leaders. We were in fact, the enemy.

As bubbly as our first boy was, the one next to me was silent. His face was drawn and traumatized. I had never seen the look of trauma before. No expression, just a deep frown line and a blank stare. His words were few. I saw that more than once during our visit. The third boy described how the three of them swam across together. One fell back, afraid he was dying, but the other two urged him on. And yes, they planned to go back. The boys could not be seen outside. They couldn't play or go to school or make noise. So, in that warm, cozy home, our Chinese Christian "auntie" loved on them, told them about Jesus and the truth about their circumstances. Who knows whatever became of any of them.

Rita and I were then placed in a small taxi for a truly unknown destination. Believe me, it takes faith to get into a cab in a remote part of China with a stranger you can't communicate with. I prayed we would reach our mysterious destination, and after what seemed like a long ride, we finally did.

We were given a few instructions. We were going to be dropped off at an apartment building where we were to climb to the top floor and knock on the door of the designated number. But when the driver pulled up in front of the building, it was still daylight. There was a long freshly dug trench stretching across the front of the building, filled with forced laborers, connected by chains.

You can imagine our pulses racing as we two very white, Western women got out of the car and made our way across the chain gang and into the building. What else could we do? There was no turning back and no place to hide.

We mounted the steps to the top floor, knocked softly and were quickly ushered in. We had only been there a few minutes when the doorbell rang and panic broke out on the faces of the residents. We hurried to the back room amid shushes and watched as our host hid behind a curtain to peer out the window. Time passed. The doorbell rang again, and thank God it turned out to be someone they knew. A major sigh was heard from all of us.

The occupants of this apartment were housing four North Korean refugees. Sitting on chairs and on the floor, we heard and recorded their incredible stories. A twelve-year-old girl sat across from me with that same countenance of trauma I saw earlier on the boy. A frown, a stare, an emotionless voice as she spoke of her grandfather. She was living with him, but they had no food. Each day she walked ten miles one way to pick up sticks she gathered to sell for close to nothing. At some point, they tried to escape. She saw her grandfather shot by police, but somehow, she got away. Because of the difficulty in translation, we couldn't understand as much as I longed to comprehend.

On the floor was a beautiful twenty-four-year-old woman with mangled legs. She made her way across the river previously, but upon returning to North Korea, she was arrested. Chinese Christians at that time set up stations along the river to feed refugees, and always gave them a small Bible along with the story of the Savior. But because Kim Il-sung hated Christians, if you were caught with a Bible, three generations of your family were killed. When this young woman was sent to prison, in order to save her family, she jumped out of the top floor of the prison trying to kill herself. She broke both her legs instead. I don't know how she got back over the river, and I can't imagine how she could ever have gotten out of that apartment to find a new life.

Imagine the risk and generosity of those Manchurian Christians who risked their own safety and spent their own time and treasure to save these people.

Can you see now why I love and admire Chinese Christians?

9/11 in North Korea

Without warning, we were offered the chance to go into North Korea. At that time in 2001, NO ONE was going into North Korea. How was this possible? Somehow our contacts got permission to send six of us under the guise of bringing in much-needed school supplies.

We went shopping quickly, and off we set for the border. Much like the Berlin Wall, the Tumen served as a natural barrier between North Korea and China. As we drove up in a van, their "Checkpoint Charlie" was a run-down building with various stations at which we were grilled and examined. When we finally passed through, we were directed to a wooden bridge connecting the two borders. Armed guards followed us from various perches with their guns as we walked across to tyranny.

Once across we boarded a similar van driven by a North Korean driver. He was joined by two "watchers." They were there to keep an eye on us and on each other. The ride was long and wild. Traveling through the thick, greenery-covered mountains, the road was crude and rough. At first as I bounced completely off the seat, it made me laugh, but after many hours, my body and arms were sore, the laughter vanished.

As we passed through various towns, we noticed huge buildings that turned out to be only facades. Imagine a rendering of a large building, held up by boards, like an easel. It was the North Korean version of the famous Russian Potemkin village, a fake beautiful building where no real building existed. A fake city, built to look nice to outsiders glancing, but hiding the reality of the horrible life lived there.

Along the road there were frequent huge "billboards" adorned with the "Dear Leader" (Kim Il Sung) smiling down on everyone. Every North Korean had to wear a pin bearing that same image each day to avoid severe punishment.

We drove to our "hotel" on the Sea of Japan and were promptly escorted to our rooms. There was no soap and little bedding. It was pitch black at night, with the elevator turned off for good measure. Welcome to North Korea.

Next morning, we rose to visit the school. We were treated to precision performances by the children. Incredibly precise, as it were. The little girls wore makeup and beautiful dresses, but as I approached them after the performance and placed my hand on a little girl's shoulder in a loving gesture, I felt her wince and pull away. We were the enemy, remember. They were just little props in another fake, but real-life, dangerous display.

We were then taken to a urine-smelling movie-like theater, curiously filled with people at four in the afternoon. As the curtains opened, dancers dressed in military uniform danced and sang ode after ode to the Dear Leader with that same precision and eerie soullessness.

On the walls of a public building, we saw renderings of Kim Il Sung posing like Jesus (reminiscent of those famous color renderings that graced American Bibles in the '50s and '60s): Kim Il Sung a.k.a. Jesus surrounded by the children; Kim Il Sung feeding the 5,000; Kim Il Sung delivering the Sermon on the Mount. Why in the world did these exist and for what purpose? We learned later that the Dear Leader's maternal grandfather was a protestant minister, his father an elder in the Presbyterian Church, but he had turned against its teachings with vitriol.

Also interesting to me is Stalin attended seminary, and Marx was baptized a Lutheran. Satan used their knowledge of Christianity to give them formidable insight which they in turn weaponized and perverted.

On our last day, we were taken on a "luxury" cruise near an odd but elegant casino. Erected for the use of Kim Jong Il, slots zinged and roulette wheels whirled as visitors from China hovered over them.

Out on the water that day, we were treated to seals and other interesting, but unremarkable sites. Putting their best forward, it was still terribly bleak. We were relieved to get out of that place.

Back to "Freedom"

Relieved at least for a moment, we finally walked back across that wooden bridge to what by contrast felt like freedom into Communist Northern Manchuria.

It was September 12, 2001.

Eager for good food, we were led to a Chinese restaurant by our Korean-American hosts. Eddie and his wife owned a successful dry-cleaning business in California but occupied an apartment in Northern Manchuria so they could come frequently and help refugees.

After we ordered, the manager came over to speak to us. Soberly, he told us through an interpreter about the planes that had, the day before, taken down the World Trade Center, the Pentagon, and sent many to their death in a field in Shanksville, Pennsylvania. "Is he crazy?" I demanded to know.

Andy, our talk show host from New York City, called his wife on a satellite phone. We watched as his countenance fell and his wife confirmed the news with more detail. Horrified, none of us could eat. We took our food and hurriedly made our way, following Eddie and his wife down a nearly pitch-dark path, up a dark stairway and into their apartment on the top floor. Quickly they turned on the news and as we watched the unedited version of planes hitting the towers and bodies dropping from the windows, I sat on my knees rocking back and forth, weeping.

My first thoughts were of my children. Was this the beginning of another world war? Would China side with our enemies? Would we ever get home? And would I ever see my children again?

We somehow made our way to Beijing where we were stranded for ten days. I watched CNN each night. With the twelve-hour time difference, the world was upside down in more ways than one.

We gathered soberly to watch the service in the National Cathedral. It was comforting just to see our people, our president, and Dr. Billy Graham speaking words of resolve and comfort.

I knew the world had changed in our absence when a CNN anchor invited a pastor, on the set with him, on live, prime time television . . . to pray.

Eventually flying through Tokyo, I finally made it back home, landing in an eerily deserted LA Airport, then headed to Phoenix first to see my dad and sister, then on to Chicago for a tearful reunion with my family and a very different world.

10

The CWA Babe

It was spring of 2001. I was speeding as usual, headed north on Interstate 355 for the thousandth time, rushing to the studio at WYLL. It was late morning and my heart and mind were absorbed in praying about a conflict with my station manager that seemed unsolvable. Once again, the cell phone rang. A familiar voice on the line from Domain Communications, at first chatted, then explained that Beverly LaHaye of the *Concerned Women Today* radio program needed to be absent for several weeks in the approaching summer months.

Would I be willing to fill in for her, and did I think my station manager would allow me to do such a thing? I hesitated, knowing my existing workload, but agreed I would ask as soon as I got into work.

Then he added, "Oh, and by the way, would you like to be president of Concerned Women for America?" My heart stopped.

Concerned Women for America was the largest women's public policy organization in the country. CWA didn't major on women's issues; they were women who addressed all the major issues of the day. Founded by Beverly LaHaye in 1978, they grew to a membership of 500,000 with chapters in all fifty states. I was the voice of their radio specials and the announcing voice for their daily radio show.

Would I like to be president of Concerned Women for America? Uproot my life and move to DC? My mind was swirling as I promised to consider it and hung up.

By that time Sasha was at Marklund Children's Home for six years. Jeremy was a junior at Wheaton College, living in our home along with a bunch of other Wheaton College Students. I loved having a house full of those wonderful young guys. How could I leave my son and his friends?

I went home that night and, standing in the kitchen, told Jeremy all about the phone call. His immediate response was, "Mom, if that's what God is calling you to do, you have to go!" I couldn't believe his magnanimity. I didn't expect it, and my acceptance or rejection of the invitation had everything to do with his response.

"Okay, son!" I responded. "I guess now that you're twenty-one, I'm leaving home!" Thus began my journey toward yet another major life change.

A Blue Dress Nearly Cost Me the Job—No, Not That Blue Dress

The vetting process took several months. I didn't officially start until 2001. No one was more surprised than I when people I trusted weighed in with letters of recommendation to Mrs. LaHaye on my behalf: Congressman Henry Hyde; Illinois Attorney General Jim Ryan; the legendary Phyllis Schlafly, constitutional attorney and founder of Eagle Forum; Joe Scheidler, the "Green Beret" of the pro-life movement, founder of Pro-Life Action League; Senator Peter Fitzgerald and State Senator and future U.S. Congressman Peter Roskam. Paul Caprio, my dear friend and comrade at arms through many battles in Chicago and the State of Illinois, who was founder of Family Pac Federal, joined the chorus and later hosted an incredible luncheon as a going-away celebration.

One by one the superlatives began to mount up. I blushed to read them, but the reason I mention this is because in reading them, I gained confidence.

Plagued by insecurity, I asked myself, *What qualified me to lead such an organization?* I was a musician and radio talk show host, not an attorney, a politician, or leader in the movement. Why did Mrs.

LaHaye choose me? Could I do everything required in this leap to a new level and a new world? These people I trusted thought I could. My son thought I could. And most of all, evidently God thought I could.

I passed muster with Mrs. LaHaye and the CWA board, but the DC staff had yet to meet with me and approve. I flew to Washington to meet them, and here's where it almost went off the rails.

Did I say I was a singer/radio talk show host? Did I say I loved fashion? I had plenty of bling, plenty of fun clothing, including a man's suit with a crisp white shirt and tie, blue jeans, cowboy boots and a hat, and lots of black—LOTS of black. But none of it seemed appropriate for Concerned Women for America. What do Concerned Women for America wear? Something conservative, I reasoned. Something like women wear in church, I thought. I carefully chose a long, sleeveless blue shift dress and pearls, completing the ensemble with beige wedge sandals fastened with cloth ties.

It makes me laugh even now to think about it. Completely unaware of the dress code or the culture in the District of Columbia, I came to the meeting looking like a church lady. Unbeknownst to me, there was severe judgment at the other end. The dress code at CWA and in DC at that time was buttoned-down and all business. Men and women wore immaculate suits and nothing sleeveless—ever. I was Michelle Obama before Michelle Obama ever exposed her muscular upper arms. Men's sleeves were never to be cuffed up, and women were never to wear open-toed shoes.

I'm sorry. I'm still laughing here.

Unaware, I flew back to Chicago oblivious of these rules or my inadequate apparel. That, my friends, nearly cost me the job.

But once Mrs. LaHaye brought it to my attention, I promised her that I could dress appropriately for DC and I did. That was a fun shopping trip. Clothing always makes an important statement, whatever field you're in. And I have dressed for lots of fields.

Those beautiful suits from Lord & Taylor served me well when night after night I appeared on television, or had meetings at the

Justice Department, Congress, or the White House. In the Old Testament, Queen Esther's physical appearance and dress were central to how God was able to use her to save her people, Israel. While it's true God looks at the heart, the Bible also makes it clear, "man" looks on the outward appearance.

In order to reach people where they are, and have impact, our appearance shouldn't be central, but neither should it be a barrier to the mission.

Flashback to North Korea

Rocking back and forth on my knees crying in that top floor apartment in Northern Manchuria, watching the bodies drop from the Twin Towers on that fateful night just one month earlier, my mind raced as I contemplated what might be the result of the event we were watching. Would there even be a DC left after this? Would CWA still exist, and would anyone care about legislation or policy if the whole world were at war?

My Beginning at CWA

When I drove to the CWA office building, two blocks from the White House, only a few weeks later, the embers were still smoldering at the Pentagon.

Staff was traumatized as they recounted to me the horrors of September 11—the fear, the gridlock, the eerie experience of looking over rooftops to see snipers and hear sirens wail. All of Washington was in a state of shock in those first few weeks, but soon jolted into action.

I arrived in October 2001 to a large, spartan office with nonexistent or mismatched furniture and chipped paint on the walls. But there were floor-to-ceiling windows, stretching the length of the room, with an equally long balcony overlooking McPherson Square. I could see the White House from that balcony. Lee LaHaye, CFO and son of Mrs. LaHaye, generously donated money to refurbish what became a beautiful office where hour upon hour was spent in work and prayer. Lee became a very good friend, and his life became a very sad story.

We began with a budget of twelve million dollars, and a staff of thirty-five. Part of that staff was producing a popular monthly magazine and the national morning radio show. Bob Knight, former reporter for the *LA Times*, was someone from whom I learned a great deal and had inspired me long before I ever got to DC. Bob headed our Culture & Family Institute, where we addressed the thorniest moral issues of the day. Peter LaBarbera, founder of Americans for Truth, also a former news reporter, was his fun and very knowledgeable sidekick. Pete probably had the largest collection of books and articles and institutional knowledge of the LGBT Movement than anyone else in the country.

Dr. Janice Krause directed the Beverly LaHaye Institute which did focus solely on women's issues, challenging academia with statistics and studies. CWA was an NGO at the United Nations and an active participant in trying to fight the export of abortion, feminism, homosexuality, and more to the Third World. Most of this began with Hillary Clinton's determination to radicalize the world. I covered the UN's Beijing Conference on Women in 1995. I knew of Hillary's special tent to teach "lesbian love-making," and of her efforts to create the notion of five genders. I also knew of her advocacy of the Convention on the Rights of the Child which included taking away parental rights on religious practice, abortion, and sexuality. Hillary Clinton believed children had a "right" to be sexually active from the age of twelve.

I came to DC with a fire in my belly to stop that in any way possible.

But heading CWA gave me the power to fight in a tangible way.

Ironically, the women of the Third World fought back. In Africa, South America, and other places around the globe, they organized and went to bat to stop this exportation of depravity. In many places, like Uganda, they succeeded. And we helped them in any way we could.

Wendy Wright, a champion in the pro-life movement, spent time in jail for her efforts to save babies. Wendy headed up our international work along with the fight against abortion advancement at home, and often hosted our morning radio show.

Our much beloved but shrewd Irish Catholic Michael Schwartz was vice president of our governmental affairs division, leading our lobbying team in both House and Senate. Michael became one of my most trusted advisors. After we both were gone from CWA, he became chief of staff for Senator Tom Coburn. During his tenure in that position, he developed Lou Gehrig's Disease, which overtook him quickly. He struggled to make the commute from Maryland for months, finally resigning himself to home. The last time I saw him alive, I visited, sitting next to him, propped up by pillows while he dictated incredible stories of his journey in the pro-life movement. Self-deprecating, no one fully understood what a treasure we had in Michael Schwartz. Each year young staffers, now adults, who worked for him commemorate his life at an Irish pub in downtown DC.

Michael spent the first week, escorting me around "town," introducing me to key players, educating me on issues, pitfalls, and people.

My first event was an awards ceremony in a relatively small hotel ballroom honoring Justice Clarence Thomas. I met so many of the people I interviewed from Chicago who became professional friends: Byron York, Michael Barone, Andy McCarthy, Jonah Goldberg. (Yes, Jonah used to be a champion for the conservative cause.) I was grateful for the ease that came in being with them in person for the first time. It was a great beginning!

First Steps

Wisdom dictates that a new leader doesn't come to an organization and begin radical changes right away. (Elon Musk is the exception.)

I had much to learn. My initial changes were hard but necessary.

First, I tackled what I knew—media. I hired Keith Appell's new company, CRC, a powerful DC PR Firm to handle our media. That was a major step that paid off in very big ways. It was my determination that our experts should be the ones featured in their areas of expertise. In many organizations, there is a designated person to handle all media, but I knew we were sitting on a gold mine of knowledge, and I wanted it unleashed.

Our media presence exploded as our managers delivered powerful punches of truth each and every time. I was a generalist on everything we were doing. They were the experts, and I was proud of them.

Jan LaRue, our chief legal counsel, was a later hire. With expertise in child pornography and pornography in general, she was a force to be reckoned with. When the Bush administration failed to prosecute pornographers or enforce laws against those distributing and producing it, Jan and I made a visit to Attorney General John Ashcroft. As we sat in his office, he explained how he hadn't gotten involved because he didn't want to view such things. Jan handed him a graphic image of baby pornography as we both not so gently admonished him that the internet had become the Wild West, and he MUST get involved, no matter how unpleasant.

It was under President Clinton that the recognition of Gay Pride Month by federal agencies began. We were appalled when in June of 2002, George W. Bush's Attorney General Ashcroft carried on with the practice.

I called his office immediately to challenge him. I was connected to the assistant attorney general, Larry Thompson, for a conversation I won't ever forget. If you think I enjoyed these confrontations, you would be wrong. I felt the Holy Spirit come over me as I admonished the Pentecostal Christian AG and his Christian assistant attorney general that they had lost their sense of righteousness. This was my job, wasn't it? As the president of one of the most prominent Christian public policy groups in DC and in the country, how could I remain silent?

General Thompson responded quietly, and steps were taken to reverse course, at least for that year. It was the beginning of a floodgate we couldn't imagine.

Television and Radio

My managers, as they were called, appeared all over the networks fighting everything from abortion to homosexual "rights," to pornography, and judicial nominations.

Each Friday we ordered pizza, met in the kitchen, watched videos from each appearance, and cheered.

My extensive exposure on television and in major media was due in no small part to the work of Keith Appell and CRC. I was featured in *Time Magazine, Christianity Today,* and did frequent interviews with the *Washington Post,* the *New York Times,* and other major outlets.

Once when I was in the airport in Boston, I got a call from 111-111-1111. I thought it was God calling, but it was the *New York Times* instead.

I learned early not to place too much trust in reporters who loved to twist your words or leave strategic ones out. It wasn't quite as hostile a press then, however, and I actually made friends with some of them.

When things later went south at CWA, one of those reporters from the *Washington Post* called in concern—and yes, for a story, but I could not give it to him.

Learning a New Skill

I debated on *PBS, MSNBC, CNN, FOX,* and the major networks. At each opportunity, I prayed for God to give me the ability to transfer my long experience in radio, speaking the truth in a way people who didn't share my faith would listen. That was my goal. Most of the time, honestly, I felt a failure. Many Christian friends were critical of how aggressive I became. But it only took two minutes to realize television debates are short and the Left is not your polite next-door neighbor. They filibuster, they talk louder, they lie, and personally disparage you. How does one enter that arena without rising to the challenge?

I think that's when I first got the nickname "The Velvet Hammer." I landed plenty of punches, but always with the idea of redemption, not condemnation.

In 2003 I debated the first openly gay Congressman from Massachusetts, Barney Frank, and I debated the president of our nemesis, the National Organization for Women (NOW), Terry O'Neill. I remembered how NOW savaged my friend Joe Scheidler during his twenty-year court case, *Scheidler v. National Organization for Women*. In the federal building in Chicago, during Joe's trial, I sat at the feet of Patricia Ireland, listening to her threaten to take his home, his car, his livelihood. I knew who the enemy was, and how wicked they were. I was no innocent in this arena.

In 2003 I flew to New York to be on the set with famous San Francisco atheist, Michael Newdow, and famous heretic, The "Reverend" Barry Lynn, founder of Christians United for Separation of Church and State. I debated Barry several times. He was cunning, convincing, and never bound by the truth. The topic for the evening was to be the Ten Commandments controversy. Michael and Barry led the movement to remove the Ten Commandments from schools and public buildings. Under the smokescreen of "separation of church and state," a phrase used only in a letter from Thomas Jefferson to the Danbury Baptist Association and never in the Constitution, the uneducated public fell for the argument that the Founders believed government should not be associated with or reflect any particular religion.

In fact, the Founders demonstrated by their words and their actions, "religion and morality" were the foundations upon which the freedoms guaranteed by the Bill of Rights and the Constitution could be fully enjoyed. Thomas Jefferson ordered Bible study to be taught to the Indians when he was president. Bible verses and biblical renderings adorn Congress, and DC monuments, while the Ten Commandments is emblazoned in marble behind the sitting Supreme Court justices. So much for separation of church and state.

One by one, monuments, plaques, and in fact the knowledge of the Ten Commandments left the public domain. If anyone wonders why many of our children have no respect for life, for parents, for other people's property, for marriage, one has only to remember they grew up in a world where the plumbline laid down by the Creator/ God is unknown to them.

There were some real challenges. Phil Donahue began as "Mister Nice Guy" on Chicago television. I was in the audience twice many years before, loving his style and this new brand of television talk show. But Phil became mean and bitter. Greater people than I met his famous buzzsaw only to be annihilated. Dr. James Dobson, founder and chairman of Focus on the Family was one of them.

Once when I was sitting in the makeup chair prior to cameras rolling on *The Phil Donahue Show*, I was facing away from the mirror. When the artist turned me around to look, my makeup was heavy, my eyelashes huge and dark, my long hair teased out into a huge wild bush à la Tammy Faye Baker. I knew what they were doing. When the artist left the room, I stood up and muted the makeup and tamed the hair.

In one of my most beautiful Lord & Taylor suits, I moved to the stage.

I was seated arm to arm between Michael and Barry. The audience was in a small half-moon configuration on risers, like a classroom. There were no women dressed in sleeveless long dresses and pearls. Hostility filled the place. Behind us, Dr. Jerry Falwell was on a relatively small television screen. It was hard to see, and he was hard to hear, so I was virtually on my own to defend the Ten Commandments. Who could do that?

In prayer and serenity, but determination, I did my very best. It was hard to get a word in between Phil, who obviously hated me, my seat partners, and the audience who jeered and sneered. I remembered something Bob Knight shared long before I ever got to CWA about being in a similar situation. He described the Holy Spirit coming over him bringing an incredible feeling of love toward his opponents.

The same thing happened to me. During commercial breaks, I found myself saying to every single hateful, sneering audience member, "God loves you. God loves you. God loves you." I felt no anger, just a deep love, understanding they did not really know what they were doing, or the eternal implications of such vitriol.

Phil never introduced himself, never spoke to me, never welcomed me personally. Tyra Banks did the same years later, but up until that time, even among those of us who debated passionately on opposite sides, there was cordiality on a personal basis. Not so with Phil.

On the Other Hand, Bill Maher

I flew to California at the invitation of Bill Maher's talk show.

No matter the subject matter, Bill, the atheist, always brought it back to the existence of God. He snarled at and degraded anyone who equivocated even slightly on their faith in God. He could smell weakness or effort to please the crowd and he savaged those who did.

Since my faith is sure, and my motivation for doing television is more evangelism than building a résumé, I gave as good as I got. And honestly, Bill's response was to give respect.

Bradley Whitford, from the mega-hit television show *The West Wing*, along with Iranian intellectual Reza Aslan, and I debated something related to Islam. Afterward, Bill asked me to join them for dinner. Bill brought a black female prostitute. I think he thought it would shock me. Added to the dinner mix was one of Hollywood's most famous movie score composers, Michael Penn, brother of Sean Penn, and a famous screenwriter whose name I could drop, if only I could remember it. The first part of the conversation was a flurry of name-dropping, but I had no idea who they were talking about so I wasn't a great audience. I realized then how insular Hollywood is—how they really do believe the world revolves around them and their work. Then amazingly, the subject turned to my faith. MY faith—did I really believe God existed? "Why did He allow suffering? Did I actually believe Jesus was the only way to heaven?" And on it went.

I prayed for wisdom, I prayed for discernment, I prayed for ways of responding that would reach them.

The night ended and back to DC I flew. As I walked down the aisle of the airplane, passenger after passenger spoke up to tell me they saw me with Bill Maher the night before.

One last Bill Maher story: Once from a DC studio, I was Bill's guest along with who I learned was Gandalf in the movie *The Lord of the Rings*, the gay actor Ian McKellen. I bowed my head on the set, from exhaustion and stress from the battle we were waging against same-sex marriage. I prayed, then looked up straight into the camera on cue as God gave me strength and courage to fight this battle too. Ironically, for months Bill used this particular clip of me from this appearance in promos for his show, *Real Time with Bill Maher*.

How I Got the Nickname "The CWA Babe"

CNN's most popular talk show, *Crossfire*, used to be aired live from George Washington University with a packed audience and great guests of diametrically opposing viewpoints. James Carville and Paul Begala rotated as the host on the Left. Tucker Carlson and occasionally I rotated as the host on the Right. The last element in the mix was a huge screen where anyone notable from Dr. Ruth to Dr. Jerry Falwell appeared larger than life on the screen behind us.

It was a winning formula, and the most popular show on cable news for a reason. Just four months after 9/11, I was the guest on the topic of public indoctrination of students regarding Islam. In the immediate days and weeks after the attack, there was natural anger and blowback toward Muslims, since they were quite clear in uncovered documents from the Holy Land Foundation trial that they wanted to, "Destroy their [our] miserable house from within." (See "Exploratory Memorandum" From the Archives of the Muslim Brotherhood in America at SecureFreedom.org)

Muslim Brotherhood operatives through their propaganda arm, the Council on Islamic Relations, or CAIR, went into hyperdrive creating the concept of "Islamophobia," "In what came to be a successful effort to silence and shame anyone who dared speak up in criticism, it was a preview of all that was to come.

No surprise, the National Education Association, jumped in to "help." Under advisement from CAIR, they created curriculum ingraining children with the notion of "Islamophobia" or fear of Islam, patterned after that other successful made-up word, "homophobia."

I was a guest that night. The very young, bow-tied Tucker, the host on the Right, was facing off with the very snarly Southern bulldog, James Carville, the host on the Left. I had debated James already on more than one occasion and come away feeling defeated. James was a fearless debater, never constrained by facts. By the time I was correcting one lie, he was four more ahead. It was impossible to debate James Carville. I knew this going in, and once again prayed for wisdom.

I loved being on *Crossfire*, and things were going well, until James introduced the next guest up on the main screen. It wasn't Franklin Graham, but a quote from Franklin Graham, which in part said something like "Islam is a very evil and wicked religion . . ." When James finished reading the quote, he turned on me and with a literal sneer, said, "Do you agree with this fundamentalist Christian?!"[5]

"Yes, I do," I responded quietly at which James stood and slammed his fist down on the large wooden table, cursing, "God-D_ _ _ _!" An inexplicable calm came over me, as I looked at James, by then, foaming at the mouth. Rather than respond, I handed him my cup, and said, "James. You're dripping—you're drooling." At that point he went into more rage. Remember this was before a live audience in the auditorium and broadcast in real time into millions of homes around the country.

Tucker's funny response made James even madder: "That really was an amazing outburst. If we can just stop and appreciate that for a minute."

I never debated Carville again, and I don't think I have to guess why.

The next morning, I came into work to find a sign on my office door that read "CWA BABE!" My staff informed me Rush Limbaugh was playing the clip over and over all morning, calling me the "CWA Babe." The staff made a Barbie doll draped in a sash labeled "CWA Babe." What fun we had!

Later, when it was time to get a Virginia license plate, in a moment of poor judgment at the humongous, confusing choices, I quickly, and to my regret, chose CWA BABE. It wasn't until later when former Education Secretary, Bill Bennett joined me in my little PT Cruiser bearing that license plate to drive to an important meeting with Chuck Colson, Dr. Dobson, and other Christian leaders, I realized it was a mistake. I was mortified as I drove into the Colson Center parking where they were all standing, watching as Bill and I drove up. It was funny, but my sense of humor surely must have made me seem shallow at times. It certainly did on this occasion.

I ordered another license plate.

It's Okay to Lead

My first address to CWA staff in October of 2001 was on the damning, neutering, culture of "niceness." We are not called to be nice. We are often called to be confrontational. In more recent years, that became the opening of my morning radio show, and it caused not a few eyebrows to raise.

Over the decades, it seems to me a culture of "niceness' has descended on Christians. "Nicer than Jesus," some have said. It is so ingrained in Christian culture it has become synonymous with what it actually means to be a follower of Christ. Lots of often meaningless smiles, paired with quiet, smiling acquiescence to all kinds of wrongs seems to equal nice. No necessary, healthy confrontations in churches or homes are "spiritual."

Being nice has become a badge, a signaling of "Christian" virtue, actually. Nowhere in the Bible do we read an admonition to niceness.

To kindness, humility, goodness, mercy, and more—but NOT niceness.

Niceness isn't about imitating Jesus, for on many occasions He was surely NOT nice.

He called the religious leaders of His day "blind guides, who strain out a gnat and swallow a camel!" (Matthew 23:24). He said their mouths were like open, white-washed tombs, and they smelled of the grave. He called them hypocrites to their faces. He took out a whip and in anger, overturned tables, and drove people out of the temple who were exchanging currencies and stealing in the process (Mark 11:15–17).

No one ever described Jesus as nice. He is described as the "Lamb of God who takes away the sins of the world!" (John 1:29). But He's also pictured as a warrior on a horse, eyes blazing like fire, with a sword coming from His mouth when He returns again to earth (Revelation 19:15).

Being called nice is actually about us and our reputation, not about Him. We want to be known as nice because it is culturally the thing to be, not because it means we are deeply manifesting the fruit of the Spirit.

That was an interesting way to begin my relationship with those wonderful people known as the CWA staff.

Being a leader is something that falls on you as a result of the way God has wired you. I certainly never set out to lead, but because I served a God who gave me guidance and wisdom, people followed. At certain points, God clearly had to show me it wasn't always my place to lead. I also had to learn to follow. As I grew in the knowledge of Him, I tried, sometimes not so successfully to keep my opinions to myself and know my place.

There was a constant "governor" in me, trying to restrain me so I would not step out if it wasn't appropriate. Each week at CWA I met with the managers in the conference room, sitting at the head of a long table. I believed in leading by listening. I spent enough time with these experts to be able to trust them. With little exception, they were selfless warriors who wanted what was best. They were not in these battles for personal triumph; they were in it for the same reason I was: to re-establish truth in a decaying culture to preserve the country we all loved.

If there was controversy about how we should handle an issue, I sat back and listened. I encouraged them to argue respectfully. I wanted to hear every viewpoint. There was such intellect in that room at times, it was no small thing to keep up. But as they were making their points, sometimes diametrically opposed, the realization hit me that now I AM the leader. It is my job to make the decisions. It isn't immoral or presumptuous, it is the role God has assigned me to take.

The conversation ended, everyone would look at me, and I would make the decision. I felt an incredible freedom and confidence. And my respectful staff, most of whom had more experience in public policy and often more education, in return showed me uncanny respect. Like a marriage, I thought, where husband and wife are designated roles. God's design for marriage and for leadership is a good one when all parties are submitted to Him.

Remarkable Moments

The first CWA convention I presided over in 2002 was in beautiful downtown DC at the historic Willard Hotel where Julia Ward Howe penned "The Battle Hymn of the Republic" and Abraham Lincoln was smuggled in by the Pinkerton brothers to stay in safety until his inauguration on March 4, 1861. Elegant and breathtaking, it was a perfect backdrop for our event.

The room was filled as I introduced Dr. Norbert Vollertsen as our main speaker. Dr. Vollertsen was a German doctor with a big swoop of thick straight, blond hair that partially covered his eyes. He looked like a stereotypical Nazi, probably because his father was one.

Dr. Vollertsen had so much guilt over that, he spent his medical career trying to make up for it. I interviewed him the first time on *Concerned Women Today*. He came in-studio fresh from a series of meetings at the UN and the European Union. In the first year after I took on the presidency of CWA, I was asked to chair the first North Korea Freedom Coalition.

Obviously, I was one of the few Americans ever to visit there, and some thought I was a natural choice. After my trip, I learned with horror and in much more detail of the atrocities practiced by the Dear Leader Kim Jong Il. People were starving to death. Cannibalism was not uncommon. Labor camps were horrendous. It was the most oppressive regime on the globe.

With that backdrop, Dr. Vollertsen made it his life's mission to help the people of North Korea. At one point, Madeleine Albright took a delegation into the country accompanied by journalists from around the world. Secretary of State Albright declared right then and there that North Koreans were free and the country was a great place to live.

Meanwhile, Dr. Vollertsen secured a van and peeled off several of those journalists to see the *real* North Korea, including the starvation and the camps.

It created such an uproar, he was kicked out of the country and consequently pursued all over the globe. During that first interview, he told me of surgeries without anesthetic, beds without sheets, hospitals without soap or medicine. He donated his own skin for grafts on burn patients. He won the trust of the government until they realized he exposed the reality.

At the UN and the European Union, his horror stories were met with shrugs. "So?" delegates responded. But when he shared those stories with me while on air, I began to cry. That simple natural response brought tears to his eyes and moved him deeply.

When it came time for our convention, I wanted him to speak. Just before I introduced Dr. Vollertsen, I was informed there were

North Korean agents in the room, even sitting at the dinner tables. Norbert was in great danger. I made an announcement telling everyone what was happening and asking every attendee to look around their table to make sure everyone seated there belonged. I told the infiltrators to get out immediately because they were not welcome. I saw figures jumping up and heading for the doors. We locked those doors, and the evening continued.

The Big Lie: *Roe v. Wade*

Bob Knight produced a documentary on the history of *Roe v. Wade*. Norma McCorvey a.k.a. "Roe" was never raped. The story was a construct by attorney Faye Wattleton and her abortion-loving conspirators. Norma became a pro-life advocate, telling the story of the deceit to all who would listen. Dr. Bernard Nathanson, the famous abortionist-turned-pro-lifer who helped form NARAL, also joined us. He revealed how the made-up numbers reported each night on CBS by "America's most trusted anchorman," Walter Cronkite, were fabricated by him and others. Walter Cronkite was a willing accomplice to the deceit and, by the way, an avowed closet Leftist.

A Funny Confession

During the Ten Commandments debates of 2003, I flew to Alabama to speak on the steps of the Alabama Supreme Court in defense of Chief Justice Roy Moore who erected a privately funded monument of the commandments on the premises. For that, he was removed from office and under incredible attack. The worst betrayal came from Christian leaders.

At first, Alabama pastors and Christian leaders were passionate defenders of Justice Moore. One morning during a crucial time, a large gathering of them were to meet at a prayer breakfast to show their solidarity and support.

Suddenly a missive went out from Dr. Richard Land, Executive Director of the Southern Baptist's policy division in DC, the Ethics and Religious Liberty Commission, and Jay Sekulow, founder of the ACLJ, withdrawing their support, accusing Justice Moore of defying the law in breach of the admonition for Christians to obey it. I knew Justice Moore to be a man of incredible character, standing alone to defend the right for courts and schools to display the commandments which our forefathers embraced and upon which our laws were based. He insisted Americans had a right to acknowledge God. Separation of church and state penned by Jefferson did NOT mean there should be NO acknowledgment of the God of our fathers, but simply that belief in Him should not be forced by a state church.

I was not happy with Dr. Land or Jay. It's easy for people to nit-pick the methods of others who are taking a bold stand, thus giving themselves a pass for doing nothing. The inference to me was "I WOULD do something about this, but as a Christian, I can't defy the law. In fact, I'm taking the moral high ground by refusing." One can't judge another's motives, but the choice they made just happened to comport with what the DC establishment wanted. Judge Moore was an embarrassment to the establishment, unwilling even to defend the Ten Commandments if it meant associating themselves with him. The Bible I grew up reading was clear, when conflicts arise between God's law and man's law, "We ought to obey God rather than men" (Acts 5:29).

Okay, so finally, here's the confession. My dear friend, Mariam Bell, Chuck Colson's right-hand "man" at Wilberforce Forum, traveled with me to Alabama on this trip. On our return flight, we were moved to first class. *How fun!* we thought. I was bound up by nerves and exhausted as we boarded the plane. When the flight attendant offered a glass of wine, teetotalling-me took it, thinking I needed something to help get some much-needed rest. In only a few minutes, the wine had its effect. I rose from my seat to wobble to the restroom, clinging to the seats on either side of the aisle.

"Mariam, I think I'm drunk," I whispered in distress. Mariam followed me home in my PT Cruiser that night, driving slowly. We laughed at the thought of the headline, "President of CWA Arrested for Drunk Driving Returning from Ten Commandments Rally!"

Mariam and I had a wonderful time together in DC. The daughter of a clandestine CIA agent, she was born in Kabul, Afghanistan, raised in South America, and spent her teenage years in Northern Virginia. Her husband, March, was an attorney with the Justice Department. Ever the society maven, she took me everywhere and introduced me to everyone on the social scene.

On my second tour of duty in Washington years later, Mariam invited me to a Republican women's event where Martha Alito, wife of Justice Sam Alito, was to speak. I arrived early to find myself among the sophisticated, elegant women of Northern Virginia. They have a look of class and brilliance. I arrived before Mariam. Not knowing anyone, I took my place in the serving line. I was wearing a pastel pink sweater. Nice enough, I thought, for this lovely crowd.

While standing in line, nodding, and smiling at everyone, a woman approached me and whispered that there was something on my shoulder. I looked down to see a bright yellow, Velcro hair roller firmly attached to the front of my pink sweater. Oh, brother.

Mariam and I laughed, we cried, and we prayed. She made my lonely post in DC as a "watchman on the wall" fun and joyful.

Financial Troubles

CWA obviously survived 9/11, but like charitable organizations and churches everywhere, donations plummeted. As we moved into 2002, only two and a half months after 9/11, the fiscal year began badly. Between the rental of the top floor of a beautiful building on K Street, salaries for staff, and other regular expenses, things got very tough.

We scheduled an out-of-town meeting with some former CWA leaders and financial experts we trusted. It was a brutal few days. We slashed the budget, which included necessary, painful layoffs. We stopped making coffee in the office, stopped buying flowers. I refused security at events, traveled on my own all over the country.

Meanwhile, I began aggressively laying the groundwork for new sources of income. I hired Phil Olsen, a great big, football player–sized man—a brother, in fact, to football great, Merlin Olsen. Phil raised millions for Family Research Council in the past, and I asked him to come help us do the same. We worked for months, held new events with new donors, met with foundations that supported Christian organizations, and received great encouragement when we showed them what we were accomplishing.

When the calendar year ended, we were exactly one million dollars below our budget. We projected our new sources would kick in, in the coming year, but nevertheless I agreed to keep the upcoming year's budget the same as the last. I asked Mrs. LaHaye for a one-million-dollar loan to CWA that would be paid back in full in the new year.

The LaHayes by this time were multi-millionaires from the sale of Dr. LaHaye's *Left Behind* series, who I thought were still vested in supporting the organization Mrs. LaHaye founded. But I was wrong. I was forced to make more painful layoffs of good people, right before Christmas 2002. Many of the staff were unhappy with me, but I could not explain my decision to them.

Standing in another airport during the Christmas holidays, waiting anxiously to see if Mrs. LaHaye would help us, I got a call saying she would donate $500,000 in an end-of-year donation. The caveat was, $250,000 was designated to the Beverly LaHaye Institute, and the other $250,000 to her son Larry in California who was brokering CWA's direct mail to a printer. Around that same time, she and Dr. LaHaye donated millions to Liberty University for the LaHaye Fitness Center and the LaHaye Ice Skating Rink. It was disheartening.

This was the first sign of trouble for me with Mrs. LaHaye. When she wanted to take away family medical benefits for our male staffers, I put my foot down. I began to feel any success I might have leading CWA was, for some reason, *not* good news to her. So . . . the struggle began.

Memorable Moments . . . Some Even Funny

I was at a donut shop in Scottsdale, Arizona, with my dad one morning, when my cellphone rang. It was Justice Clarence Thomas. I moved quickly to the exit, mouth full of chocolate glaze, to have a conversation outside the store. Returning inside, the irony of the intersection of just plain life and this great man, made me laugh.

Later Justice Thomas, and especially his wife, Ginni, became very dear friends. Familiarity often breeds contempt, but in this case, I was able to see exactly why these two principled warriors had risen to the heights they had achieved.

Karl Rove

Karl Rove was the King Swing of Washington in those days. The "Architect" was his moniker. After managing George W. Bush's successful presidential campaign, he became chief of staff to the president, and wielded his power like an iron rod.

As president of CWA, it was my job to get to know Karl and have conversations whenever necessary. All of Washington seems filled with human beings full of bravado and verbal command, but I was never one of them. When my heart was full of passion on an issue or whenever I felt God compelling me to speak, I was fierce, but it was never natural to me. That's why this story is so funny.

The first time I had to call Karl in November of 2001, I was a nervous wreck. I wrote out my thoughts, called, and left a message. Hours went by. It was a Friday evening, and I was back in my apartment, lying on the couch. Exhausted, I took a Tylenol PM to help me relax and sleep while I took in the news. I was watching Air Force One land, then Karl Rove, pacing back and forth on the tarmac, when my cellphone rang. It was Karl. Jumping up from my drug-induced state, I frantically looked for my notes and tried to clear my head. I'm sure I made a great first impression. That is how my friendship with Karl Rove began.

I liked Karl, but he was a bully. I watched as he manipulated, humiliated, and worked his dark magic on conservative Christian leaders time after time. Karl would say horribly insulting things, and they would cower and do his bidding. This is what got me into a great deal of trouble—but more on that later.

You have to understand power to understand DC Power and money run the place, and most who operate there swirl around it jockeying for position. Christian leaders were no exception.

The White House Christmas Party

I was at the White House Christmas Party in 2002. My date was my future husband, Bruce Rather. (But more on him in chapter 12!) It was the most magical night you could ever imagine. We entered a long corridor decorated with Christmas trees made of poinsettias to the wonderful sound of four madrigal singers performing Christmas carols.

Entering another marbled floor atrium, the Marine Band/Orchestra, dressed in their gorgeous cherry-red and gold uniforms, were playing beautiful Christmas classics. Could I just say there's no place in the world like DC at Christmas, no better music than that created by the U.S. armed forces bands and singers.

Bruce and I wandered through the rooms, trying to control our obvious awe at their beauty. From the ornate, detailed crèche on a brilliant blue background, to the incredible bounty of not just good food, but beautiful food—we were enthralled by it all. We were fascinated by portraits of former presidents and their wives, gilded furniture handed down through the centuries, and . . . Karl Rove.

We were standing in a very long line to have our portraits made with President and Mrs. Bush in front of a giant Christmas tree, when we saw Karl trying to make his way through the sea of people. Like flies they descended on Karl, and he was only advancing by inches.

Karl was the center of power—the closet person to the sitting president.

Watching otherwise sane people swarm him was another kind of jaw-dropping moment. Karl saw me and slowly made his way to us. I actually hugged him in sympathy. But maybe he loved all the attention and didn't need my sympathy.

One more White House Christmas story. Just after we had our photos made with the president and first lady, we sat down on a satin settee in the next room with our backs to the wall. Close to the end of that very long line, we sat there, marveling at it all, when, from behind us, through the opening of the Christmas tree/photo room, came the first lady, Laura Bush, calling out "Bushie! Bushie!" as she walked through the room. Next followed the president who, when he realized we were sitting there, gave us that famous impish grin at the private moment we had just humorously observed.

No Such Thing as a Coincidence

Once in the middle of the raging battle over same-sex marriage in the fall of 2003 my friend Judy and I decided to meet for a twenty-four-hour R&R. Judy was my dearest friend. Mother of five children, she and her husband, Lynn, were missionaries in Zimbabwe for fifteen years. When Lynn took an administrative job at TEAM headquarters in Carol Stream, Judy and I became very close. Our kids grew up together, we did life together.

When I moved to DC, Judy had earlier moved to North Carolina where Lynn led the missions program at Westover Church in Greensboro. They were five hours away, and whenever I needed my friend, we would jump in the car and meet halfway to laugh, cry, and pray.

As I barreled my car south toward North Carolina, my phone rang constantly. All of those calls were incredibly important, all of them from people whose names you would know, discussing strategy. With each call, my stress level went up.

Judy and I didn't have a place to meet, we were just going to call each other along the way as we got closer to determine the best exit.

Suddenly I lost cell service. Blessedly, that meant I could get a reprieve from phone calls, but not so blessedly, it meant I had no idea where Judy was. I called out to God for help and took the next exit. How in the world would we find each other?

Pulling into a McDonald's parking lot—still no service—I asked a man in a truck if there was any way he could let me use his phone. Graciously he said "yes." The strange number came up on Judy's phone, but she answered anyway. She also had prayed—then took the *same exit* and was sitting in a parking lot just across the street from McDonald's!

We had a joyful reunion, understanding it had only been possible by a loving heavenly Father who hears our prayers and often grants them in real time!

And about the Bush White House

It's an old story now, but conservative presidents often have rotten staff. More than once, we caught them undermining what we at least thought were President Bush's positions on important issues. I can't tell you how many bad policies we blocked by White House staff who had no interest in the moral issues we pressed. It was a block and tackle often not so private.

One morning, the Eisenhower Building (White House) auditorium was filled with black pastors, Christian leaders, and others when staffers proceeded to stand on stage and mislead—no, *lie*—about what was actually in the African AIDS bill Bush was championing. When I explained to Dr. James Dobson what Bush staff were trying to slip through, he and I tag-teamed a challenge. First Dr. Dobson stood up and then I followed. The room came unglued as we explained the deceit, and the staffers were forced to stand down their subversion.

There were also great aides to President Bush, not the least of whom was a young Matt Schlapp, who served Bush as deputy assistant and political director. Matt was a champion then and he is a champion now as head of the American Conservative Union. Only history will show what Matt and his beautiful wife, Mercedes, have done to save this country.

It is not true there are no heroes left in Washington. One of the greatest joys of my life is having the privilege of working with many of them right now. Matt and Mercedes are two of the most courageous!

By 2003, Concerned Women for America had become a powerhouse, but unbeknownst to me, things were about to change.

11

My Green Face, and the End of It All

On June 26, 2003, I turned on the television in my office one morning just as news of the *Lawrence v. Texas* decision hit like an earthquake.

Sodomy was outlawed in many parts of the country, but LGBT activists rightly reasoned that taking down Texas law forbidding homosexual sex would set a precedent upon which they could begin their long-term plan to legalize gay "marriage." Using a word erroneously does not change its meaning. Marriage as ordained by God was between one and one woman. It will never mean two men, two women, three people, a man and his dog, or any other perverted variation.

I tuned to *Fox News* just in time to see not one, not two, but THREE attorneys all cheering on the decision. Fair and balanced? I think not.

I quickly called Bill Shine, *Fox News* vice president. I repeated to him what I'd just observed and he responded by asking me to come on air that night to make the case on why *Lawrence v. Texas* wasn't a good decision.

I was booked on *Hannity & Colmes*. I had been with Sean and Alan a "million" times, but on this night, I sat and waited, wired up and in the chair while the minutes ticked by. With just five minutes left to go, they turned to me for my response. I don't remember what I said, but I do remember what happened the next day when I went to my office.

As soon as I got in, staff swarmed to tell me during that appearance, as soon as I was introduced, my face turned green. Not a subtle color shift, but an outright, Wicked Witch of the North putrid green—only my face, nothing else.

Our executive director, George, called Fox immediately. Bill Shine tried to convince us it was a technical problem, not a sabotage by one of the technicians/producers. Nice as Bill was, I knew better.

Out of those interactions with Bill came a good friendship and later an offer to be a *Fox News* contributor. "What man meant for evil, God meant for good!" (paraphrase of Genesis 50:20).

That juvenile attempt to humiliate me was just one of many by LGBT activists. I received death threats in Chicago, vile, demonic e-mail, and later horrible tweets. I say demonic because the authors were able to think of the most degrading, upsetting things no human could imagine—sometimes about my disabled daughter, Sasha.

But honestly, from the death threats to the green face to the vile verbiage, I never let it bother me. Demonic forces were no strangers to me, and the apostle Paul's admonition in Ephesians 6:12 (KJV) that we "wrestle not against flesh and blood, but against principalities, against powers, against the rulers of the darkness of this world, against spiritual wickedness in high places" had long ago shaped my understanding. Satan is in fact referred to in the Bible as, "the prince of this world" (John 12:31; 14:30; 16:11 NIV). The youngest disciple, John, the only one who died of natural causes after writing the last Gospel from the perspective of old age, wrote, "He who is in you is greater than he [Satan] who is in the world" (1 John 4:4).

I didn't take it personally when later, in June of 2015, I stepped down from a stage after speaking and purposefully walked through crowds of gay men at the Supreme Court the day the Obergefell decision making gay "marriage" legal, as they hurled personal insults. My heart was filled with compassion because I knew many spent a lifetime fighting their urges, longing for someone to say those urges are normal. For me to stand and say, however gently I might say it, making it legal does not make it moral and God has a "more excellent way" for us to live out our sexuality, made me their enemy. And it stirred the demons within to try and destroy me.

I'm not invincible. I knew they could do harm, but I learned not to fear those who could hurt me physically, but those who could actually destroy my soul (Matthew 10:28). My mind is stayed on Him (Isaiah 26:3). It is well with my soul, and I trust Him. And in spite of what they thought, I cared about them deeply.

Little did I know how the *Lawrence v. Texas* decision would affect my own life. As the gavel fell in Texas, the greatest battle of my life in DC began.

My Greatest Battle

The Arlington Group which came to fame in the early 2000s was birthed in my apartment building's elegant conference room in Arlington, Virginia. Formed shortly before the sodomy decision came down, it was made up initially of a small group of the heads of the major Christian policy organizations. Dr. James Dobson of Focus on the Family, Dr. Richard Land of the SBC Ethics and Religious Liberty Commission, Lou Sheldon of Traditional Values Coalition, Don Wildmon, president and founder of the American Family Association, and a few others.

Almost every day when my kids were young, I drove to McDonald's, Sasha firmly in place next to me in her portable wheelchair, little Jeremy in the back car seat. We ate and listened to Dr. Dobson as he gave marvelous advice and encouragement on how to raise your children.

During the glory days of the television show *All in the Family*, I remembered seeing a Southern preacher frequently on television taking on Hollywood—Norman Lear, in particular—for the decadence creeping into our homes via his clever but shocking sitcoms. The Reverend Don Wildmon was bold and articulate. He spoke with the passion of a pastor and a father, and when he spoke, I listened. Decades later I went to work for the organization he later founded, the American Family Association. But that story comes later!

Imagine me, then, sitting as a peer among those great men. But it was my place to lead with them and not acquiesce to their opinions because of my admiration and respect. And so, I did.

Because of the foresight of men like Matt Daniels of Alliance for Marriage and Professor Robert George of Princeton, a federal amendment to the Constitution to prevent homosexual marriage had already been crafted. But when *Lawrence* came down, we all felt the urgency of moving it forward.

But what language would we adopt? The current version, while banning same-sex "marriage," left room for interpretation that would inevitably allow civil unions. Would we embrace that amendment, or would we insist on language prohibiting the legalization of any kind of same-sex relationship?

Sometimes it's hard to go back and reimagine the atmosphere and attitudes of decades before. Ever changeable, human beings more easily slide into immorality than they hold fast to moral absolutes. And since the beginning of time, we are all, in varying degrees, influenced by our culture. That doesn't make the "slide" any less immoral. Since the deceptively named "Respect for Marriage Act" was passed by both houses of Congress and signed into law by President Joe Biden on December 13, 2022, gay marriage has been codified now in law as it was codified by the SCOTUS *Obergefell* decision in 2015. Gay couples are everywhere, on television, at PTA meetings, in our neighborhood. It's hard to imagine that just twenty years ago American voters were not ready for that.

Some of the Arlington Group came down in support of the compromise language. I fought vehemently against it. It was my position that it didn't matter what name we called a same-sex relationship—"marriage" or "civil union"—we should NOT codify same-sex relationships in law. I argued that if the issue were slavery, we would not outlaw slavery while legalizing it under another name, "chattel." It would be a meaningless gesture to ban "marriage" yet allow "civil unions."

Despite false flag arguments in favor of same-sex "marriage" that lesbian and gay persons could not buy homes together, visit the hospital and make health decisions for their partner, there were in fact numerous laws already on the books to provide for all of that, just not in the context of marriage.

If the union between one man and one woman, established by God in creation, and practiced all over the world for nearly two millennia, were to morph into some provision allowing men to lawfully unite with men and women with women, what possible difference did it make if we didn't call it marriage, but civil unions?

"The federal government has never gotten involved in regulating marriage. It's a state issue." I was told. But that wasn't true either. Utah was prohibited from joining the Union until it outlawed polygamy in 1896. Multiple partners or same-sex partners, what was the difference?

America's legal system was based on marriage between one man and one woman. Social Security benefits, retirement, taxes, family and divorce law, property rights, all of it based on the centuries-old foundation of British Common Law and the Ten Commandments. Common sense alone would dictate a weak amendment like this would create chaos in law as well as in society.

From June of 2003 until spring of 2004, my managers and I were on television constantly making the case. Privately I began to lobby key people. Michael Farris, founder of Patrick Henry College, and currently head of Alliance Defending Freedom, attorney, and great thinker, was the first key person I persuaded. At last convinced, he joined me in the fight. Former secretary of education, Bill Bennett was a tougher sell, but then to my delight, joined us too. Leonard Leo set up a small but powerful forum at the Federalist Society, inviting some of the greatest conservative legal minds in the country to debate the issue. Highly esteemed legal scholar, Robert George, who authored the current version was there. We sat around a table each sharing our views. I sat across from Robby, gifted but humble, and reasoned my heart out to bring him along with us. I was thrilled when he came.

Meanwhile divisions grew. Karl Rove was also lobbying. The White House wanted the compromise amendment and Karl was doing a full-throated "Karl" to make sure it happened. We had meeting after meeting, expanding our "group" to include other conservative leaders. One fateful night, we were in a conference room at FRC sitting around a large, U-shaped table trying to come to some agreement. An amendment would never pass if conservative leaders couldn't agree on the language. After much discussion and much pleading by me, one by one, we went round the table to declare our position. Paul Weyrich, a lion of the conservative movement, who had among other things co-founded Heritage and the Free Congress Foundation, from his wheelchair, made an impassioned statement. There was powerful prayer and many tears. I couldn't believe my ears as, slowly and deliberately, each person at that table decided to go "all in" for the stronger amendment. God intervened miraculously that night and we reached unity.

Well, all but one. As all of us were intently listening and praying, Richard Land was paying precious little attention, coming in and out of the room while talking on his phone. He missed Paul's statement and the outpouring of the Spirit at that table, and when he returned to sit, he was very upset at our decision and expressed his opposition. It wasn't the first time I did battle with Dr. Land and certainly not the last.

The Story Didn't End There

The next step was to present our case to the leaders of Congress. Dr. Dobson, Bill Bennett, Michael Farris, and I met for lunch in a room, around an elegant dining table, in a house close to the Capitol to coordinate our presentation. Over lunch, Dr. Dobson told me he changed his mind. I suspect he was under enormous pressure from Karl Rove and his own staff to embrace the compromise amendment. Why would I say that? Once, during one of our earlier meetings, the wall phone rang and I answered. It was Karl's assistant asking to speak to Dr. Dobson. I suspect it was Karl, doing "Karl."

But back to the luncheon. When Dr. Dobson told me he changed his position, my heart sank. We were due to meet with the leader of the Senate, Bill Frist, and Speaker of the House Dennis Hastert in just an hour. As I sat next to Dr. Dobson, that man who I admired so much, I broke down each and every reason not to support a compromise. I prayed fervently as I spoke to him, excluding really everyone at the table for the time we had.

"Dr. Dobson, you have never compromised on anything. It was you who confirmed in me the conviction to hold fast no matter what," I pleaded. To my amazement, he changed his mind sitting there at that table, and we went into that history-making meeting unified again.

Each of us had our assigned presentation. Mine was to present a recent poll showing how Americans felt about homosexual marriage and same-sex unions. At that time, in 2002, overwhelming majorities were opposed to both. It was politically as well as morally sound to pass a strong amendment, I argued.

But It Still Wasn't Over

The day after that meeting, we were scheduled for a press conference and public statement of our decision. I noticed immediately the Focus on the Family Team, under the leadership of Tom Minnery, was unfriendly and standoffish. Bizarrely, I was shunned. I knew something bad was in the works. In contrast to our previous open and honest meetings, this seemed like a secret power move I couldn't quite figure out. Eventually it became apparent conversations had been had with Dr. Dobson, persuading him once again to change his point of view. The press conference and our unity were sabotaged.

As a result of that, I pulled CWA out of the Arlington Group. I could not sit at the table with people who did not operate in good faith. If Christian leaders can't do that, then who can? I would not play games on this issue or ignore this betrayal in order to proceed with business as usual.

There was one final meeting, convened by Chuck Colson at his new offices in Virginia. Could I just pause to say how I loved Chuck Colson, his story, his leadership, Prison Fellowship, the Wilberforce Forum—all of it. Whatever I may say here is exactly what happened. People are not necessarily defined by a few bad moments and this episode did not define Chuck Colson for me.

Nevertheless Chuck Colson, the Marine, showed up on that day. Chuck had been absent in this battle. He was never part of the discussions or decision-making process so many of us devoted endless hours to.

In the fall of 2003, out of the blue Chuck called a meeting, inviting a wider swath of church leaders, most of whom knew precious little about what was before us. Father John Neuhaus sat on one side of me, Joe Stowell, president of Moody Bible Institute on my left. Maggie Gallagher, a highly respected writer with a strong voice within the Catholic Church and around the country, actively lobbied to allow civil unions, and was given the floor to make her case. Without fanfare, Chuck proceeded to declare we had to adopt the weaker language, making allowances for civil unions. When I tried to present the arguments against that, he talked over me in his powerful, resonant voice, dismissing me like a fly on his shirt. Bill Bennett and a few others tried to speak up, but Chuck and Maggie and Father John had made up their minds, so case closed.

I can only surmise the purpose of this meeting, or whose idea it was to call it. Let me just say that being part of the Republican Party apparatus was never my focus. While for the most part then, and now always, Republicans were the only ones willing to fight for moral issues, supporting those positions was not the same as loyalty to the party.

That was not true for many conservatives and it's not true today.

Republican Party loyalty is the great divide between social conservatives. It certainly was in this particular fight, and it would be the common thread for decades to come, leading to bad decisions by "conservatives" eager to please party leadership.

Chuck was firmly connected with Republican leadership and the White House. Could it be possible that Karl Rove reached out to Chuck to orchestrate this grand meeting to wrest back control of where social conservatives were headed on the Federal Marriage Amendment? Very effective if he did.

That was sad to me then, and it is sad to me now. Chuck was a thoroughly "born-again," new man in Christ. His books were already standard classics for Christendom. How could it be this man who wrote about and sought after the heart of God could, with the same force, declare a compromise on an issue of such profound moral consequence, striking a blow right at the heart of creation?

Let me repeat. It is as natural as breathing for man to veer off the path of God's righteousness. Far more difficult to hold fast in an ever-changing culture, and certainly in the political arena. It is a constant fight to hold the line.

I lost that hard-fought battle. And I have the scars to prove it.

By the way, during my tenure at CWA, we were beginning to recognize the concerted effort taking place on Capitol Hill by gay activists to populate conservative office holders with gay staffers.

Senator George Allen of Virginia was the first Senator to hire a chief of staff who was openly gay, but many, many followed. Soon after that, the previously stalwart conservative Senator Allen caved on the issue of same-sex "marriage." After I left DC, George W. Bush's director of political affairs, Ken Mehlman, came out as a gay man. Not only was *Fox News*, which was watched religiously by social conservatives, populated by gay activists, so were conservative organizations and offices everywhere. Log Cabin Republicans who were gay but allegedly conservative flourished in the process.

To be clear, I don't object to gays or lesbians holding office or being hired for any job apart from Christian ministry. If we were to stand against that, we would have to do a morality test for every employee for every job. Who could pass? Should adulterers be allowed to hold office? Men addicted to pornography? We live in a fallen world, so moral tests aren't possible. The problem I've observed with gays and lesbians is, at least in politics, eventually, their homosexuality trumps all other considerations. They might be conservative on all other issues, but in time they turn their focus on advancing their lifestyle.

Considering their warm embrace, still clandestine at the time, at the Bush White House, it's no wonder Karl Rove pushed so hard for a compromised marriage amendment.

Conservative Christians seem too easily morally confused when a friend or family member declares their homosexuality, or now their transgenderism. I will never forget when Dick Cheney's daughter, Mary "came out." Suddenly, the very conservative Cheney was embracing gay marriage, even when no other conservative politician was. His daughter was a lesbian, and for him the moral law had to bend to accommodate her.

But the moral law does not bend. Adultery is still wrong. So is lying—so is stealing—and so are same-sex relationships, as are faux gender changes, regardless of your last name. "Male and female, He created them" (Genesis 1:27). Two sexes only—marriage between one man and one woman, only. If we love people dear to us, we won't watch as they destroy themselves spiritually and often physically, coloring outside of the lines from God's design for human sexuality. We don't have to preach out of some moral superiority, for heaven knows, we are all sinners. But "practicing" and approving sin is another thing. We speak truth to them out of love, not condemnation, remembering our own forgiven sins in the process.

We can love our gay and transgender friends and children and family members without approving of their lifestyle. Real love requires we do.

Another Front in the Battle

Massachusetts was moving forward aggressively to make same-sex marriage legal. New Hampshire, Vermont, and Massachusetts were all on the cutting edge of homosexual rights, legalizing civil unions,

And chipping away at existing laws to set the stage for full-blown "marriage."

"Out-Right Vermont" was already hosting seminars for middle school girls, showing slides to illustrate the removal of healthy breasts. Homosexual activists were gaining power in schools and in legislatures in New England, and weak legislators were folding one by one.

In February of 2004, I flew to Massachusetts to help the opposition there. I met with Governor Mitt Romney's staff who assured me Governor Romney was standing firm in his opposition to same-sex marriage.

I spoke at a packed event at Faneuil Hall in Boston to encourage people to stand strong. On February 9, I joined Boston Cardinal Seán Patrick O'Malley on a makeshift stage on Boston Commons speaking to the thousands of concerned citizens who gathered to listen.

What unfolded in Massachusetts was a precursor of what was to come. Before the Massachusetts Supreme Judicial Court issued any decision, Governor Romney sent out letters to town clerks ordering them to issue marriage licenses labeled "Partner A" and "Partner B." Same-sex marriage licenses were NOT legal when Romney did this, but only a few of us had any knowledge of what he did.

As a side bar, Mitt Romney was made CEO of the Salt Lake Organizing Committee in charge of the Winter Olympic Games in 2002. He was the first American leader to kick out the Boy Scouts, who served the American Olympics for decades, because they refused to allow gay scout leaders (at the time).

Later, when Mitt was running for president in 2008, he came to a private meeting in Chicago to get our support. There were twelve of us sitting at a table as he stood to make his pitch. Impressive and impeccably dressed, he made a good impression on most everyone. But then we were each given a chance to ask a question. I knew he would not like my question and honestly, I decided it would be better if I didn't ask it. But then my good friend, Paul Caprio, who convened the meeting, turned to me and said, "Sandy, didn't you have a question?" Oh, brother.

"Isn't it true, Governor Romney, it was actually you and not the Supreme Judicial Court in Massachusetts who authorized gay marriage?

"Isn't it true you sent out letters to clerks demanding they issue such licenses before the court even reached a decision?" I asked.

Romney exploded. Like James Carville previously on *Crossfire*, he began to shout at me, calling me a liar. Condescendingly, he asked if I, in fact, was a lawyer, then announced out of the blue with great bravado, "I have a degree from Harvard Law School!"

Joe Morris, a highly esteemed attorney in Chicago and former assistant attorney general under President Reagan, and a good friend, looked across the table at me and said sardonically, "Maybe that's the problem." At that moment, Romney's aide physically took Romney's arm and pulled him out of the room. It was an amazing moment.

The people at that table knew and trusted me for years.

Nevertheless, I went home and sent each of them a copy of the order to the clerks signed by Romney to issue marriage licenses to "Partners A & B" to confirm my veracity.

All Good Things Must Come to an End

I didn't realize it at the time, but my last television appearance as president of CWA was to be a guest on James Robison's show in Texas. James is a godly man who, after a powerful conversion to Christ, began his life as a Christian evangelist. I remember hearing him preach in my home church in Illinois when he was only nineteen, and I was just a girl.

James extended the invitation to come, but as it turned out, he had another motive as well. Unbeknownst to me, he was very involved in Texas politics, Karl Rove's political birthplace. He took me into his private office for a chat. Out of the blue, he warned me that I had become a terrible threat to the powers that be in Washington, and they were afraid of me—Karl, in particular.

I was flabbergasted. Never once, in all the battles I fought did I consider myself to be some force to be feared. If anyone was afraid of me, it was God's power within me they feared, certainly not me. I was just an exhausted, vulnerable woman, alone and burdened by the load of a long, hard fight.

Just a few days after that conversation, I was back in my office in DC. It was March of 2004, and Mrs. LaHaye was flying in from Palm Springs for a visit with the staff for the first time since I became president. We were scheduled to meet late morning, but when I went to her beautiful office to greet her, she tersely instructed me to join her instead at 9 a.m. When I explained that would be during our daily morning show, she was unmoved. Whatever guests we had or plans we made didn't matter to her. Major red flags went up.

Mrs. LaHaye's Past

Before I came to CWA, during my long vetting process, there was an executive with Domain assigned to walk us through it. Richard was open and honest with me that Mrs. LaHaye was a difficult personality.

She went through at least two picks for CWA president in the few years preceding me. (I learned later there were others.) Janet Parshall was brought to DC to be groomed for the position, but after hosting *Concerned Women Today* for a few years, suddenly left. Carmen Pate, a pro-life activist from Texas, was then brought in and named president. But Mrs. LaHaye perceived Carmen to be disloyal, ordering her computer to be examined without her knowledge. When that search turned up emails that Mrs. LaHaye felt were critical to her, Carmen was unceremoniously dismissed, tremendously hurt by all of it.

These things I knew. The difference this time was the CWA Board requested that Mrs. LaHaye step into the role of chairman of the board, move back to Palm Springs, and let the new president run the place.

Richard warned me it would likely be a bumpy ride, but if I could hang in there, the new model could succeed. I agreed to that and went to DC with no illusions. So the morning Mrs. LaHaye flew in, I was certain it meant trouble.

Back to That Last Morning

I scrambled to get a manager to host. It was obvious Mrs. LaHaye was there on a mission. I steeled myself and went back to her office.

Sitting at her desk, she proceeded to open a large folder and tell me she had seventeen reasons I needed to step down as president of CWA. I watched her carefully as she read first one, then another. But underlying all those charges, the real reason emerged when she looked up and, for the first time, with real emotion said, "Sandy, you're running away with CWA!"

Running Away with CWA

Going back in time, I knew exactly what she was referring to. From the moment I took on the role as president, there were issues of trust. I treated Mrs. LaHaye with the utmost respect, but still she was cold and distant. The last thing I ever wanted to do was to hurt her. She built a great organization, and what I really wanted was to make her proud. My success was her success, I tried to tell her. But the strife continued. I'll give an example.

One of my many jobs was to host the national morning radio show. But Mrs. LaHaye had great difficulty giving up that role. She would call our producer, Angela, and make last-minute changes without telling me. Mrs. LaHaye was in and out and in and out and miserable, I think, in the process.

Finally, I asked her if she would just please take back the morning show and work with Angela directly. I had my hands full learning the rest of my responsibilities and it would be a tremendous help. For a few weeks she did take it back, but then suddenly quit.

She didn't really want it, but she just couldn't let her "baby" go, and I understood that.

Each week Mrs. LaHaye would join our CFO, Lee (also her son), George, our executive director, and me by phone to go over expenses and budget. I appreciated her input on this as I was learning. But when our finances became the problem I described earlier, I realized I was going to have to take a more active role in that too.

I hired an outside auditor to go over our books. We discovered expenditures above the norm and I set about to find out why.

We were cutting everything to the bone at that point and were not receiving much financial support from Mrs. LaHaye. I was happy to build different sources of revenue, but then, I had to have more to say about our budget. Like many Christian ministries, CWA had in many ways morphed into a family business.

Lee LaHaye was the CFO and even though it sounds strange, we had a wonderful relationship. Lee was very competent and professional, but troubled. I knew before I arrived he was gay, and later when the time was right, asked him if he was engaged in the homosexual lifestyle. He assured me he was not, and I chose to believe him. There were gay activists ready constantly to "out" him, and for his sake as well as ours, I had to establish the boundaries.

When the outside auditor came in, Lee held nothing back. I think in many ways he was weary with his job. When I began to discuss moving him into a different role, he was relieved. I kept in touch with Lee for a long time after I left CWA. Within a few years, he tragically died before his time. I grieved for him and know, in spite of his struggles, he is now whole in every way in the arms of Jesus.

George, our executive director, was fluent in French and very knowledgeable about educational issues. During this same time frame,

I decided to move him from his executive director role to oversee our United Nations NGO and head up a new CWA department focused on education. But George was not happy about that. While I was making these changes, Lee came and begged me to fly to Palm Springs to talk to his mother, whom he always addressed as "Mrs. LaHaye," even to me. Reading between the lines, I knew this was a warning.

Dr. and Mrs. LaHaye occupied the entire top floor of a luxury condo building. It was spacious and beautiful. The ceiling was painted in a fresco, the furniture lush and lovely. We sat around the dining table as Mrs. LaHaye expressed her anger at my changes. Calmly, I responded with my reasoning, but she wasn't having it. She insisted I go into the back room and fire the two people I just hired, reinstating George and Lee to their positions. I did that, making each difficult phone call at her request. Hard as it was, she was so very upset, for the sake of CWA's stability, it wasn't worth it to refuse.

I flew back to DC thinking we made peace, but it was only a week or so later she made her fateful trip from Palm Springs in March 2004.

Back to That Morning . . .

I listened carefully as Mrs. LaHaye completed her list. Honestly, I can't remember any of the reasons except for one. I fired a staff member for reasons she was well aware of, but I couldn't make public. It was the only time in the years I served her when I got angry with her. She and her son, Lee, assured me this particular hire was fully vetted and so in trust, I made the offer. It came to my attention later there were serious moral issues they were fully aware of—serious and potentially criminal. I was the president of the organization, tasked with running CWA. It was my face and my name and my reputation on the line if the details became public. It would have been the height of hypocrisy and a dereliction of my duty to ignore this problem, and I wasn't about to.

A few months before, after receiving a phone call alerting me to the situation, I called to confront Mrs. LaHaye. How could she put

CWA and me in this position? I was truly angry with her. However qualified this person, I could not allow them to represent us. But Mrs. LaHaye in return was angry with me for the firing.

She completed her list and then told me I could either resign or she would fire me. Since we were currently in the middle of so many important battles, I told her I would not quit. She would have to fire me. And so she did. She gave me three months' severance with the threat of withdrawing it if I discussed any of the details of my firing.

I was given until five o'clock to clear out my office and vacate the building. Meanwhile, my beloved staff was ushered into the conference room and given the news. They sent word that they would resign in protest. I told them emphatically "no!" They had too important a role in the battle to leave the field just to defend me.

I sat at my desk stunned. I looked around at the office I decorated and made my home—at the portraits of Sasha and Jeremy on the wall, the bookcases filled with books and memorabilia from DC, my moon-shaped couch where I spent countless hours studying and praying, eating breakfast and lunch there in-between.

Then I looked at my large stack of unfinished tasks. Then, my usual ill-timed sense of humor kicked in. A smile came to my face as I realized nothing in that huge pile, that the day before overwhelmed me, mattered any more. The burden was gone. My dear friend, Mariam, came to help me pack. I had to turn in my cell phone, load up a cart, and head to my car. Like a criminal, I was walked out of the building as though I had something to be ashamed of. I have many things I am ashamed of, but the tireless work I did and the decisions I made at CWA were not among them.

I learned in short order as board members began to contact me that Mrs. LaHaye fired me without their knowledge. I had a good relationship with the board and with CWA leaders around the country who began to reach out. But my signed agreement to silence made it impossible for me to explain.

There were some really fine people on that board, who without exception treated me with great respect. But many of them were family members. Two of Mrs. LaHaye's daughters along with Lee and others with business ties to the LaHaye family made it hard for them to think or act independently.

I went to DC alone, sold my home, left my children, my friends, and my life in Chicago. I gave nearly three years, 24/7 to CWA and to my beloved country. I felt like a freight train moving at max speed down the track, suddenly derailed and inert.

Still . . . even though I could not understand it at the time, I knew God was in this too.

12

The Blessing of Bruce

Bruce and I were married in a purple palace in lovely St. Charles, Illinois, on January 31, 2009, surrounded by dear friends and family. It was the most beautiful night of my life. As Bruce, in his deep, resonant voice, began his vows, I looked at his face realizing that this man, this FBI agent meant every word of them.

We had traveled a long way, Bruce and I, to get to this point. Looking back, we both agree we were an unlikely pair. How, then, did this marriage come about? It's the chapter I've most looked forward to writing—how did I meet the man who would become my husband?—so sit back and relax, and I'll tell you about God's hand in the midst of a wild ride!

Post-9/11 in the District of Columbia

It was spring of 2002 and I was in my first months of serving as President of CWA. Each morning I got up early to work out in the gym before going to work. It was a habit I acquired long ago. I always said Diet Coke was the secret to my success, but really, aerobic exercise was the thing that gave me energy and added ten much-needed points to my IQ.

There was a beautiful gym in my apartment building. My Scottish friend, Morag, talked me into taking the place, despite its pricey rent, because she felt I would be safe. It was a great call from a loving friend.

As I mounted the elliptical, I proceeded to read a mound of single sheet printouts, tossing them onto the floor as I finished. Workout done, I gathered them up, threw them in the trash and left the gym. Unbeknownst to me, this strange ritual was noticed by an FBI agent named Bruce Rather. This is his story to tell, but I'll try to do it justice.

Just before 9/11, Bruce received orders to transfer from the FBI's LA bureau to the Chicago bureau to be the associate division counsel. The planes hit the World Trade Center only days after he put his home up for sale in Huntington Beach. In the aftermath of that disaster, Bruce drove across the country to Chicago for his new assignment, only to be immediately sent to FBI headquarters to be part of the Osama Bin Laden Terrorism Unit. Military and law enforcement personnel converged in DC collectively going into overdrive to protect our country and bring the attackers to justice. Tensions were high, but so was patriotism and a common goal Bruce was also in that gym every morning. While I saw nothing, he observed everything— including me. He wondered who in the world this woman with such strange behavior was and determined to find out. One Saturday I was in the gym alone, watching the dreadful news, trying to get a workout in before going to my first annual CWA picnic.

Bruce had just come in from a long bike ride, when he saw me alone and decided this was his chance. Not wanting to be a stalker, he carefully chose which machine to use—not too close—not too far. I was oblivious. I was focused on the news report of a recent bombing, when a man from behind me asked if I was from Chicago. I was wearing a baseball shirt featuring the Chicago Skyline. I gave a dismissive "yes." He persisted, adding this time that he was with the FBI and working on those bombings. Now he had my attention. We chatted briefly and I left for the picnic.

Turns out, Bruce WAS a stalker. He found out my last name, located my mailbox, to which he attached a Post-it Note asking if I would like to go out for a Diet Pepsi.

Red flag! WHO drinks Diet Pepsi?

Somehow, we communicated enough for me to tell him I was busy for the next three weeks. Eventually we set a date, but in the process, I had to explain that I appeared often on television and never knew until that day if I would be called or not.

The day came, and sure enough, I got an invitation to appear on the MSNBC show *Alan Keyes Is Making Sense*. I left a message for Bruce at work to explain. Curious, when the hour arrived, he tuned in to watch. The topic was a book called *Harmful to Minors* which laid out the case for children as young as twelve to have a RIGHT to have sex. In other words, it was in fact "harmful" to withhold it from them. Dr. Joycelyn Elders, former surgeon general for President Bill Clinton, was my opponent. Bruce would say she looked and sounded very grandmotherly as she began to praise the book. When Alan turned to me to respond, I did what I always did. I didn't make it personal, but I unleashed a tirade. I let her have it with both barrels. This was disgusting—unthinkable—how could she support sex for minors? When she denied that was in the book, I jumped in to give page numbers and quotes. She was stammering as the interview concluded.

Again, this is Bruce's story, and he would tell you from that moment on, he called me "Tiger."

I, on the other hand, was thinking something quite different. The last thing I wanted to do was start down the road with a much younger man. I had no idea how old Bruce was, so I decided in that moment, on national television to announce my age so, if he was watching, he could just stop pursuing if that was an issue. "As a fifty-two-year-old woman . . ." I began one of my statements.

Ironically on one of our first days together, shopping in a mall, I inadvertently saw his driver's license. I thought I was seeing things when I realized we have the same birthday, but different years. And that has been one of the joys of our lives together. More on that later.

We eventually did have a real date. And after that night, he called me the next day to ask if it was too early to go out again. Morag was visiting me and since she didn't drive, I was to take her back to

Maryland. As she was listening to the conversation, she was mouthing to me, "Ask him to come along!" Morag got me in more trouble!

I did ask and he seemed happy to join us. So during the first twenty-four hours of getting to know Bruce, he was drilled by Morag, then Mel, an NSA analyst, and a house full of kids and grandkids who had become my family.

Bruce and I only had about three weeks together before he was transferred back to Chicago. During that time, he often laid plates of chocolate chip cookies in front of my door. After we said our final good-bye, he sent me a bouquet of roses with a card with a note, "To a woman who is as beautiful on the inside as she is on the outside."

There were two major problems. Bruce grew up in church and knew about and respected God, but had not experienced God's power or the life change of making Jesus His Lord. It was impossible for me to spend serious time with a man who didn't share my deep commitment. "Unequally yoked," the Bible calls it (2 Corinthians 6:14). Our relationship to God determines everything—how we spend our money, our time. What we watch and listen to, and of course, how we conduct our lives. This relationship was impossible.

Second, while I had been divorced for years, Bruce was fresh from a painful divorce. He needed time to heal and recover. It was better he moved back to Chicago.

In spite of the distance, we kept in touch by phone. For the first few years, I maintained my home in Wheaton where Jeremy and his fellow students still lived. I traveled home once a month to see Jeremy and Sasha, and more often than not, see Bruce in the process.

I urged him to try Moody Church in downtown Chicago, only a short distance from his condominium. To my surprise, he agreed. He didn't have a good impression of Moody Church. "What kind of place is that?" he used to ask himself when he lived in the city, working as an assistant Cook County state's attorney. Nevertheless, he went. His earlier experiences in church seemed dominated by pitches for money. He was disgusted by that, so it was ironic when on that first solo visit to Moody, Dr. Erwin Lutzer, senior pastor, who rarely preached on giving and money, spoke on—you guessed it—giving and money.

Bruce called me in DC feeling angry and justified: "See! That's all they care about in these churches!" I talked him down from the ledge and he agreed to try again. Gradually he began to listen to Dr. Lutzer's teaching. He loved the music and in time rarely missed. One weekend when I was home, with Bruce's permission, I made an appointment for him to talk with Dr. Lutzer in his office.

I just thought he needed good counsel, but instead Dr. Lutzer led him to recognize and confess his personal sin and ask forgiveness from God through His Son, Jesus.

Church words, I know, but believe me, this experience was powerful and real.

Even though Bruce is a lot of fun, his spirit is actually a quiet one. You're never sure what he's thinking or how he feels. One day when we were worshipping side by side at Moody, he leaned over to me and said, "There is no place on earth I would rather be than right here in this sanctuary, right now." I knew then his commitment was real.

Getting to Know This Man

Through the next few years, I continued the fight in DC and was absorbed in my work. Even though Bruce and I were not in a committed relationship, I was grateful for his companionship. In spite of the great rewards of the job, the loneliness was at times unbearable. And as we talked and spent occasional time together, I began to see what a treasure he was.

In the fall of 2002, after Bruce had returned to Chicago, I was asked to speak at my former church in the western suburb of Wheaton. Bruce decided to come and listen. He still didn't really know much about my job or the depth of my spiritual commitment, but as I saw him in the crowd, he listened in rapt attention. Once the presentation was over, people surrounded me with questions and comments.

As I stood there engaging for what seemed like forever, I felt a gentle hand touch my arm. I turned to see Bruce offering me a Diet Coke he ran out to buy from McDonald's. He waited patiently as I finished engaging with everyone.

On another occasion, I was speaking on the temporary wooden platform at the "Hike for Life" in downtown Chicago, when I heard a disturbance behind me. I continued to speak, but then realized a man had jumped up on the stage behind me, followed by another man who jumped up there to pull him down. That second man was Bruce.

What kind of a man would do these things? The kind of man God prepared for me.

After CWA

I remained in Washington, DC, for the next three months after the firing. I expected another opportunity to come my way there, but none did. While I was unable to speak about my ending at CWA, I am not sure Mrs. LaHaye felt such constraint. Nevertheless, I decided not to dwell on what people thought about me, and once again, tried to live in such a way as to disprove my critics.

I was offered a job leading a new organization back in Illinois called "Culture Campaign." Two young businessmen, both new believers, put their own money into beginning a real effort to turn Illinois around. They had a great start laying the groundwork and coalescing a stellar team. I accepted the offer and headed back to Chicago.

I must publicly say my heart just wasn't in this new job. Khalid and Mike worked so hard to build a grassroots effort, but I was still somewhat in shock and mental transition, exhausted from my experience in DC. I felt removed from the battle I was best equipped to fight. I left my heart in DC and had difficulty being content in suburban Chicago trying to build grassroots.

Building a grassroots movement is incredibly hard work. It was just not my gift. I knew how to work hard in other ways, but not at that. I proposed we start monthly events to draw lots of people and build our organization in that way. From Canada, we brought in conservative MP Jason Kenney on religious freedom. Phyllis Schlafly lectured on the downward plunge of public education, Dr. Al Mohler, president of Southern Seminary spoke on the theology of our sexuality, a precursor to the discussion of gender and homosexuality. We hosted former Republican Majority Leader in the House, known as the "hammer," Tom DeLay and the controversial but wildly popular Ann Coulter.

These events were a good success, much more in my bailiwick. But I don't think they were what the leadership team of Culture Campaign hoped for. I shall forever regret that I couldn't give them what they deserved.

Not Again . . .

One day out of the blue, in July of 2005, I got a call from Yechiel Eckstein, the president and founder of Fellowship of Christians and Jews. I interviewed Yechiel many times on radio in Chicago and we reconnected in DC, so I was very interested when he offered me the job of vice president of programming at the Fellowship.

I can't say I felt convinced I should take this job, or that this phone call had the hallmarks of the earlier, God-sent ones. I liked Yechiel, I loved Israel and the Jewish people, and I needed a job, so I took it.

I rode the train into the city the first day and walked to the office. Yechiel greeted me along with George Mamo, the other vice president, representing the Christian side of the Fellowship.

My job was to organize tours to Israel and other relevant activities. But then something strange happened. Other Christians in the office began to whisper to me that the name of Jesus could not be spoken in the office. We were not to pray in Jesus's name at lunch and certainly no mention of Jesus was to be made on tours to Israel. Christian staff were not happy about it. Welcome to the first day.

The second day I took the train, made the walk, came into the office to learn there was a conference meeting with *New York Times* contributor Zev Chafets, who was writing an article about the organization. Yechiel was concerned about being criticized by the Jewish community for trying to work with Christians and wanted to make sure Jews everywhere were clear that Christians were NOT out to convert them to Christ.

That was the groundwork he laid as we sat around that conference table. It was only my second day and it seemed to me very inappropriate for me to enter the discussion. Yechiel began the conversation trying to convince Zev that Christians don't really want to convert Jews. Gary Bauer, on by phone, was asked by Zev about the end-times belief that the Jews would return to Israel, followed by a mass conversion to Christ. Gary dismissed it as an "odd belief" of an insignificant minority. George Mamo joined in with the same theme. I couldn't believe my ears, and I couldn't stay silent. To be clear, I think I should have stayed silent, but the words came spilling out as I declared Jesus died for all men, but first and foremost for the Jews. Of course, Christians wanted Jews to know their Messiah!

The expression on Yechiel's face and George's face told me everything I wanted to know.

The third day I took the train into the city, walked to the office, and was promptly greeted by George who wanted to speak to me in the coffee shop downstairs. "Do you really believe Jews need to accept Jesus to be saved?" he asked. "Don't you think there is another path for God's chosen people?" I was flabbergasted.

"George! What are you talking about? What about the book of Romans or the book of Hebrews, both of which lay out the unique role of the Jewish people in God's plan of salvation through His Son, Jesus? What about the fact God sent His Son, it says, to the Jew first and then to the Greek (Gentile). The entire story of God's Son rests on the redemption of God's chosen people. Jewish believers in Christ WERE the early church. The Bible says they are the real branches upon the root of Jesse, who is Jesus. We are only grafted in. Only

Gentiles and Jews who accept Jesus are what Paul called, "The True Circumcision."

On and on it went.

George then proceeded to fire me. We were absolutely, irredeemably incompatible on the issue of Jesus. And there was no way on earth I could not pray in the office or on any tour without mentioning the name of Jesus.

I left the office and called Bruce. I was mortified to be in this same position only a few months after leaving CWA. I dreaded his response, and I was not disappointed. He was unhappy with me. He didn't understand on any level why I had done what I had just done. I just couldn't find the right words to explain it to him.

Bruce was flying to Florida to see his mom and dad for the weekend and asked if I would like to come along. I was grateful for the invitation. Bruce was still in process of growing as a new believer, so when he suggested we read the Bible together while sitting on the beach, I was amazed. I felt weak and wounded, embarrassed, and hurt by the situation and by his response. He opened the Bible randomly and began to read Jesus's words in Matthew 5:11, "Blessed are you when they revile and persecute you, and say all kinds of evil against you falsely for My sake." He paused and looked at me as though he were seeing me for the first time. "That's you!" he exclaimed with sudden understanding. And in that moment God used Bruce to bring healing and comfort to me in a very unexpected way.

When Zev's *New York Times* article was published in July 2005, I was once again mortified and embarrassed. Zev rightly criticized me for speaking up when I should have been silent, but he attributed harsh words to me about the Jewish people I never uttered.

I wrote him a long letter, not really of rebuke, but of conviction. I reminded him of what I'm sure he knew. I never said those things. But regardless what he wrote or how he slandered me, I would continue to long for the day when he and my Jewish friends would accept Jesus as their Messiah. It didn't matter what he or others said or did. Even if Christians had to lay down their lives for their Hebrew brothers, we would take the blows if it meant they would listen.

Back in Chicago fifteen years later, at a celebration for Dr. Lutzer and Rebecca's fiftieth wedding anniversary in 2021, I barely made it in the door when Dr. Michael Rydelnik, vice president, dean, and professor of Jewish studies at Moody Bible Institute came over to warmly greet me. "Sandy! Did you see what Zev Chafets wrote about you in his new article, 'The Rabbi Who Loved Evangelicals'?" he asked. I hadn't, of course. As Michael proceeded to repeat words of praise for me written by Zev, my former nemesis, I couldn't believe it.

After all those years it was a wonderful gift.

Radio . . . Again?

Upon my return to Chicago in summer of 2004, WYLL station manager Dave Santrella reached out to invite me to come back to host the drivetime show. Back to WYLL? Back to drivetime? I couldn't imagine it. I politely said "no."

A few months later, Dave reached out again repeating his offer. And once again I told him "no."

But just before Christmas of that year, I was sitting in the sanctuary at Moody Church one Sunday morning, struggling with a decision. A tremendous financial need was presented at the church, but my bank account was low, my savings diminished, with no good prospects for a well-paying job. I bowed my head in prayer and in trust and gave what I had. I've never told anyone this story, but in the context of this book, perhaps it's necessary.

The next morning, Dave Santrella called me for a third time, asking me to return to WYLL. Nothing changed about my desire to do that, but I felt this time that God was telling me to go back, and providing for me financially in the process.

Bruce loved hearing me on radio! It was all new to him and he was my biggest cheerleader. Ironically, right after we first met, he mentioned to one of his college buddies how he was dating a girl named Sandy who had been on the radio in Chicago in the late '90s. "SANDY RIOS?!" Joel asked. He was a regular listener during my first stint on WYLL.

Bruce helped me decorate my tiny new office. It was beautiful. So inviting that staff members used to like to come in and just sit with me. So much fun! Bruce was able to experience radio events, remote broadcasts, joining as my partner in all of it.

As the audience grew and I learned to enjoy it again, a few more years ticked by as Bruce and I continued our courtship. In November of 2008, Bruce was sent to Afghanistan to conduct polygraphs on terrorist suspects and informants. He was gone for thirty days and I missed him very much.

It was December 31, 2008. We were sitting in my beautiful apartment on the top floor overlooking the snow and enjoying the ambience of the Christmas lights, when Bruce suddenly got on his knee and asked me to marry him. We had never actually discussed it, but for some reason, I wasn't surprised. And it was surely no surprise to him when I said, "yes." The next day EVERYTHING in our relationship changed.

The Thirty-Day Wedding

Bruce wanted to get married in a private ceremony then have a big reception in the summer. I felt deeply that we must have a wedding ceremony in the presence of our family and friends. But when? My daughter-in-law, Liesel, was pregnant with our first grandbaby, due in March. We would have to wait until summer. Or we could get married in THIRTY days. Thirty days it was!

First we called Dr. Lutzer who was visiting family in Missouri. "What are you doing on January 31?" I asked. In his wonderful, deliberate voice, he responded, "Where would you like me to be?" We laughed as we told him our news. We couldn't believe Dr. Erwin Lutzer had a free Saturday evening only days away.

We hung up elated! We had our dear friend and pastor to marry us, but now no venue. I bought a spiral notebook and we headed for our favorite breakfast place, Einstein Bros. Bagels. And there we sat for the next few hours, planning our wedding marathon. Moody Church? A restaurant? None of those seemed right.

The next night, we had pre-arranged plans with a couple we had just gotten to know. Jeanne and Bern Bertsche were members at Moody. Jeanne was a regular listener to my show, and somehow, the four of us gravitated to each other.

As soon as we sat in the restaurant, Jeanne noticed my engagement ring.

They were the first friends we had a chance to tell. We told them about Dr. Lutzer being available, but then Bern asked if we had a venue. We explained "not yet." Before we could finish the response he offered, "What about our house?" I knew Bern was a successful businessman and they had a lovely home but we had never seen it. He insisted we come and look right after we finished dinner.

As we drove up the circular drive framing their big stone house, it was apparent this was more than nice. We entered their home, jaws dropping as we saw large rooms, each decorated in a shade of purple. The living room was two stories with long, white sheers floor to ceiling on one side, and a balcony complete with a white grand piano on the other. The couch was purple velvet. The kitchen counter was made of thick, clear bubbled glass, and was shaped like the deck on the starship *Enterprise*. The light fixtures were art deco, crystal, and glass. In short, this purple mansion was cutting-edge gorgeous. Would we like to have our wedding there? I think so!

As a wedding gift, Bern hired a wedding planner also named Sandy. For the next four weeks, the five of us met weekly to make the impossible happen.

A cake decorator from the Culinary Institute of Chicago who attended Moody agree to make, yes, our purple cake, covered in breathtakingly detailed white flowers.

Jeanne knew a gifted caterer. My talented artist friend, Karen, my fellow awkward dancer from Willow Creek days, who was by then married herself, created our purple, satin finish programs. Our good friends, Charles and Donna Butler, musicians also from Moody Church, agreed to come and sing. So did my singing buddy, Harry, and another professional singing friend, Kate. Larry, my long-time accompanist of purple suit fame, agreed to bring his keyboard for the main floor entertainment. Piece by piece it came together.

Snow was piled high and deep, so Bern hired a bus so people could park a few miles away and shuttle to their home. The ceremony and the dinner were all to take place there. Imagine that? Jeanne carefully calculated seventy-six to be the largest number of people she could accommodate. It was a terrible challenge to create that guest list. Bruce and I had many, many friends and family. How in the world could we make such decisions? We pushed Jeanne to the limits adding more people as we went.

As it turned out amazingly, only one couple was unavailable to come. As the list grew bit by bit, Jeanne managed to fit ninety-six people for dinner in that house. We gave each room an elegant name, and placed people carefully with other people they would enjoy.

Choosing My Dress

Then there was my wedding dress. Bruce and I made a quick run to Nordstrom's one night to find a purple, knee-length cocktail dress that would do.

With only days remaining before the wedding, I tried one last time to find something more beautiful. This time I took my good and stylish friends Shelly and Lorraine to help. I'm so glad I did. Somewhere in that huge store they managed to find a long black, bell-shaped taffeta skirt with large flowing ruffles at the bottom. Separately they found an elegantly beaded, black and silver sleeveless, fitted top that matched perfectly. I was SO happy. I was especially happy when, on our wedding day, our wedding planner, Sandy, came dressed in my original purple dress!

The Union of Friends

Sandy became a great friend. With just days to go, she connected unexpectedly with a florist friend who stepped in to create a wonderland of flowers. My bouquet was spectacular. (More about that bouquet later.)

Thursday night my son flew in from Vancouver, British Columbia, where he was attending divinity school on the campus of UBC. Founded by J. I. Packer, it was called Regent. My father had sadly passed away the previous October, and Jeremy was stepping in to walk me down the aisle and "give me away." LaDonna, my "big sister," as I have called her since childhood, flew in from Scottsdale with her husband to be part of the celebration.

Ironically, Bruce's best friend from grade school, Chris, and one of mine from junior high, Teresa, came, bringing identical elegant Waterford champagne glasses as gifts. Each special occasion we think of each of them with a smile.

Bruce's mom and dad came in from Florida. My dear friend Judy came in from North Carolina. On Thursday night, we took our respective families/friends out separately for a joyful celebration. After everyone was settled in at their hotels, Bruce came by to meet me in the lobby of mine. There were all kinds of last-minute stumbles, but Bruce took me in his arms and assured me that no matter what happened, we would work it out.

The Big Day Arrived

Jeremy drove me to my hair stylist, Andre, who proceeded to style my hair as beautifully as I have ever seen anyone's. Meanwhile Bruce was running all over the place, picking up flowers and people, and wine. He carried the burden of the stress to enable me to relax and enjoy. Honestly, I had no idea how much stress he was under until after the wedding. His mom by that time was living in a nursing home and his dad had his own physical challenges. They both required help. Bruce was doing his best to juggle his wedding duties while caring for them. We hired someone to bathe and get his mom ready, another to style her hair, and my makeup artist from FOX to do her makeup. However incapacitated, Mrs. Rather was a beautiful woman and she looked lovely on that purple couch beside her husband as the ceremony unfolded.

It was a cold, winter night on January 31, 2009—with heavy snow that had accumulated the night of the wedding. Because of the shuttle, the arrival time began long before the ceremony. People filed into the basement—the beautiful basement, might I add—where Bruce's hilarious college roommates discovered the wedding wine. Before long, the basement was rocking and the wine was gone! Bruce had to get his mom and dad dressed and in place, run to the store for more wine, then hurry back to get dressed.

Laughter peeled from the basement, as, for the first time, my friends met Bruce's and the party began!

The Ceremony

Five o'clock came as Donna Butler stood up to sing the old Negro spiritual, "Who'll Be a Witness for My Lord?" in her powerful voice. I walked down the aisle with Jeremy, feeling more beautiful than I had ever felt in my life.

Dr. Lutzer prayed, and it all began. Charles led us in worship with "God of Wonder" as we sang repeatedly "You are holy! Holy!"

The two-story living room was filled top to bottom with the sound of singing. Those of us who were Evangelicals, lifted our voices in praise, as those who weren't joined in in other ways, feeling, I think, the presence of the Spirit in that room.

Dr. Lutzer and Rebecca offered us their wedding vows for the ceremony. They were beautiful and we were honored. Dr. Lutzer did what he always does. He delivered a powerful message on marriage and on the importance of Christ in each partner's life. He would later ask us often, "Did I tie a good knot?"

Safe to say, everyone was moved in some way. There was much laughter and tears. We dismissed then, to our separate dining areas, enjoying conversation surrounded by the beauty of every room.

Then It Fell Apart

We reconvened in the living room for the entertainment. I knew we were in trouble when Harry took his place on the second row, right in front of me. The first thing on the program was to be Harry, Kate, and me singing some worship songs we did in our Willow Creek days. "Harry! Where's the music?" I asked. He was looking at me with a blank stare when horror came over his face. "I left it in my car!" That would be his car parked miles away down a road covered in waist-high snow. Scratch that.

Next, I planned to sing a medley of old love songs Larry and I performed a thousand times. But we didn't have a chance to rehearse before the wedding, so as he began the intro, I realized "Let Me Call You Sweetheart" was in a key that would have placed my voice in the stratosphere. We tried again—then stopped. Tried again—then stopped. It was all wrong no matter what song we attempted. Scratch that.

Next up was Kate who launched into a great rendition of Aretha Franklin's "Respect." She was in it about ten bars when a fuse blew, and the sound went out. At this point, Bruce came up and, putting his arms around me, he whispered, "Why don't we just cut the cake?"

Suddenly, up sprang Dr. Lutzer to save the day. He did a stand-up routine, delivering the "news," imitated Billy Graham, and told corny but hilarious jokes. The night was saved!

We gave up and cut the cake!

Oh, but We're Not Done . . .

The next day was Super Bowl Sunday. After enjoying breakfast with all our friends and family, it was time to make the hour drive back to Chicago. Bruce left first with his mom and dad. Jeremy and I, my sister and her husband, Jeff, followed shortly after.

Bruce's home, now "our home," was located in a "transitional" area of Chicago.

What that meant was, there was a row of refurbished homes in the midst of the "hood." There was a large, stone, crack house across the street from us. A drug-dealer, who was continually "meeting friends" in cars that randomly drove up, lived three doors down. One evening police sirens and rotating bright, flood lights, filled our living room as a raid was conducted on the crack house. Not long after that, the drug dealer and his mother were murdered.

One morning Bruce was sitting in front of his house in his incognito bureau car, when he noticed a large black man coming up from behind on the driver's side, headed toward him. Bruce put his right hand on his gun and cautiously prepared to draw, when a cheerful voice introduced himself as "Eddie with the Secret Service!" They both had a good laugh to realize they were neighbors, two houses apart, in the midst of this "transitional" neighborhood.

"I hope you know I just racially profiled you," Bruce quipped.

"I don't blame you," Eddie good-naturedly replied.

The home was a typical "row" house on a skinny city lot. It was spacious with three finished floors, but long and narrow and surrounded by a fence on all four sides. In order to get in, you had to climb twelve concrete stairs to enter the first floor.

Bruce had fallen into an exhausted sleep after managing to get his parents inside, when the doorbell rang, unmercifully waking him, and his bride's entourage arrived.

We began to unload boxes, filled with gifts, quickly through that frigid air. Bruce ordered me inside as he left one last box, sitting by the car with my beautiful purple and white wedding bouquet placed on top. In the time that it took to take one box into the house and retrieve the next one, the bouquet vanished.

Welcome to the neighborhood!

I was moving into Bruce's house on this first day of marriage. And on that same day, I made chili and snacks for everyone. Together, Bruce and I made beds all over the house, and we all sat around the fire watching the Super Bowl and having a wonderful first day!

I forgot to mention we did this wedding thing in thirty days without taking time off from work, with the exception for me on Thursday and Friday, and Bruce only Friday before the wedding. If you're boasting about your insanity, is it okay to boast?

The next morning, Bruce began shuttling everyone separately, to O'Hare Airport. One by one they left. I was his last passenger, flying to New York City to appear on *The Tyra Banks Show*. He ended that day going to my apartment in Wheaton to move what he thought were just a few final things before midnight when the lease was up.

It turned out to require not one, but two one-hour roundtrips into the city to load and unload. Do you think by midnight that second day of marriage, Bruce was still happy he married me? You'll have to ask him!

Life in the City

It was exciting to live in the city. I really loved our home despite its challenges.

In warm weather we took Bruce's boat out on beautiful Lake Michigan, often setting anchor off Oak Street Beach. We crossed over the locks on the Chicago River winding down and around the huge, majestic buildings for miles.

We were close to our beloved church, Moody. During the Chicago Marathon one year, the course wove in and around the streets of Chicago, surrounding the church, making it impossible to get near. Trying to get to the service, Bruce and I parked several blocks away and began to walk. In the distance we could see the large brick façade of Moody Church, fashioned one hundred years before in the likeness of the Hagia Sophia in Istanbul. As we came to an impassable street, filled with marathoners, we waited for the herd to thin, then jumped in to run along with them, moving at an angle as we ran forward, in order to make our way to the other side of the street. We laughed as we heard someone say, "Look! There's a woman running in high heels!"

A downside for me was the driving distance to my radio studio which was located off the Kennedy in the Northwest Suburbs. Driving to work wasn't a problem, driving home was a nightmare, especially on Friday nights. It would sometimes take me two hours to make the eighteen-mile drive.

It was Sasha's 35th birthday on one of those Friday nights. I SO wanted to be with her, but Marklund Children's Home was at least an hour the opposite direction. It was such a quandary for me. Tired, as usual, at the end of the week, I reasoned I would drive out the next day to spend time with her.

Early the next morning, Bruce and I were sleeping peacefully in bed, when his cell phone rang. Marklund had been trying to reach me all night, but for some reason, the ringer on my phone was off. Bruce took me in his arms as he told me my sweet Sasha passed away in the night.

Floods of grief welled up in me as I realized she died alone after midnight on her birthday, without me by her side. The guilt and the sorrow overwhelmed me. While I was in DC, serving at CWA in 2003, Sasha developed a serious sepsis infection. By the time they called me, she was already undergoing a six-hour surgery where they removed parts of her stomach and intestines. I took the early morning flight out of DC, rented a car, and drove like a demon to be by her side. It was touch-and-go for a few days, but with the care of a loving doctor who knew her for years, she survived. But it took its toll on her young body, as it swelled unrecognizably from heavy doses of steroid. In spite of my grief in the moment Bruce delivered the news,

I was grateful to God He brought her home. Grateful that at last she was whole. After the funeral, my friend Kathy, was sitting in Shelly Mazzenga's dining room, overlooking a preserve when a brand-new fawn was birthed. She watched as he struggled to stand on his wobbly, new legs. It occurred to her then, that was exactly what was happening with Sasha. In heaven, my child who was never able to walk, was finding strength for the first time in her new legs.

> *Then will the lame leap like a deer,*
> *and the mute tongue shout for joy.* (Isaiah 35:6 NIV)

Bruce and I got ready quickly and made our way over an hour to Delnor Hospital in Geneva. My good friends from Berlin days, Seth and Ruth, who lovingly helped me care for Sasha through the years, were sitting in the room next to her, as we entered. My heart breaks all over again to remember that scene. I signed papers. I donated her cornea. And I said good-bye to my precious Sasha, at least to the body she left behind.

Twenty-five years earlier, Vern and Joanne Hultgren, owners of Hultgren Funeral Home, bought shares in a limited partnership to make it possible for me to record my first album, *Sasha's Song*. Their son, Tim, subsequently treated me with incredible grace and tenderness. We chose a casket, planned the funeral at Wheaton Evangelical Free Church where I raised the kids, and where Sasha noisily interrupted so many services with her "singing."

Harry and other friends jumped in to sing. Jack Schrader, of John Wilson Singers days, played piano. Shelly and Myrna White helped get photos and a video of her life produced, using the first album's title song "Sasha's Song" as background. (You can view these at www.sandy rios.com.) Jeremy and Liesel and four-month-old baby Moses flew in from Vancouver for Jeremy to deliver a poignant message. It might have been his first funeral to preach—ever. Bruce in his own eloquent way added profound words on the value of her life, however damaged.

People who cared for Sasha for the fifteen years she was at Marklund lined up to pay their respects and offer sweet stories. Sasha was a bit of a celebrity for those who knew my musical life, and it was a wonderful tribute to that little, silent girl who taught us all so much without words.

You might think it was a somber service. It was not. Joy filled that room. Taking Sasha's place to interrupt a service, my first grandson, Moses, loudly filled his diaper on several occasions. We all laughed, but I felt God was helping me understand He was bringing this new baby boy into my life to bring new joy, and I must look to the future.

We buried Sasha in Carmi, fittingly next to my mom and the new grave of my father as well. How they loved and cared for her.

My dad would have had the last laugh, as this was a reminder that twenty years earlier, he purchased two grave plots for his ungrateful daughter for her fortieth birthday. In his own loving, practical way, he once again provided for us.

God kept Sasha alive for a very long, difficult time.

But in the interim, He provided for me a loving, selfless husband to share my grief when the time of her death actually came.

13

Shouldn't This Story Be Over?

Honestly, at this point, I need a break from telling my own life story. It just goes on and on. Shouldn't I have died in my sleep or in a dramatic plane crash by now?

In all seriousness, more than once in my life, I have come to the place where I thought God was done with me in public ministry. I said "good-bye" to professional singing, I said "good-bye" to radio three times. I said "good-bye" to CWA and life in DC. I said "good-bye" to television when I left FOX. I said "good-bye" to being a wife, then a mother when Sasha died and Jeremy left college to spend the next twenty years and counting to live in a foreign country.

Then another call would come, bringing a completely different opportunity or perspective. Sometimes in times of discouragement, I would leave my studio to fly to events only to discover that people were actually listening to me, greeting me with more respect and accolades than I ever deserved.

I have always understood that whatever role I was asked to play was only temporary. "He must increase, but I must decrease," said John the Baptist when the adulation of the people for him began to turn toward Jesus (John 3:30). Time moves on and others take your place. Nothing in this life is permanent. Hold loosely to whatever it is you are holding. It was never about you nor was it yours to keep.

241

There WILL be someone else who can do the job as well or better. It is a privilege to serve, and it is NOT your story.

Understanding this brings great freedom and courage and minimizes competition and jealousy, I think. "Set your mind on things above, not on earthly things," urged the apostle Paul in Colossians 3:2. In the Sermon on the Mount, Jesus Himself instructed:

> *"Do not lay up for yourselves treasures on earth, where moth and rust destroy and where thieves break in and steal, but lay up for yourselves treasures in heaven, where neither moth nor rust destroys and where thieves do not break in and steal. For where your treasure is, there your heart will be also."* (Matthew 6:19–21)

Back to DC

After a little more than a year of living in the "hood," in the fall of 2010 Bruce was transferred back to Washington, DC, to be an adjudicator in the FBI's Office of Professional Responsibility (Internal Affairs). He would be adjudicating FBI agents who ran afoul of or were accused of running afoul of FBI regulations or criminal law. It was an interesting post and almost every day he came home with stories which I can't repeat.

I left my second stint at WYLL in October 2010 and was happy to return to DC where I felt I had unfinished business. I stayed current by attending a few of the weekly gatherings of "conservatives." Ironically, my first time back to an insider luncheon was the day Congress was considering the "Don't Ask, Don't Tell Repeal Act" which when eventually passed, lifted all restrictions on military service by gay, lesbian, and bisexual personnel. I was stunned to hear no one in that meeting pushed back in any way. Where were Christian conservative leaders who might have stopped it? Except for Elaine Donnelly of the Center for Military Readiness and Phyllis Schlafly and Eagle Forum, I don't know of any real fight. That doesn't mean there was none, but if there was, it was so quiet the thing passed with hardly a ripple.

It's just true that when we don't hold firm, things don't stay static. Next comes more compromise, then more, and finally you don't recognize yourself—or your organization—or your country.

After attending a second, larger meeting of "conservatives," hearing people advocate for legalizing marijuana and often featuring a member of the Muslim Brotherhood, whom I saw on video reciting, "We love death more than they love life!" I had enough. I sat through each meeting trying desperately to hold my now famous tongue, angry at the deception, angry at what the "conservative" movement had become.

Obama's DC at Christmas

The first Christmas back, Bruce and I were eager to enjoy the beauty of DC. During our courtship, we spent many nights driving around the District (City in Chicago terms), moon roof open, listening to music. Washington, unadorned was beautiful. Imagine all of that decorated for Christmas. Between the legendary stone, carved-out bridges spanning the Potomac, the White House, Congress, and the monuments, we were eager to take it all in. Except there was nothing to take in.

Obama began a "War on Christmas," and DC went dark. According to Obama, Americans, after all, weren't overwhelmingly Christians. In various order, he inferred they were Muslims, Hindus, Jews, and atheists—with some Christians. There was one dwarf Christmas tree on the vast Capitol grounds. The Obama White House Christmas tree was ordained with an ornament featuring Chinese Communist Leader, Mao Zedong. Precious few businesses downtown bothered to put up lights and the bridges were just stone. It was depressing.

Contrast that later to the Obama White House being lit brightly by rainbow lights after the SCOTUS decision legalizing gay "marriage" in 2015. What a dreadful place DC had become.

Another Life-Changing Phone Call

In January of 2011, I went to work as vice president of Family Pac Federal, representing my dear friend Paul Caprio in DC, and FOX was keeping me busy as a contributor out of the DC bureau.

In February 2012, *The O'Reilly Factor* invited me to come in and discuss the selection of comedian and talk show host Ellen DeGeneres as the spokesperson for J.C. Penney. The problem was Ellen wasn't just gay in her private life; she was a gay activist. A family-friendly company like J.C. Penney was virtually endorsing gay activism by this choice.

Everyone loved Ellen. She was funny and engaging. How in the world could I oppose ELLEN DEGENERES? I prayed as I always did for the right words that didn't personally attack but called out the issue.

Sitting in the chair in the *Fox* DC bureau before we began, Bill O'Reilly from New York spoke into my earpiece, warning me not to say anything bad about Ellen. I appeared with Bill a million times. He always treated me with respect but was still a verbal bully. Only one time did I see Bill let a guest express their viewpoint without interruption. In a long form interview with Rosie O'Donnell, who was advocating convincingly for gay parenting, he treated Rosie with great deference and without challenge.

Not so for me. The segment began. Bill set up the premise and turned to me. What did I think? As I started to speak, Bill interrupted. I began again as Bill interrupted. He managed to block me from completing a thought or finishing a sentence. When the segment ended, I was upset.

As I got into the car where Bruce was waiting for me, I started to cry. "I have been on television for years. I am not interested in doing that to be seen, I'm doing it to make a difference. If I can't even share my thoughts, what in the world am I doing?" We drove home in deep thought.

The next morning, once again, the phone rang. This time it was Tim Wildmon, president of the American Family Association. He saw my appearance with Bill and asked if I would consider doing the morning show for American Family Radio. I recognized the timing of that call was miraculous, but an early morning show? There was no way I wanted to do that.

Then my sweetheart, Bruce, spoke up. He told me how much he missed me on radio and how he felt I needed to be out there once again speaking on the issues of the day.

Sometimes the person God sends to you doesn't say what you want them to say. Sometimes they are in fact the voice of God speaking to you.

I accepted the job and the next chapter began.

Some Use Clocks to Tell Time, I Use Apartments!

We lived in yet another high-rise near the Pentagon this time around, and in the seven years we lived there, we moved five times within the same building! Trust me, there were reasons. We had it down to a science. We used grocery shopping carts and were able to settle FIVE times in new spaces in good order.

Each apartment was different. The eighth floor one was warm and cozy. Not working full-time, I was able to invite guests for Easter, the Super Bowl, Jeremy and Liesel and little Moses for Christmas. Life was almost normal.

Can Double Hip Replacement Really Be Funny?

The next apartment was a townhouse on the ground level with a long hallway and set of stairs leading up to the second level. We did our efficient move in just a few days, settling every room in neat order, just in time for me to have both my hips replaced at Mayo Clinic in Rochester, Minnesota. I wouldn't tell this story except it is funny.

I was in terrible pain from the time I left CWA but didn't quite know what was causing it. Let's just say I went lots of places for help, tried working harder in the gym, but the result was always more pain. I had trouble walking and couldn't lift my leg even over a low fence. These are embarrassing but necessary details.

Just after our marriage, Bruce insisted we join the executive health program at Mayo Clinic. We both had a female doctor, Dr. Stephanie Faubion, whom we really liked. We joke, but it's true, we spent our first trip—just a month into marriage—preparing for a colonoscopy in our hotel room. I'll leave that to your imagination.

Dr. Faubion changed our lives. She diagnosed my pain as a hip problem and began lobbying me to have surgery. I didn't want to have surgery. But the next year I gave in as Dr. Faubion brought another miracle worker into our lives, Dr. Robert Trousdale. He was a no-nonsense, bottom-line surgeon who assured me he could replace both hips at the same time so I could get back to DC in short order and resume my work.

In December of 2012 he delivered on his promise. The first thing I mumbled to Bruce when I came out of anesthetic was, "I don't feel any pain!" A snowy two days later, we drove to Rochester airport to board a plane. I was in a wheelchair, trying to get through security, when the TSA dude asked me to stand. I couldn't stand. Bruce, the FBI agent, assured the guy I wasn't an international terrorist posing as his wife and not currently posing any danger. Nevertheless, after swabbing and scanning my threatening wheelchair for explosives, we began to board the plane. Well, we tried.

It was a small plane connecting us to Chicago where we would board a second plane to DC.

SO . . . it wasn't a standard walkway, it was a narrow gangplank, with only flimsy chains to hold on to. Slowly, I got out of my wheel-chair and began to "walk" like Frankenstein over that walkway, grasping at the chains. Bruce followed right behind, unable to help. When I got to the doorway of the plane, I desperately grabbed the facing of the door, then the curtains. The attendant took one look at me and sat me down in the first of two single seats across from the little kitchen. I plopped down in relief and cold sweat.

Meanwhile, there were other patients trying to get on board. One of them looked like Yasser Arafat's twin. Dressed in a red-and-white checkered scarf, escorted by a woman in full burka, they sat a few rows behind. Trust me, I was oblivious and saw nothing, but as usual, Bruce saw everything.

The burka-ed woman got into an argument with the attendant for trying to place a huge rectangular suitcase underneath the seat. They went back and forth communicating by exaggerated hand motions, until the female attendant prevailed.

Once we landed in Chicago, wheelchairs were brought for me and "Yasser" who ran ahead of me to grab the first one, as I stood and waited. Finally, the second one arrived and I sunk down in relief. The worst part of this journey was over.

Meanwhile, the huge suitcase appeared again and once again the burka-ed lady got into an argument. This time with the wrong person. Mrs. Yasser proceeded to snap her fingers and point down at the heavy bag, engaging with a very tough, Chicago TSA employee who happened to be black. As Mrs. Yasser snapped her fingers and motioned to the employee to pick up the bag and bring it to her. Ms. Chicago placed her hands on her hips, and moving side to side barked, "I don't think so!!" It was hilarious.

Apartment Number Four!

Back to the townhouse, walking up and down that long hallway and up and down those steep stairs to the second floor was how I made my recovery after double hip replacement surgery. It changed my life. I was never able to run again, but I got back into the gym and on my bike soon after, and for the first time in years was not in pain.

But while I was still recovering, a beautiful but small eighth floor apartment opened and we jumped at the chance to move up from the lower level. Apartment 817 had only one bath, but the master had a long, curved wall with unique floor-to-ceiling windows. Sometimes when the stars were out or a storm was raging, we opened the curtains to watch in wonder from our bed.

The American Family Radio technical team came to install my first AFR Talk studio in the 8' x 10' bedroom that doubled as Bruce's closet. Each morning I would rise in the dark, hobble to a chair, and struggle to get dressed. First one sock, then the other, slowly, carefully. There was no hurrying. I hobbled into the "studio" competing with Bruce's clothes, equipment, files, and folders. It was a crowded mess, but that's how it started.

Mother Superior and the Spiral Staircase—Apartment Number Five!

Not long after, we got another call from the girls in the apartment building office, who had become our friends, that a two-story loft on the top floor had become available. Once again, we grabbed the chance to get into more space and enjoy a wonderful view from the two-story, floor-to-ceiling windows. We moved the studio to the loft where I could gaze out over the Village of Shirlington.

One Christmas, when Jeremy and Liesel came with their growing family—Moses, Cates, and baby Asa—we watched as the snow fell and blanketed the whole village. It was magical.

Into that space, I was able to invite many wonderful guests to come in person.

One unforgettable one was a Mother Superior from Syria who was serving in one of those ancient mountain-side monasteries you see in photos, overlooking a deep and craggy ravine. Syria was in the midst of conflict, and the Mother Superior was in the States to bring attention to the dangers of radical Islam as she experienced it.

When I learned she was in her seventies, I worried how she might navigate the tiny, spiral staircase leading up to the loft. But when she arrived in her long robes, as though stepping out of time, she climbed them like a gazelle. We settled in as she gave me the most astounding interview about life inside the monastery and attacks by jihadis.

Ann Coulter and friends like former Congressman Fred Grandy of *Love Boat* fame and his wife, Katherine; Sebastian and Katie Gorka; and other, fascinating guests graced those stairs, as the years ticked by. I SO enjoyed it.

Dual Birthdays on September 17

Each year on our birthday, Bruce and I planned something special. One year we invited his college buddies and their wives to come to DC and celebrate. These six guys remained close since they were young. I had, by then, heard all their stories, and loved each and every one of them and their wives.

The first night, we prepared dinner in our beautiful loft apartment. After dinner we surprised them with a long limo for a nighttime tour of the monuments. Next day we toured the district on top of a red double-decker bus. We visited the Ford Theatre Museum, walked the streets of Georgetown, took the amphibious Duck on the Potomac, wore ridiculous matching sweatshirts, and enjoyed our great friendships.

What a gift from God for our birthday!

Sparks Fly at a Meeting with President Trump

Another important chapter opened in DC on that second assignment. I wasn't the only person disillusioned and upset by the "conservative" leadership in Washington. Ginni Thomas, Justice Clarence Thomas's wife, and I and a few other stalwarts decided it was time to form another group with a different flavor.

We hand-picked people we knew to be uncompromising and serious about the mission of saving the country. We called ourselves "Groundswell." We determined to be off the record, behind the scenes.

As we met around a table each week, like the Founders, we pledged our lives and our fortunes. Many there had already paid a big price for holding fast. There was courage, passion, and selflessness in that room.

When President Trump was surprisingly elected, a small army of patriots were vetted and prepared to staff his agencies. Thinking he was making a smart move to unify the Republican Party, President Trump further surprised everyone by nominating Reince Priebus as his chief of staff. But those great résumés never saw the light of day and instead, establishment Republicans from the Bush and Cheney world, and the John Boehner and Paul Ryan worlds, populated the agencies and began to undermine the president.

The few managed to get through like Steve Bannon and Stephen Miller who were the exceptions. And the many fine appointees President Trump still managed to make were stalled for months—some over a year for confirmation by House Majority Leader Mitch McConnell. Many withdrew their names in frustration.

Other appointees, especially in national security sphere were just plain Leftists. Jared and Ivanka Trump, both registered Democrats, also had a lot to do with who ended up "serving" in the Trump Administration.

After President Trump was elected, a representative group of us met with him in the Roosevelt Room at the White House on January 26, 2019. Kelly-Anne Conway, Ivanka Trump, and many of his top aides sat in chairs surrounding us. We knew firsthand that President Trump was being actively undermined by staff. We tried to warn him, but somehow those messages were intercepted.

As we sat down, Ginni asked me to open in prayer. I was directly across the table from President Trump when I asked if I could pray for him. We bowed our heads. We decided to conduct this meeting with President Trump as we conducted all our meetings. That meant opening in prayer followed by frank discussion.

I'm guessing no one ever held a meeting like that with President Trump. One by one we presented our concerns to him. When we told him he was being undermined even by people in this room, President Trump was stunned and asked us who. One of our members pointed out Johnny DeStefano, sitting at the head of the elegant table. Johnny was senior advisor to former House Speaker John Boehner, who hated Donald Trump. Now Johnny had somehow been placed in charge of hiring for President Trump! Johnny became very angry when the president turned to him and ask if it was true. He denied it, but a month or so after that meeting, DeStefano was gone.

After that bit of fireworks, we then handed the president a more complete list of names of people we knew were sabotaging him. It was a meeting none of us would ever forget.

We agreed we wouldn't discuss this private meeting, but suddenly an article appeared in the *New York Times* laying it all out—at least their twisted version of it. Maggie Haberman claimed we had people praying throughout the meeting and ridiculously, that one of our members, herself a former Marine, declared to the president that women shouldn't serve in the military.

From that *New York Times* article, fodder then grew to lay groundwork to either force Justice Clarence Thomas to recuse himself on things alleged to be his activist-wife's positions, or further to impeach him because of his marriage to her. Funny how the *NY Times* never showed the same concern for Ruth Bader Ginsburg's personal radical activism while a sitting justice.

Groundswell became an integral part of my activist life. Through that trusted group of friends, many, many things were accomplished that shall never be written about—not even here.

Bruce's Last Act at His Beloved FBI

Bruce retired from the FBI just before his fifty-seventh birthday, September 17, 2013, which was mandatory for all agents. But it was a great loss to him. As a ten-year-old boy, he toured FBI headquarters with his parents and watched as agents did trick shooting in the basement firearms range. Enthralled, Bruce told his dad if they paid people to do that, he wanted to be an FBI agent. Years later at Quantico, he won the quickdraw competition in his class—and he DID get paid for it.

Bruce graduated second academically in his class at Quantico and second academically in Polygraph School as well. Hilariously, he did finish first in one major category: driving in reverse at high speed in tactical driving school. He was a trained hostage negotiator, served on the Evidence Response Team, and later as a special U.S. attorney.

He served for twenty-four years in Huntsville, Alabama, Los Angeles, California, Chicago, and DC. In addition to being a polygrapher, he worked bank robberies, kidnappings, street gangs, drugs, surveillance, public corruption, terrorism, presenting evidence in the now famous FISA court, murder-for-hire, and finally OPR (Office of Professional Responsibility). It was a long, distinguished career.

As we saw the date approaching, Bruce became irritable. He warned me not to have any kind of party or celebration. But I had to do something. I drove to a McDonald's parking lot, which was often my place to pray and read my Bible, and asked God what I should do. It meant too much to him for me to ignore this mark in time.

Suddenly, it occurred to me that Bruce's mom and dad were the most important people in his life. When they were both seriously injured in a car wreck years before, he transferred from LA to Tampa temporarily to live with and take care of them for months. They were in turn devoted to him and very proud of his accomplishments. What if I could fly them in as a surprise?

There in that parking lot, I called the airlines to check flights. Amazingly, I found a perfect one! I called Mr. Rather, then Mrs. Rather, who by that time was living separately in a nursing home. In spite of their limitations, they were excited. I called Bruce's best friend, Pat, from Dallas. "Can you come, Pat?" Not even a pause—Pat was all in.

Next was the tricky part. Bruce's boss at OPR, Candace, was an assistant FBI director I didn't know well. I was hoping and praying she could help. When I called and told her about the surprise guests, she went all-out to plan an in-office luncheon, order a beautiful FBI emblem–decorated caked and helped me scheme. It was great fun, until the day before the party, Bruce decided he wanted me to spend the day driving to Quantico with him for one last look while he could still enter the premises. Oh, dear. I was trying to clean and cook and organize everything without him noticing. I couldn't say "no" to this important trip, so off we went. But as we were driving around Quantico in the car, my phone rang. It was Candace. I could NOT let him know she was calling me. SO incredibly awkward, I managed to fake my way through the conversation, and Bruce was none the wiser.

That night, I asked if he could hang a few pictures that had been lying around the apartment. Uncharacteristically, he barked at me, warning again that I better not be having a surprise party. Thankfully, he hung them anyway.

The next morning, Bruce went to work. I went into overdrive making beds and finalizing everything. I drove to the airport, parked, and went in to greet Mr. and Mrs. Rather. Speeding down the long corridor, I saw Mr. Rather pushing his wife's wheelchair slowly toward me. They rose at the crack of dawn, moving heaven and earth and their tired, worn and injured bodies to make this difficult trip alone. Meanwhile Pat landed and ran to join me and help.

We had just enough time to drive down to the District in time to surprise Bruce.

We had to make a trip to the bathroom, lifting a tired Mrs. Rather in and out of her wheelchair. When we opened the car door to sit her inside, the corner of the door raked across her shin and blood began to run into her stockings. Such a beautiful, elegant woman, she so wanted to go back and change, but we just didn't have time.

We drove from Reagan to the J. Edgar Hoover Building as fast as we could. Pat got out as together we re-loaded Mrs. Rather into the wheelchair and they hurried into the building as I parked the car.

Candace had by then gathered everyone in the conference room for the luncheon, where I had hurried ahead to join Bruce. When the door suddenly opened, in walked Bruce's mom and dad and his best friend, Pat. Bruce's face lit up with joy, and his party was filled with laughter and tributes to his service.

What another wonderful memory from that loft apartment, when we think of their final visit with us.

This Could Have Been MY Last Act . . .

Bruce and I loved to take long bike rides into DC along the George Washington Parkway, often to the Lincoln Memorial. One beautiful spring day in 2020 we were riding around the Washington Monument, as hundreds of people were enjoying the same by foot on sidewalks and walkways. We were riding on an old stone sidewalk near the White House, weaving in and out of the crowds.

I was following Bruce as he drove onto the grass and back onto the pavement, but as I turned my front wheel to get back on, they didn't turn at all, and I was thrown head-first onto my face on the stone pavement. I pulled myself up slightly, face down, as I realized blood was running over the pavement and into my hair. I got up on my knees, leaning forward on my arms, head down, as I heard people gathering around me. In that moment, I was strangely calm and aware of God's presence. "My life is Yours. I trust You, Lord." Then I heard Bruce's voice, asking me if I was alright. I told him I broke out my two front teeth. I heard a man call for an ambulance, then felt a woman take my hand and speak to me gently in an Asian language. Through my bloodied hair I could see she was in her native dress. I felt her compassion and believed she was praying for me.

The White House uniformed Secret Service saw what happened and came right away to assist. They called an ambulance to take me to

George Washington University Hospital, a miracle since other hospitals in DC were notoriously bad.

The SS loaded our bikes onto the ambulance as the paramedics loaded me. They were young, GWU students, so very caring. Nothing in that experience was remotely a typical DC response.

My nose and my jaw were broken, one front tooth was half gone, the other knocked out completely. My lower lip had a deep laceration which required many painful stitches. Beautiful, life-giving conversations were had with the staff as they attended me. Finally, after many hours, we were free to make a visit to our dentist, who graciously agreed to meet us at 10 p.m. the night before Mother's Day. There were so many mercies that day.

It was three full years before I finally had two proper front teeth. In the interim, I had temporary ones with varying degrees of success. Remember I was on the radio every morning, trying to communicate through those teeth.

It wasn't until years later I realized how much damage was done to my ability to speak. Between my altered lower lip from multiple stitches, to my altered or missing two front teeth, it was difficult to recapture my once, clear speech for which I was often hired to do voiceover and radio work.

I mourned for about five minutes, then started to retrain myself to over-enunciate. To this day, my speech often sounds lazy and some days I just can't get my lower lip to cooperate, but I think it's just another example of needing to let go of what was and look toward the future and what is to be!

Fleeing Hillary

As the 2016 election approached, I worked tirelessly to try and keep Hillary Clinton from becoming president. Whether it was on the air, or working at election precincts, I must admit I was weary—very weary. Often Bruce would come home from his contractor job to find me on my back on the floor in exhaustion.

Bruce determined we should make a new start somewhere else. When Donald Trump actually won the 2016 election, no one was more startled and thrilled than Bruce and I.

By then, we only had a few days before our scheduled move to Florida where a new home and a new life was waiting for us.

14

When COVID Came Calling

For the next four years I hosted *Sandy Rios in the Morning* on AFR Talk, covering the news every single day. I traveled back and forth to DC, while attending and speaking at various events. In May of 2021, Jeremy and Liesel, Moses, Cates, Asa, and three-year-old Lucy came back from St. Andrews, Scotland, where Jeremy completed his PhD and moved in with us for five months while in transition. We were thrilled to have them and life was never dull. Little did we know we were in for a drama that could have ended in life or death.

In January of 2020, I was conducting interviews on Radio Row at CPAC in DC. Immediately when we returned home, the world began to hear about this new contagious respiratory infection called COVID. The headlines in the U.S. more than inferred that CPAC, the largest gathering of conservatives in the nation, was a spreader of the disease. And thus, it began.

At first, we all just watched with dread and without understanding. We were horrified to see videos of people collapsing in the streets in China, all the while being told it was coming our way. Footage from Italian hospitals added to the fear, showing overcrowding and further scenes of the outbreak where workers from Wuhan, China, the place of origin, were numerous.

The entire world went into panic and eventually lockdown. As a talk show host people listen to and trust, it was an incredible burden to try and make sense of it all. The visuals looked terrible, but there was something not quite right happening with the messaging, then the shutdowns. Something untoward, unseemly, about the barely disguised pleasure new medical stars like Anthony Fauci and Deborah Birx seemed to get watching the world hang on their every arbitrary rule. But it wasn't just the medical community. Regular people in our neighborhoods, in stores, and in church seemed to enjoy keeping these new "rules," and shaming others who didn't. *What in the world?* I struggled to comprehend.

And then the vaccines were introduced. The elderly were dying en masse. They were the most at risk so seniors hurried to be vaccinated. Then people of all ages rushed to get the vaccine, clinging to the promise they could get their lives back. But that didn't happen. Next they were led by these new medical gods to turn on people, even family members, who didn't want the vaccination. A new phrase was coined, "The pandemic of the unvaccinated." How sad and ironic, that in time, the worm should turn so that the vaccinated, having lost their natural immunity, replaced by the mRNA in the "vaccine," consequently had no immunity to fight the new COVID variants. At that point it became and still seems to be, at this writing, "the pandemic of the *vaccinated*."

I was still in the throes of trying to understand it all when in July of 2021, our little grandson, Asa, caught something at Vacation Bible School. The most active of the four, he went down for the count. He lost his taste and described his legs as wobbly. Healthy kids do, despite what the manipulator-experts were saying, recover quickly. Asa soon bounced back to his normal self.

But Bruce began to feel bad. Not one to complain, my first clue was his grumpiness. We were scheduled to attend CPAC Dallas later in the week, so he agreed to go to the doctor. Unbeknownst to me, he was diagnosed with pneumonia in both lungs. The doctor gave him a shot and lots of medicine, and off we went.

During a long delay on the plane, he began to feel worse. I felt we should get off the plane, but he wanted to persevere. I began to feel unwell myself, so when we landed in Dallas, we headed straight for an urgent care where I got a shot and some antibiotic. We went to an outdoor Mexican restaurant, but by that time, Bruce couldn't hold his head up. He was resting on the table when I brought our food back on a tray. When he excused himself to the bathroom, I sat and waited with knots in my stomach. And when he didn't return in thirty minutes, I was out of my mind. I asked someone to check the men's room. I watched anxiously until finally Bruce appeared at the table with marks on his face and head. He had fainted, hitting his head on the bathroom wall and laid on the floor, unable to get up. Finally, he stumbled his way back to our table.

For the first time, I was thinking the "C" word. But what in the world could I do?

I couldn't get him back on a plane, and by then I already knew enough NOT to trust hospitals. If I put him in a hospital there, I knew the dangers of the ventilator, the forbidding of wives and family from coming in. I might never see him again. I got him to the hotel room, lying in the bed, administering meds and liquids, hoping and praying that could restore his strength. I went to CPAC during the day and returned to bring food and check on him. He was sleeping constantly, and by Friday night struggling to breathe. The night after that was a nightmare as I listened to him labor. "Dear God," I prayed. "What should I do?"

By Saturday morning, he was able to walk around. We managed to get to the airport, get him on the plane and back home. He was so sick he couldn't lift anything—so sick—I took him directly into the house and helped him lie down on the bed. When I returned to the bedroom after unloading, he lay quietly, his body now half off the bed.

Still, I knew hospitals in our area were following the same routine: putting patients on ventilators which ultimately led to their deaths. No spouses allowed in the room or in the decision-making process.

The next morning was Sunday. I took him to an urgent care clinic, back to the doctor who diagnosed his double pneumonia. I thought perhaps Bruce was dehydrated so they gave him a full liter of liquid through an IV. We both took a COVID test which were both, of course, positive. After another bad night, I got him up early, steeled myself, and drove him to a hospital nearly an hour away with a reputation for better patient care.

After checking him in, I ran to the car to get his personal items, but when I returned, they had already taken him away without giving me any chance to say good-bye. How cruel COVID made the medical establishment.

I called Frontline Doctors and was connected to a no-nonsense female doctor from Chicago who proceeded to explain to me exactly what needed to be done and what not to do. She instructed me to urge my doctor to follow that protocol.

Later that afternoon, his doctor called to give me his assessment. It was bad. If he didn't turn a corner soon, they were going to put him on a ventilator. "Dear God in heaven," I prayed. And as we talked, Dr. Koo identified himself as a Christian. He was very kind, and we ended the call praying together.

It was a restless night as I tossed and turned in worry. I got up early and wrote a letter to Dr. Koo. *Not too long or complicated*, I instructed myself. Basically, it said, "Dr. Koo, I am not a medical professional, so I am NOT trying to tell you what to do, but I am in the information business. And in that business, I have access to knowledge about COVID. Would you please, I beg you, use Ivermectin and these other protocols listed here on Bruce? And if not, why wouldn't you? What have we got to lose?"

I drove to the hospital early in the morning and sat in the parking lot praying. I folded the note with the doctor's name on it and proceeded to the entrance. I was blocked from entering except for the first few feet. I asked the tall man who approached me if there would be any way he could get this to Dr. Koo in the COVID ward.

The next evening, Dr. Koo called again. In spite of his great kindness, he felt Ivermectin was a mistake. They were instead administering Remdesivir, a nightmare drug that causes organ failure and death, but I didn't fully comprehend that then.

After much pleading, Dr. Koo agreed to ask the infectious disease doctor. It had to have been prayer, because for some reason that doctor acquiesced. Later, angry and resentful about it, the infectious disease doc stood over Bruce's hospital bed, as sick as Bruce was, railing about Ivermectin and President Trump.

They began the Ivermectin on Wednesday and by Saturday, I was able to bring Bruce home. It would be an exaggeration to say he was well, he was not. But the worst was over. What amazed me was how the hospital didn't seem interested in keeping or even treating him until the pneumonia was gone. He was released with only a few days of antibiotic and oxygen. I took him back to the same urgent care clinic to get more Ivermectin, prednisone, antibiotic, and gradually nursed him back to health.

It Was Partly Angus's Fault

This will sound like a made-up story, but it isn't. Bruce got COVID amid a series of accidents and surgeries that lasted three years. It began with a freak accident in 2017 when he broke his hip. He drove himself to the hospital and called me in DC where I was at the FRC Values Voter Summit. I left the event, frantically gathered my things, making Reagan Airport in time for a flight just ninety minutes after Bruce called.

Early in the morning on Memorial Day of 2020, I was sorting boxes in the garage. We went shopping and came across a four-foot-tall suit of armor we mischievously thought would be a great gift for Jeremy's upcoming graduation from St. Andrews. We named him Angus.

Before Angus ever made it into the house, Bruce thought on that early Memorial Day morning it would be funny to place him in my "water closet" as a surprise. But the surprise was on him when, while lifting Angus from the car, the sheet metal handily sliced through the tendon of his left thumb. Several stitches and one more surgery later, that was a "Memorial" Day we won't soon forget.

During a surfboard accident in California back in the '90s, Bruce broke his right shoulder. The clavicle floated in pieces for years and the joint became ever more painful. We found a brilliant, young surgeon who had a new method of repairing shoulders. In September 2020, after the Angus incident, Dr. Baker performed a miracle on that shoulder. Adding tissue, grafts, and a smaller than usual device, he restored Bruce's shoulder to near perfection.

On December 31, a few months into his recovery, I was adding finishing touches for our New Years' Eve party, while Bruce decided to go for a bike ride. Gone longer than expected, he eventually made it home, apologizing profusely.

In a freak accident, he was thrown over his handlebars, landing directly on the newly repaired shoulder, breaking his humerus in what we would learn later was nine pieces.

Back into a cast already after months of immobility, he began to lose the use of his right hand, his dominant hand, his gun hand. After three surgeries in succession, July of 2021 brought Covid. We waited as long as we dared as he lost more and more strength and dexterity in his right hand. Finally in August of 2021, a hand surgeon performed an intricate surgery, connecting and grafting and transplanting other nerves, predicting that in a year's time he MIGHT regain use of it.

After many months of pain and recovery, his left shoulder, by now was also in tremendous pain. In July 2022, the same surgeon, Dr. Baker, replaced it.

In all of that, I never heard Bruce complain or observe him get mad at God—ever. He bore it with grace and perseverance, and I learned even more about the man God sent into my life thirteen years earlier!

Warning!

As more and more injuries were reported, and death rates in the United States increased dramatically, it became apparent the untested vaccine was injuring and, in some cases, killing people. Stillbirths and difficulties with unborn babies have greatly increased, as has blood clotting, heart problems, and cancer. Like a wave of the plague, young men in and out of the military, often fit and active in sports, have begun dropping dead unexpectedly. More of them have been subsequently diagnosed with myocarditis, a serious lifetime condition of the heart.

For months, I held back on giving an opinion on the "vaccine." I told my audience Bruce and I were not going to take it, but I could not, would not advise them on their decision. But as the numbers of injury and death began to rise, I could no longer remain agnostic.

As a non-medical person, it's not appropriate for me to give medical advice, but I can and will issue a warning. Do NOT get another vaccine or booster until you have taken the courage to read the almost completely censored opposing view.

Doesn't the fact that anyone speaking negatively of the vaccines is immediately shamed and silenced tell you something? Contrary to the medical tyranny Dr. Anthony Fauci has imposed, real science actually welcomes opposing views. The few doctors who dare to oppose the medical establishment have often lost their positions and most certainly their reputations yet persist to speak what they believe is the truth. Doesn't THAT tell you something too?

Dare to look at the writings of Dr. Robert Malone or *Conservative Review* senior writer Daniel Horowitz to name a few. Or sign up to receive and read the *Epoch Times*, an outlet begun by Chinese dissidents who, at this writing, seek to tell the unwavering truth.

Do NOT bury your head in the sand. Even if you or your family have taken the vaccine, you must find out the truth. If the danger is as real as I believe it is, don't you want to stop your children and grandchildren from taking the mRNA shots and boosters? There is no satisfaction taken from these stats for those of us who refused to take the "vaccine." Many of our friends and family, our children and grandchildren did take it. Our grief will be as great as yours if more and more of the ones dear to us die before their time.

As you read this part of my book, the issues around the COVID-19 vaccines may have passed into relative silence. The greater lesson I learned from this experience, and that of many of my family, friends, and colleagues, is to think critically about everything—especially anything the government says and does.

Untold harm was thrown over our nation and the world by people who were far less interested in help than building and keeping position and power. There was also a massive amount of money made capitalizing on the suffering and fear of the American people.

God's people in particular should never trust people more than His sovereignty and love.

15

Quite the Coda!

A coda is the portion of a musical composition that brings it to an end. It can be short or long, but it must be beautiful, well-crafted . . . worthy of the piece itself.

This is the "Coda" of this book which will begin the telling of the "Coda" of my life. The God who called me and wrote the overture and every single movement thereafter will take this work of my life to completion. And by His grace, I will not mar it by failing to do my part to make it a worthy ending.

I came into this world at the end of an era—the Second World War. God called me during peace, grew me thru the turmoil of Civil Rights, and the strife of another war, Vietnam. He made my roots grow deeper in the belly of God-less Communism, and commissioned me for service during the decline and degradation of my beloved country.

He gave me adventure. He protected me from many dangers. He provided for me and He gave me Hope.

I am just an ordinary girl who God called to do extraordinary things. I tried to make right choices every step of the way. My choices were not always good ones, but I never failed to confess them and repent. I know who it is I serve. And I know that I cannot live without His presence in my life.

As I write, the world is in turmoil. I could write about that turmoil, for I have been speaking about it and bringing my thoughts and opinions about it for years. But instead, I choose to offer, in this short Coda, the secret to navigating it all.

In everything God has called me to do, I have tried to bring Him into the forefront. In each controversial issue, each television appearance, each commentary, I sought His counsel. "The law was our tutor to bring us to Christ," wrote the apostle Paul (Galatians 3:24). I always felt, and still do, that Truth leads people to the God of all Truth.

By speaking truth, we are awakening in men's hearts the knowledge of God. I've seen it happen time and time again. And as things have gotten darker in our world, I have seen people I would never have thought would deign to be open to bringing God into their life show an openness to hearing about Him . . . right now.

Why does that matter? What difference would it make to what we're facing? In the words of a Thai man I interviewed in a Buddhist refugee camp who had just embraced the truth of Jesus, "It has changed the way I think about everything." My own husband said much the same. After living a good life as a "good" man, he too embraced the truth of Jesus and later said to me, "It makes everything make sense."

During the Black Death (Bubonic Plague) of 1347–1351 in Europe and North Africa, 75–200 million people died. Everyone was in fear and mourning. As pagans carried their dead, they wailed in grief.

But as Christians buried their dead, they sang songs of praise. THIS was the tangible difference Jesus brought to the world that people could see. No fear of death.

"Where, O death, is your victory? Where, O death, is your sting?" (1 Corinthians 15:55 NIV).

In my many trips to China, I observed terrible oppression and hardship. But as I wrote earlier, let me repeat, I saw with my own eyes, the inexplicable joy and courage of Chinese Christians, who— in the face of possible imprisonment and death, and certainly poverty without a future—were even bolder to proclaim this mysterious thing we call faith in Christ.

"If you declare with your mouth, 'Jesus is Lord,' and believe in your heart that God has raised him from the dead, you will be saved" (Romans 10:9 NIV).

That's how it happens and that's when our perspective on everything changes. We take on the "mind of Christ." Much deeper than "What would Jesus do?", we conform our minds and our thinking to His Word.

When we do, the power of God is unleashed in our lives, as it was in mine to face the most difficult circumstances that come our way.

I don't look forward to what comes next right now. I have moments of fear and anxiousness, but because I've gotten to know God so well through His Word and thru His steady, faithful guidance in my life, I know now I can trust Him.

Trust Him to do what, you ask? Will He save me from my doorbell ringing with a hostile government on the other side? Will he save me from losing my home, my life savings, my livelihood? Will he spare me from cancer or heart failure? Sometimes He does. But sometimes He doesn't.

Then why would we serve Him? Because He gives inexplicable strength, He brings comfort, and He gives a peace that "surpasses all understanding" (Philippians 4:7).

As to the world situation we find ourselves in, understanding Him helps us understand that too. He is clear in His Word that the world will get more and more wicked:

> *You should know this, that in the last days there will be very difficult times. For people will love only themselves and their money. They will be boastful and proud, scoffing at God, disobedient to their parents, and ungrateful. They will consider nothing sacred. They will be unloving and*

unforgiving; they will slander others and have no self-control. They will be cruel and hate what is good. They will betray their friends, be reckless, be puffed up with pride, and love pleasure rather than God. They will act religious, but they will reject the power that could make them godly. (2 Timothy 3:1–5 NLT)

You might not find that comforting, but I do. This and other passages warn us about the future. We are not surprised then, when we see everything unravel.

But along with that warning is the promise of hope and a future.

Here's where the skeptic reading will struggle, because this is the supernatural part. Interesting to me that many world religions or beliefs feel the need to hide their doctrine, but Christians don't.

We claim that there is only one God and that He created the heavens and the earth in seven days. The oceans . . . the mountains . . . every single animal . . . every fish in the sea . . . and man himself. We believe that.

We claim further that He had a Son by a woman named Mary with the help of NO human man, that His name is Jesus, and that God actually allowed His Son, who was fully God, to be crucified—brutally murdered and publicly humiliated on a cross—so that He could bear the sins of the world and forgiveness could be offered to every man and woman from every tribe and nation.

And we believe that He is coming again to judge the living and the dead. We believe He will descend from heaven with a shout of the Archangel to lead a great battle called Armageddon, win a great victory over the armies convened for that final conflict, destroy this earth, and bring about a new heaven and a new earth.

Did you ever notice that no matter how your body changes—in puberty, in maturation, and in aging—your mind always stays the same? Not your opinions, but the essence of you—from birth to life—the unique living being that you are is the same. On your death bed when you can no longer utter a word, in your conscious mind, you will still be the same person. Could it be that that's our soul? The part that never dies? Christians believe in eternal life for every person. But your eternity with God the Creator is not assured unless you accept His beloved Son, Jesus.

"For God so loved the world that He gave His only begotten Son, that whoever believes in Him should not perish but have everlasting life" (John 3:16).

But I love the next verse too:

"For God did not send His Son into the world to condemn the world, but that the world through Him might be saved" (v. 17).

You may have rejected God because you had the impression that He has rules too stringent for you to follow. Or perhaps you're not willing to give up something even though you sense this is all true.

God didn't send His Son to impose rules on you; He sent Him to forgive you. Would you give your firstborn son as a literal sacrifice for anyone? No. But that's exactly what God did for you. When you finally get that, you can't help but serve Him, and nothing that you cling to now will be worth separation from Him.

That was exactly my battle when God renewed my faith before going to Berlin. I didn't think He could forgive me. I didn't understand His grace and mercy, and I didn't understand His power to transform my mind.

So Now . . .

I have thought so many times that God was finished using me publicly. Truthfully, my heart's desire was to have lots of children, raise a family, and nurture and care for them and my grandchildren in my later years. But God had another plan.

And He still seems to have one. After ten years on American Family Radio hosting an early morning show, I stepped down to launch a podcast in January of 2023, called *Sandy Rios 24/7.* I interview newsmakers as I always have done, but this time I add my former

FBI Agent/Cook County Prosecutor-husband for his timely perspective on all that is unfolding. I still serve as Director of Governmental Affairs for the American Family Association and my work in DC still continues.

THIS, then, is my Coda . . . To finish well and make it beautiful. But meanwhile I'll be listening for the next call!

Acknowledgments

It was just about one year ago from this writing that my husband, Bruce, and I were in the car driving home from Mayo Clinic. I had just been diagnosed with Stage 1, Level 1 breast cancer and we were in deep conversation. I began to tell him stories of my life—funny, hilarious stories and we began to laugh . . . and laugh . . . and laugh some more.

Finally he said to me, "You need to write a book. You need to write TWO books—one serious and one funny."

It's not the first time Bruce has encouraged me to do something as you read in this book. He is God's gift to me.

A selfless husband who loves and respects me and WANTS me to write and speak and travel and be out there fighting.

When I went back to Mayo for five days of radiation, we spent every single day talking through chapters, writing and strategizing together. This book is a product of those five days.

I want to thank my publisher, Gary Terashita. Gary reached out to me twenty years ago when I was President of CWA to see if I would be interested in writing a book. I never forgot his professional manner and his kindness, but I was too busy "doing" to sit down and write about it. Then in 2022, in separate interviews with my friends Lt. General Jerry Boykin and Congressman Steve King, I saw they had the same publisher . . . Gary Terashita and Fidelis Publishing. I reached out to Gary and, amazingly, he responded immediately with great affirmation. I don't think these things are coincidental.

Through the years, many people have suggested I write a book. Early on they wanted me to write about my severely disabled daughter, Sasha. I didn't want to write that book and live that heartache all over again. But at this time in my life, I felt the need to recall and record, not just the sadness, but in retrospect, the great things God did in the process.

I want to thank my dearest DC friend, Mariam Bell, who walked through much of the storms I faced in my Concerned Women for America days and out of the blue recently said to me, "You should write a book!" I want to thank Cleta Mitchell for asking me to tell her my story over lunch at a conference a few years ago, and was so motivated by it, launched into a campaign to get me published! But the timing wasn't right just yet. We became good friends from that exchange.

I want to thank my new but very dear friends, Bobbie and Al Brecher, who each have their own great story to tell. Jewish and from New York, they came to Florida and found the Messiah, Jesus. Al was born in Russia and lived his early life fleeing from the Communists and the Nazis. They are incredible friends and incredible Bible teachers who have fervently prayed for and supported me, my radio show, my podcast, and now this book.

I want to thank my dear friends in the class Bobbie and Al teach in my home church, for their constant support and prayers. Bruce and I are often overwhelmed by their encouragement and kindness. It's been hard through the years to plug into local church life as I loved to do before my travel life began. But I have always believed that connecting to the local body of Christ not only gives you strength, but also the accountability every Christian in the public eye needs.

I want to acknowledge my dear, sweet friends, Nancy and Tom Spaman, who have given great feedback on *Sandy Rios in the Morning* and now *Sandy Rios 24/7* and really lived through the past years sharing life, and even unselfishly sharing their children and grandchildren with Bruce and me. Cheerleaders always, godly people who love unconditionally but hold us to righteousness.

I shall forever be grateful to Adam Sudduth, my producer, for the countless times he has dropped everything to rescue his frazzled boss, from the technology beast.

I have my gifted friend Alan Terwilleger to thank for spending countless inconvenient hours taking the photos over the finish line.

And finally, I want to thank my "Big Sister," LaDonna who tirelessly searched through old photos to use in this book. Age difference and the miles between us have kept us from sharing our lives the way we both wished for. It means so much to me that she has loved the idea of this book since its inception, and cheerled her "Little Sis" on every step of the way.

Endnotes

1. Though Hope Publishing seems to be the publisher, no registration could be found.

2. Andrew Glass, "Senate opens Clinton impeachment trial, Jan. 7, 1999," *Politico,* January 7, 2018, https://www.politico.com/story/2018/01/07/this-day-in-politics-jan-7-1999-324974#:~:text=Henry%20Hyde%20(R%2DIll.,are%20the%20president.%20

...

3. In September of 2022, a UN Tribunal finally convicted three members of the Khmer Rouge for their atrocities. Most of the guilty died of natural causes in the ensuing decades.

4. We weren't in any danger of being shot or harmed, just deported. But our friends who helped us surely were.

5. "What Will Children Learn about September 11?" Transcript from *CNN Crossfire*, August 20, 2002, http://www.cnn.com/TRANSCRIPTS/0208/20/cf.00.html.